D1528311

COMMUNITY ENGAGEMENT IN HIGHER EDUCATION

Edited by Dan W. Butin

This series examines the limits and possibilities of the theory and practice of community engagement in higher education. It is grounded in the desire to critically, thoughtfully, and thoroughly examine how to support efforts in higher education such that community engagement—a wide yet interrelated set of practices and philosophies such as service-learning, civic engagement, experiential education, public scholarship, participatory action research, and community-based research—is meaningful, sustainable, and impactful to its multiple constituencies. The series is by its nature cross-disciplinary and sees its readership across the breadth of higher education, both within student and academic affairs.

Dan W. Butin is an associate professor and founding dean of the School of Education at Merrimack College and the executive director of the Center for Engaged Democracy. He is the author and editor of more than 70 academic publications, including the books *Service-Learning in Theory and Practice: The Future of Community Engagement in Higher Education* (2010), which won the 2010 Critics Choice Book Award of the American Educational Studies Association; *Service-Learning and Social Justice Education* (2008); *Teaching Social Foundations of Education* (2005); and, most recently with Scott Seider, *The Engaged Campus: Majors and Minors as the New Community Engagement* (2012). Dr Butin's research focuses on issues of educator preparation and policy, and community engagement. Prior to working in higher education, Dr Butin was a middle-school math and science teacher and the chief financial officer of Teach For America. More about Dr Butin's work can be found at http://danbutin.org/.

The Engaged Campus: Majors, Minors and Certificates as the New Community Engagement
Edited by Dan W. Butin and Scott Seider

Engaged Learning in the Academy: Challenges and Possibilities
By David Thornton Moore

Deepening Community Engagement in Higher Education: Forging New Pathways
Edited by Ariane Hoy and Mathew Johnson

Deepening Community Engagement in Higher Education

Forging New Pathways

Edited by
Ariane Hoy and Mathew Johnson

palgrave
macmillan

First published in 2013 by
PALGRAVE MACMILLAN®
in the United States—a division of St. Martin's Press LLC,
175 Fifth Avenue, New York, NY 10010.

Where this book is distributed in the UK, Europe and the rest of the world,
this is by Palgrave Macmillan, a division of Macmillan Publishers Limited,
registered in England, company number 785998, of Houndmills,
Basingstoke, Hampshire RG21 6XS.

Palgrave Macmillan is the global academic imprint of the above companies
and has companies and representatives throughout the world.

Palgrave® and Macmillan® are registered trademarks in the United States,
the United Kingdom, Europe and other countries.

ISBN: 978–1–137–31991–3

Library of Congress Cataloging-in-Publication Data is available from the
Library of Congress.

A catalogue record of the book is available from the British Library.

Design by Newgen Knowledge Works (P) Ltd., Chennai, India.

First edition: September 2013

10 9 8 7 6 5 4 3 2 1

Contents

Part II Developmental, Engaged, and Educational Partnerships

Part III Faculty: Exploring New Epistemologies for Academic Community Engagement

Illustrations

Figures

Tables

Foreword: Reflecting on Bonner's Journey

Wayne Meisel

When I arrived in the fall of 1988 at the library at Bertram F. Bonner's home on 36 Rosedale Road, Princeton, I was not exactly sure what to expect. I had written a letter to Mr Bonner the month before telling him about my work with college students and campus–community service programs. He had responded, asking if I would come and see him. How hard could it be to take a paid trip back to my old hometown, I wondered.

During that conversation, Mr Bonner shared with me that he and his wife, Corella, wanted to take what they had earned and saved over a lifelong successful business career and create a foundation. Mr Bonner had visions, vague and undefined, yet strong and with conviction. He wanted to "help the person who was hurting" and to "displace despair with opportunity."

Hence, these became the two principles from which to work as we set off on the course that launched the Bonner Foundation and the Bonner Scholar Program. If one now looks at the Bonner Scholar and Bonner Leader Program and the efforts required to build comprehensive community engagement centers, it can all be traced back to these two simple, perhaps vague, yet powerful concepts.

So how did we get from here to there? The success of the Bonner Program has been based on three ingredients.

One is that we have not imported anything to the institutions with which we collaborate. Rather, we were the ones who were inspired by the great histories and foundings of the colleges and universities that we have worked with for decades.

What prophetic witnesses could be more daring, courageous, and compelling? Consider the abolitionist John Gregg Fee who founded Berea College or Charles Finney who served as the second president of Oberlin College. Or how about Horace Mann, an early president of Antioch College who made his expectation clear when he said "Be ashamed to die until you have won some victory for humanity." And then, there were Harriet E. Giles and Sophia B. Packard who launched the Atlanta Baptist Female Seminary, which later became Spelman College.

Guided by these aspirations, we took the stories and mission statements and sought to be partners with each institution. We sought to affirm and strengthen bold ideas and important roles that these schools were created to play. This meant that we were never pursuing an outside agenda. When others got suspicious about what we were up to, we would always bring our focus back to the school's mission. We would return to our shared purposes—to help create institutions that live out their missions for educating students who contribute to our society and democracy, to supporting institutions to live their public missions. This was affirming the soul of the school.

What we found was that oftentimes an outside voice could lift up issues and challenges in a way that no insider could or would. This role continues to this day.

Some have referred to the colleges and universities that have a Bonner Program as Bonner schools. Whenever I hear that, I correct the statement by explaining that there is no such thing as a Bonner school. Rather, there are schools that have invited the Bonner Foundation to partner with them, over years and even decades. We are the supporting cast, and it has always been our pleasure and honor to work with these schools that are defined by their integrity and mission.

The second ingredient to our success has been our focus on student leadership and development, not merely as individuals but collectively as a team. There are many strong community engagement initiatives that do not have a service-based scholarship program like the Bonner Scholar Program or put a priority on student leadership. The fundamental principle that we have held firm from the very beginning and that is at the heart of our work is our *belief and expectation that students would be at the heart* of the operations, not merely as bystanders or on the sideline, but true partners in building the program and executing the vision.

Strong student roles have enabled the schools to develop comprehensive programs that are much larger than an institution could afford. Key staff roles were being played by students, rather than paid professional staff. Yet, this approach can only work if (1) a school is committed enough to have students in such positions of responsibility and (2) if the students are trained and supported to play the kind of role that other institutions would hire college graduates to perform. Indeed, the programs operate in this way.

Unlike many scholarships that merely affirm or even dote over their recipients, Bonner does anything but that. Yes, it is an honor to be a Bonner but as Stormy Gillespie said, "being a Bonner is not merely a duty but a fulfillment." We ask a great deal out of these students and when well coached and supported, they deliver. Support for student development and leadership is a key part of the success of the program model.

Yet, it was never just about the students. The program is about providing students a chance to be a part of someone else's lives and at the same time enriching their own. While it was always important that students had a good experience, that was not the end of the story. Just as important as his or her service work, the commitment of any Bonner Scholar or Leader is to engage "Everybody, everyday." In other words, a Bonner's primary role is to engage the campus, not just each other. We aspire to the vision of creating a culture of service where the work of the Bonners permeates every aspect of the campus life, including academic life and the curriculum.

The final principle that has led to our success to this point is that we have never claimed success. We have never been satisfied with what we have accomplished. As a network, we have invented, we have created, and we have achieved, but we have never arrived. If an important aim of our work is to create a healthy and lively democratic culture for our society and all that goes with it, then we still have a long way to go. We have been successful at different turns, but we have never declared it permanently.

To this day, we have committed to how to advance the work of campus–community engagement, what we need to do to be stronger, what we need to do to help the person who is hurting, and how we might displace despair with opportunity. When we launched the Bonner Program, most of the student activity was invested in tutoring and coaching, worthy activities to be sure. However, as we continued in our work, it became clear that the needs and the possibilities increased. As our expectations rose, it required that our imagination, standards, and accountability move along with it. Volunteering gave way to community service; community serve was replaced with service learning. Now, we seem to live in the language, the challenge, and the promise of civic engagement and deep service.

As part of this transition from simply volunteering to civically engaged students and faculty, we have attempted to engage the highest levels of critical thinking and resources, including in ways that address issues and problems. The foundation, under Bobby Hackett's leadership, led the charge for vision and practice around community-based research and other strategies to leverage the intellectual and institutional assets of our higher education institutions for sustained engagement in addressing the root causes of challenges facing our communities and fostering systemic change. Bobby's charge since the tenth anniversary of the Bonner Program was to "turn best practice into common practice." We have encouraged innovation and the Bonner community has responded and when excellence was obtained, it was shared and incorporated throughout the network. And, as a result, we have grown and changed. What was exemplary five or ten years ago, in many cases, is no longer cutting edge or even noteworthy.

Having recently celebrated our twentieth anniversary as a program, we are both humbled and inspired by what the next 20 years will bring. One thing we know for sure is that the next two decades will challenge us, our ideas, models, and assumptions. So while we enjoyed some successes and been connected with programs that are exemplary, we are not ready to stop here. There is still much to do and as long as there are people who are hurting and there is despair, we have a job to do. This book helps to share the highest levels of achievement and innovation that we have reached as a community of higher education institutions connected with and leveraging the Bonner Program to achieve their aims as educators and in service to the public. We celebrate the innovation, courage, and achievement. We will use it as a source of inspiration to continue to foster broader and deeper community engagement in higher education.

Preface

Ariane Hoy and Mathew Johnson

The Inspiration of a Place and a Walk

There is a special place in New Market, Tennessee, called the Highlander Research and Education Center. On the side of the building is a mural in many colors. It depicts Dr Martin Luther King, Jr, Caesar Chavez, and Rosa Parks and reads (in both English and Spanish): "without action, there is no knowledge"; "sin accion, no hay conocimiento." The place, founded in 1932 as the Highlander Folk School in Grundy County by educator Myles Horton and James Dombrowski, a minister, bears significance. Its legacy offers many lessons. Indeed, Dr King, Rosa Parks, and others to this day gathered at Highlander to be trained as organizers for movements and social change. This recognition—that the capacity for courage, strategy, planning, teaching, action, and leadership—can be *developed* is critical for education and community engagement.

As lifelong students, we both came to community engagement through a journey, the inspiration of family and mentors, the insight and wisdom shared with us not only by professors but by people in the community, and the vision of an education that puts knowledge into practice for the improvement of our communities, nation, and world. We look to practice as a fundamental part of knowledge creation. In "We Make the Road by Walking: Conversations on Education and Social Change," two remarkable educators, Myles Horton and Paulo Freire, talk about their notion of education, one that is framed by place, by action and reflection, by circles of people coming together to address and solve their own problems. It is in the spirit of these educators, and others like them that we are glad to share the pages of this volume, that we write. We recognize that we make the road by walking, and that our paths are deeply shaped by those who have come before us and, even more, by the students who walk them now and will continue to shape the future.

The community engagement *movement* in higher education, or some might say *field*, is at a critical moment. As the chapters throughout this volume make clear, scholars and practitioners reflect on both the achievements of this collective work and the obstacles that lie ahead. Whether it is harbinger reports like *A Crucible Moment: Civic Learning and Democracy's Future* or *Stewards of Place*, volumes like *The Engaged Campus* or *To Serve a Larger Purpose*, monographs such as *Civic Provocations*, or other works, what is clear is that civic work, its scholarship, and its practice and potential impact for higher education are strong, vital, meaningful, and significant. As we have worked on this volume, in tandem with an effort to bridge engaged learning and community engagement we call the Bonner High-Impact Initiative, we have facilitated strategic planning with nearly twenty colleges and universities seeking to forge community engagement that is deep, pervasive, integrated, and developmental. In an effort to also foster a national learning community among not only campuses involved but also key national partners, we have attended the conferences of and met with leaders from Association of American Colleges and Universities, the American Association of State Colleges and Universities, Bringing Theory to Practice, Campus Compact, the Council for Undergraduate Research, Imagining America, and the Center for Engaged Democracy, to name several. In every context, we observe not a plateau but the *rediscovery and imagining* of civic work, now connected with other vital questions such as its importance for student persistence and retention, usefulness for communities in measuring and improving their civic health, and *place* of community engagement (both philosophical and geographical) in affirming the importance and relevance of liberal arts education.

In this process, we have observed several trends that now shape our emerging and changing field. In fact, these trends tie with the themes to be explored in chapters in this volume.

1. *Assessment*: Beyond the growing body of discrete studies of service-learning, centers of community engagement and institutions of higher education now seek to document and measure student learning. Many institutions, as well as higher education associations, are involved in articulating learning outcomes, including for personal and social responsibility and civic engagement. There is a recognition that this work can and should be acknowledged as academically rigorous, and hence connected to the work of the curriculum. Assessment of student learning and finding what truly works is also part of the foundation community, aided now by new

technologies and the platforms—like e-portfolios and badges—that they afford.

2. *Engaged teaching and learning*: Research—whether reports by Liberal Education and America's Promise, high-impact practices (Kuh, 2008), or the Bonner Foundation's own study of outcomes of the four-year cocurricular program—clearly suggests that students' learning is enriched by involvement outside of the classroom. Engaged learning—whether first-year seminars tied to place, community-focused research projects, learning communities focused on issues of power and privilege, internships in international nonprofits, or capstones during which students forge new programs and curriculum for local organizations—yield better results, not only for students but also potentially for communities.

3. *Impact*: The maturing of our field also supports its examination and reorientation towards community impact and evidence-based program design. The Corporation for National and Community Service, which oversees AmeriCorps, signals this shift with its current articulation of service areas and metrics for community impact assessment. At the same time, higher education associations, nonprofit funders and foundations, also affirm that centers and institutions (as well as nonprofit organizations) must find ways to demonstrate their qualitative and quantitative results.

4. *Changing pedagogies*: As engaged pedagogies and high-impact practices have taken hold, and new technologies are transforming classroom practices and courses, so too is a reexamination of effective teaching and pedagogical practice taking place. It suggests what community engagement has long held true: *knowledge resides in other places*, like the community, and empowered students learn from engagement and application. Moreover, a changing professoriate—which is also younger, more racially and ethnically diverse, increasingly female, and not tenured—wants to be engaged. As Sturm, Eatman, Saltmarsh, and Bush (2012) articulate in *Full Participation: Building the Architecture for Diversity and Public Engagement in Higher Education*, civic engagement interrelates with the work to support diversity (both of students and faculty) and public scholarship. Eckel, Hill, and Green (1988, 2001) offer a model for how engagement must be made more pervasive, deep, and integrated with the core of the institution. Saltmarsh, Hartley, and Clayton (2009) suggest that institutions can reframe what has largely been technocratic community engagement into more democratic engagement, a practice that will require a rethinking of pedagogies to value the knowledge that is produced outside the bounds of traditional disciplines and courses.

5. *Consolidation and positioning*: Since the mid-1980s, which saw the founding of COOL and Campus Compact, public service has witnessed several iterations, suggested in part by the evolution of common language. What started as voluntary "community service" later became "service learning" with discrete ties to courses, then "community-based learning" with ties to projects (some of which might transcend a semester course through problem-based initiatives), then "academic community engagement" (as institutions forged new ways to link and transform curriculum). As this consolidation occurs, many institutions are beginning to bring together and revalue as rigorous in their own right the functions of academic yet noncurricular student engagement into single student engagement center. These include community engagement, undergraduate research, domestic diversity and global/international programs, career and professional development, and so on. This positioning of student engagement as a significant academic task values active knowledge creation outside the traditional classroom as much as the knowledge consumption inside it.

6. *Trusting and centering student leadership*: Moving to the next levels of community engagement relies inherently on drawing on what helped engagement and engaged learning reach the depth and breadth it has already achieved—the commitment, talent, interest, passion, and leadership of students. The growth of infrastructure on campus at times lost sight of the powerful roles that students played and continue to wield for community engagement. Today's students can and want to be engaged in new ways, both in place and online. Their higher levels of experience with community service in the K-12 levels suggest that they can and want to play more challenging roles—including those that connect to politics, advocacy, and activism; analysis of root causes; and working toward systemic solutions. The next phases of engagement again rely on students to play critical roles in leading the relationship building, networking, design, innovation, and direction of our work.

How This Book Is Organized

For the Bonner Foundation and Network, accepted wisdom and practice are the core aspects of our work in community engagement, which are mutually reinforcing: student development and learning, community partnerships and their impact, engaged teaching and learning, and campus culture and infrastructure. Hence, this book is organized into four parts, with these frameworks in mind. In a longer introduction, first, we share the important developmental frameworks that guide.

Part I: Students as Civic-Minded Professionals: An Approach for Student Development

The chapters in this section explore key aspects of student development and its interconnections with civic work. Saylor, Gruber, and Nix provide a review of psychological theory and research and its application to what practitioners of community-engaged learning know and do to support the developmental and psychological needs of emerging young adults. In addition, they integrate their perspectives as center director, program coordinator, and community partner to share examples of student leadership in multiple campus and community contexts, drawing on their work at Carson-Newman College. Cochrane and McNew Schill, drawing on the deep experience of Berea College's commitment to engagement and its Center for Excellence in Learning Through Service (CELTS), explore the lessons and challenges for supporting students' cascading leadership development and how to organize center and program leadership in ways that support students' development. Meisel describes the powerful role that exploration of faith and spiritual beliefs can play in grounding and guiding students' development, particularly in the context of community service and engagement.

Johnson, Levy, Cicetti, and Zinkiewicz provide an overview of the National Assessment of Service and Community Engagement (NASCE), an instrument developed to provide a more accurate picture of the depth and breadth of campus-wide student engagement in service and civic activity that address unmet human needs. Implemented on more than 30 campuses to date and with more than 15,000 student respondents, this assessment suggests that student engagement is by no means plateauing. In fact, the data suggest that 75 percent of community engagement is being performed by roughly 10 percent of students. Far from being at a ceiling, this developmental approach to students' work in community engagement suggests that there is much that can be done to deepen and expand this work. This and other research suggest that as educators (and students), we can intentionally craft the kinds of experiences, in and out of the classroom, that shape graduates who are meaningfully involved in strengthening their communities, and our nation and world.

Part II: Developmental, Engaged, and Educational Partnerships

The chapters that follow explore how partnerships themselves can also grow along a developmental framework, presented in the Foreword. In particular, they focus on how institutions can create sustained reciprocal campus–community partnerships through an infrastructure that links service through curricular and cocurricular life of the college in a sustainable and strategic way. Roncolato discusses the essential characteristics of high-functioning, community-centered partnerships. Stanley focuses on the importance of place, the critical pedagogical approach necessary to embracing partners as coeducators in the Freirian tradition, and the challenges of this work. Hackett and Donohue explore innovative partnerships that involve public policy and the potential of these partnerships for community change. Finally, Behrend and Starr, drawing on an international immersion, contemplate what higher-level international partnerships might look like and how students play a vital leadership role in them.

Part III: Faculty: Exploring New Epistemologies for Academic Community Engagement

The chapters in this section explore innovative strategies for engaging faculty in public scholarship, civically focused projects, and in rethinking teaching and learning in light of engagement. Schadewald and Aguilar-San Juan describe a successful model for faculty development that they have used at Macalester College. Kane, Nigro, Alcorn, and Lasagna focus on the models for creating disciplinary and interdisciplinary pathways that connect community and coursework. They draw on examples from Bates College. Blissman explores the motivations and obstacles for faculty to move into community-engaged teaching and scholarship, drawing on the metaphor of gardening. She shares some of the important literature and current scholarship about faculty development, including the Publicly Engaged Scholar research by Timothy Eatman of Syracuse University and Imagining America. McGowan and Siracusa explore an approach that one institution, Rhodes Colleges, took to internally assess and transform its academic community engagement, applying a reading of Ernest Boyer's conception of scholarship.

Part IV: Staff and Centers: Integrating the Work of Institutions

The chapters in this section explore the structure, roles, and importance of campus centers for the coordination of community engagement. Welch and Saltmarsh draw on a survey and analysis of over 100 successful applications for the Carnegie Foundation for the Advancement of Teaching elective Community Engagement Classification. Using these data, they present an overview of critical components and infrastructure that may guide campus administrators and center directors as they establish and continue to advance community engagement. Ellis and Hart present a case study, focused on the 17-year history of the development of the campus-wide center at Washburn

University, drawing lessons from this evolution. In particular, while Welsh and Saltmarsh note that more study is needed to understand the role of student leadership in a center's growth, Ellis and Washburn chronicle ways that student leadership has been and is critical to institutionalizing and augmenting community engagement. Kiesa and Hoy share lessons from the Bonner Network's experimentation with social media platforms as tools for recruiting and engaging students, building partner capacity and programs, and increasing coordination on and off campus. In particular, they share strategies for the application of Facebook, videos, and wikis for program management as well as emerging potential for deeper student learning. Finally, Hoy and Johnson describe how long-range (three to five year) strategic planning can enable centers to craft strategies to make community engagement deep, pervasive, integrated, and developmental. Besides supporting program quality, clarifying structure and roles, connecting civic work to the institution's priorities, garnering visibility, and helping secure financial and human resources, planning helps centers address common challenges—such as academic linkages, faculty engagement, coordination, consolidation, and truly integrating with the current and future needs of surrounding communities (and the institution).

Finally, an introduction offers the integrative developmental frameworks upon which much of the work for student development, community partnerships, faculty engagement, and campus infrastructure relies. Then, in conclusion, we share what we believe can help shape the future of community engagement in higher education, the intentional design and linking of engaged learning and community engagement through what is emerging as high-impact community engagement practices.

Part V: Critical Insights and Reflection

In Part V, three outstanding educators and practitioners in the field—Dan Butin, Abby Kiesa, and Tania D. Mitchell—offer their reflections on the chapters in this volume. Each of these authors provide insights and probe at what may be the next frontiers or barriers to consider to deepen civic engagement in higher education. Butin highlights the tensions inherent in this work and the challenges for moving individual illustrations of best practice to truly transform institutions and pedagogies. Kiesa examines the issue of political engagement, an area that we in the field often aim to but struggle to fully integrate and build not only into students' developmental experiences but into the fabric of our institutions' programs. Mitchell looks to the potential for community engagement to address power as well as social justice. All three, we believe, offer important themes and critiques that must be addressed to move civic engagement forward.

Part VI: Conclusion

Finally, in conclusion, we share with you the origins of our network's current work to move engagement forward by intentionally linking engaged learning and high-impact practices with well-designed and intentional high-impact community engagement. We call this the Bonner High-Impact Initiative. While just at the beginning, we believe that the strategies of transforming curriculum, approaches to engagement, and institutional structures and practices can be informed by the thoughtful, steady work of teams of community partners, faculty, students, and administrators working together. We share briefly the seeds of our thinking about high-impact community engagement and how it can be a powerful vehicle for helping our institutions to achieve their missions and maintain their relevancy in cultivating and contributing as stewards of place, civic learning, and agents of change.

References

Butin, Dan, and Scott Seider. *The Engaged Campus: Certificates, Minors, and Majors as the New Community Engagement.* New York, NY: Palgrave Macmillan, 2012.

Eckel, Peter, Barbara Hill, and Madeleine Green. *On Change: En Route to Transformation.* Washington, DC: American Council on Education, 1988.

Eckel, Peter, Madeleine F. Green, and Barbara Hill. *On Change V: Riding the Waves of Change: Insights from Transforming Institutions.* Vol. 5. Washington, DC: American Council on Education, 2001.

Harward, Donald. *Civic Provocations.* Washington, DC: Bringing Theory to Practice, 2012.

Horton, Myles, and Paulo Freire. *We Make the Road by Walking: Conversations on Education and Social Change.* Philadelphia, PA: Temple University Press, 1990.

Hoy, Ariane, and Wayne Meisel. *Civic engagement at the center: Building democracy through integrated cocurricular and curricular experiences.* Washington, DC: Association of American Colleges and Universities, 2008.

Sturm, S., T. Eatman, J. Saltmarsh, and A. Bush. "Full participation: building the architecture for diversity and public engagement in higher education [White paper]. New York: Columbia University Law School." Center for Institutional and Social Change (2011).

Saltmarsh, John; Hartley, Matthew; and Clayton, Patti, "Democratic Engagement White Paper" (2009). Boston, MA: *New England Resource Center for Higher Education Publications.* Paper 45. http://scholarworks.umb.edu/nerche_pubs/45

The National Task Force on Civic Learning and Democratic Engagement. *A Crucible Moment: Civic Learning and Democracy's Future.* Washington, DC, Association of American Colleges & Universities, 2012.

INTRODUCTION

Deep, Pervasive, and Integrated: Developmental Frameworks for Students, Partnerships, Faculty Engagement, and Centers

Ariane Hoy and Mathew Johnson

Introduction

The chapters in this book explore how a multitude of colleges and universities engage their students, staff, faculty, and institutions more broadly in serving a larger purpose: partnerships with places, people, and organizations in communities nearby, and sometimes far away. The institutions represented—Allegheny College, Bates College, Berea College, Carson-Newman College, Emory & Henry College, Macalester College, Oberlin College, Rhodes College, Saint Mary's College of California, Siena College, The College of New Jersey, University of Richmond, and Washburn University—are just a handful that are connected to Bonner Foundation and our national network. Moreover, our work benefits and relies on the wisdom and partnerships of many organizations, local and national. Some that we credit for helping to inform this volume include the Association of American Colleges and Universities, the American Association of State Colleges and Universities, CIRCLE (the Center for Information and Research on Civic Learning and Engagement), Imagining America, Jefferson County Juvenile Court, Peacework, the New England Resource Center for Higher Education (NERCHE), and the Center for Engaged Democracy. It is a commitment to sustained, developmental partnerships—between campuses and communities, campuses themselves, and even national organizations—that helps us deepen our work. In this foreword, we share some of the critical frameworks that guide and integrate the work of engaging students, partners, faculty and staff, and centers. These also tie to the parts of this volume.

Part I: Students as Civic-Minded Professionals: An Approach for Student Development

Engaged Learning

Well-documented benefits of college attendance include knowledge (especially in one's major), autonomy, social maturation, personal competence, verbal and quantitative skills, cognitive complexity, and religious views, as well as decreases in prejudice, political naiveté, and dogmatism (Kuh, 1995) (Figure I.1). Building on the *involvement principle* first articulated in 1995, Kuh and others expanded a research agenda using the National Survey of Student Engagement (NSSE). Among the insights emanating from that research are two key lessons for community engagement in higher education. First, findings make clear that institutions can and should intentionally craft students' learning experiences, including through understanding and incorporating sociological and environmental dimensions like mission, culture, and ethos. These intentionally crafted experiences manifest in particular parts of the curriculum coined "high impact practices."

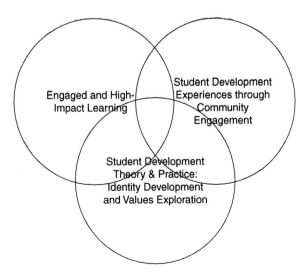

Figure I.1   Students.

Second, NSSE researchers have found that student learning is significantly positively impacted by educational experiences that happen outside of the classroom. Notably, (1) students develop practical competence from leadership responsibilities; (2) students clarify vocational goals; and (3) students increase abilities in interpersonal competence, humanitarianism, and cognitive complexity (Kuh, 1995). This second insight confirms two decades of research that clearly demonstrates the power of community engagement as a significant educational experience.

Related publications, such as those through the Association of American Colleges and Universities (Kuh, 2008; Brownell & Swaner, 2010), have become critical guides as institutions today seek to reform their curricula, intentionally build an ethos for learning and student success, and promote persistence and graduation—especially among students of color, low income, and first generation. This intentional engaged learning is now at the core of many institutions' efforts to craft developmental, integrated experiences and focus on *high-impact practices* like first-year experiences, intensive writing, service learning, project-based learning, internships, learning communities, immersions in US and global diversity contexts, undergraduate research, and capstones. More recent work suggests that "the benefits are especially significant for students who start farther behind. But often, these students are not the ones actually participating in the high-impact practices" (Kuh, 2008, 5). As higher education rethinks the importance of cocurricular academic learning, and in particular the corollary high-impact practices outside the classroom, one place to look for guidance can be the work of the Bonner Foundation and network, as we work to articulate high-impact community engagement practices.

Engaged Practice

The Bonner Foundation began the work of discovering, refining, and spreading high-impact community engagement practices in partnership with colleges and universities in 1990; Berea College was the first to begin the program. Foundation leaders drew as much on lived experience in community service and engagement as on developmental theory. Wayne Meisel and Bobby Hackett, who founded Campus Outreach Opportunity League (COOL) in 1985 as a platform for college student voice and leadership for community engagement, always championed students' involvement and leadership. COOL's early publications included "Building a Movement" and "On Your Mark, Go, Get Set" reflecting a commitment to experiential learning.

From its inception, the Bonner Scholars Program rested on a developmental model describing the aspiration and potential of an intentional educational experience that students could, by design, have throughout a four-year undergraduate experience. This student developmental model is at the core of the program's vision, required by all programs in its implementation, and borne out by the Bonner Student Impact Survey for its effectiveness. The model provides a backbone that articulates learning and leadership trajectories for undergraduate students who are involved in intensive, multiyear civic education and engagement experience, at each stage articulating the skills, knowledge areas, and roles that students assume in their cohorts, community-based positions, peer leadership roles, and in the classroom.

Student Developmental Model

The model was tested and refined by *practice*, shaped by the lived experience of Bonner Programs at campuses across the country that strove to support the engagement and success of the students (now numbering more than 6,000 as alumni)—generally low-income, first-generation, and often students of color—that committed their years to participate. In a 1996 paper, "The Bonner Scholars Program: A Four Year Community Service Scholarship Program," Wayne Meisel captured a version of the model, at that time drawing on the five-year experience of 22 campuses running the program.

Meisel outlined the Foundation's vision for how the Bonner Scholars Program could operate as a four year program to transform the lives of individual students, beginning with preparation, followed by action, reflection, discussion, and finally spirally again to renewed action. Mirroring developmental theories and approaches (such as Kolb, 1984), this process could be integrated into an intentional four year program corresponding to the academic life-cycle. Hence, the four E's were named as follows: Freshman Year—Exploration; Sophomore Year—Excellence; Junior Year—Example; Senior Year—Expertise (Meisel, 1996).

This structured, intentional, scaffolded model aligns well with the emerging research about engaged learning. Over 23 years, campuses have shaped the model, refining it through a process of moving "best practice to common practice." For instance, weekly cohort-based meetings were created and used by programs at Davidson and Emory & Henry College; later, based on a recognition of the power of cohort-based learning communities, this became a standard practice for programmatic excellence. The Foundation formalized the model through collaboration with the original campuses running Bonner Scholars Programs. Utilizing focus groups with students, community partners, staff, and faculty, campuses that were operating a four-year developmental program articulated and refined learning outcomes, skills, and (later) knowledge areas that students needed to successfully engage in increasingly complex community-oriented problem solving. Table I.1 captures that progression.

Table I.1 The Bonner Student Developmental Model

Level	Skills and actions	Values	Knowledge	Institutional practices
Expectation: previous service experiences	Interest/ethic for service and community	Student engages in increasingly complex understanding of and experience with *Bonner Common Commitments:* community building; civic engagement; diversity; international perspective; spiritual exploration; and social justice		Orientation
Exploration: intentional immersions into service	Time management, active listening, communication, goal setting, reflection		Place (place-based learning)	First-year experience; service-learning
Experience: commitment to place, issue, and partner/community	Balance budgeting, teamwork, conflict resolution, planning		Issue-based learning (i.e., literacy, poverty)	Learning communities; diversity; core curriculum; writing intensive experiences
Example: leadership roles for partner/community and program	Delegation, event planning, peer management, fundraising, project management		Poverty (i.e., economic development, analysis)	Undergraduate research; writing intensive experiences; diversity and global learning; deliberative democracy
Excellence: integrated application of experience and learning	Public education, public speaking, marketing, networking, research, and evaluation		Politics and civic action (i.e., voting, policy analysis)	Capstones

During each semester, students typically participate in regular, structured training, education, and reflection, often occurring weekly or bimonthly. The settings can vary, including within cohorts (i.e., first- or third-year students), community partner sites (i.e., the team that works at the Boys & Girls' Club), and program-wide (often with 40–80 students).

Many cocurricular aspects—such as roles within service and related skills and actions—stem from the types of experiences that engagement of students with the staff and clients (i.e., children, youth, families, etc.) at community partner sites rely on for effectiveness. Because Bonner students will work with these sites for nearly 300 or more hours each school year (eight to ten hours per week during all terms) and often full time in summer, students have the opportunity to truly develop professional, personal, and leadership skills. In the early 2000s, another Fund for the Improvement of Post-Secondary Education (FIPSE) grant focused the Foundation and many participating colleges on articulating a model for a civic engagement minor, certificate, or major. This resulted in the architecture of an academic program, including coursework in place-based learning, politics, economics, and other disciplines. Programs and faculty sought to deepen students' academic connections, scaffolding them across semesters. This academic infrastructure has deepened the learning of highly engaged students (i.e., Bonners), exposing them to needed civic skills and knowledge like systems and critical thinking, writing, and community development. Students find opportunities for students to integrate participatory civic learning and more traditional classroom learning.

Structured reflection opportunities magnify the learning that students are doing in informal settings (i.e., in the van on the way back from service or at evening talks during an overnight service trip that happens every year). Results from the Bonner Student Impact Survey and longitudinal Alumni Survey suggest that frequent, structured education and reflection magnify the impact of the program and amplify unstructured reflection. In 2009, Keen and Hall (2009) documented key findings including: (1) that students acquire key skills and knowledge areas, bolstered through intentional training; (2) that four years in the program make a difference, especially for outcomes such as respect for diversity and commitment to social justice; and that (3) financial support (for these low-income students) does not diminish outcomes. In 2011, Richard, Keen, Hatcher, Beane, and Pease presented findings from the 2010 Alumni Survey at the International Association for Research on Service Learning and Civic Engagement. Drawing on Hatcher's Civic Professionalism scale, these researchers suggest a powerful set of ingredients—service, courses, reflection, dialogue, and advising—that leads to results and documents how structured reflection magnifies unstructured reflection for students involved in civic learning. Bonner graduates vote at significantly higher rates than peers nationally (49.2% vs 26.3%). All of them stay engaged civically. They show the characteristics of civic-minded professionals and civic-minded graduates, defined as social trustees of knowledge with a commitment and capacity to work with others in a democratic way to achieve public goods (Sullivan 1995, 2005; Hatcher, 2008; Bringle & Hatcher, 2009). A civic-minded graduate:

> has completed a course of study (e.g., a bachelor's degree), and has the capacity and desire to work with others to achieve the common good. "Civic-mindedness" refers to a person's inclination or disposition to be knowledgeable of and involved in the community, and to have a commitment to act upon a sense of responsibility as a member of that community. (Steinberg, Hatcher, & Bringle, 2011, p. 20)

Moreover, they are more likely to be involved in other civic actions, such as joining organizations in support of a cause, boycotting or buycotting a product because of company values, contacting a public official, or working for a campaign. A 2010 Alumni Survey suggested that one-third work for non-profits, one-third for government, and the remaining in for-profit (25%) or self-directed careers (Arum and Roksa, 2010).

Part II: Developmental, Engaged, and Educational Partnerships

Stewards of Place

There are three provocative trends happening in the United States that those of us who care about the health and welfare of our nation and world must address (Figure I.2).

Sectoral Growth and US Economic Health

We continue to experience growing enrollment in higher education. As Duderstadt notes (2000), since 1930, while the American population has only doubled, higher education enrollment has increased tenfold. The link of economic growth and prosperity to the products of higher education, particularly research, has also fueled diversification. Arguably, the research university is a "cornerstone of our national effort to sustain American leadership in science and technology, thereby underpinning both our economic prosperity and military security" (Duderstadt, 2000). Today, according to

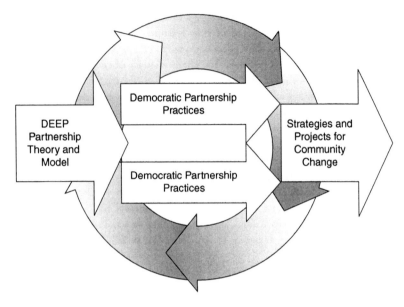

Figure I.2 Partnerships.

the *Chronicle of Higher Education*, there are roughly 4,096 colleges and universities in the United States.

This decade we have experienced dramatic economic changes, including a collapse of financial and housing markets, worldwide recession, and the emergence of new technologies that challenge old economic and social relations. Income inequality is a troubling trend. Astonishingly, as a report in the *Huffington Post* noted, in 2011 the gap between the richest and poorest residents of 20 states increased the year before, while remaining about the same for the remaining 30, according to newly released data from the US Census Bureau (Bradford, 2011). Politicians and business leaders alike have made clear that expanding higher education to prepare workers and more intentionally expand the role of higher education to tackle these challenges directly is a priority for moving the country forward, as it has been in prior decades.

Sectoral Transformation
Even as higher education is called on to be a significant part of the solution, there are serious questions about higher education's effectiveness as it is currently structured. Unemployment rates among college graduates has increased, contributing to dwindling public confidence in higher education. Moreover, public documents like the 2006 Spellings Commission and

Academically Adrift point to disturbing news about the success of higher education in promoting student learning. Assumptions about how students learn best are beginning to crumble, especially with the growth of assessment and so-called disruptive technologies and innovation (Christensen and Eyring, 2011). The Documenting Effective Educational Practice (DEEP) study found that what matters to student learning is a lived mission, a focus on teaching and learning, pathways for success, and engagement, including with peers, faculty, and communities (Laird et al., 2005). Again, it is suggested that these practices are especially vital for underrepresented populations, such as first-generation students and students of color, also the groups where enrollment is most projected to grow in coming decades.

A New Mission

In 2002, the American Association of State Colleges and Universities published an important report entitled *Stepping Forward as Stewards of Place: A Guide for Leading Public Engagement at State Colleges and Universities.* This "strategic, ground level guide for presidents and chancellors and other campus leadership that offers a working definition of public engagement, provides exemplars of campus-wide commitment to engagement initiatives, and proposes concrete actions for institutions, public policymakers, and the association to promote an even fuller commitment to the concept of engagement" (Votruba et al., 2002, foreword). Defining public engagement with four key attributes—*place-related, interactive, mutually beneficial, and integrated*, the report notes that a "publicly engaged institution is fully committed to direct, two-way interaction with communities and other external constituencies through the development, exchange, and application of knowledge, information, and expertise for mutual benefit." Examples include applied research to solve a problem; technical assistance by faculty and students to address or understand a problem; demonstration or service-learning projects that model or apply best practices; impact assessment designed to measure the effectives of programs and services; policy analysis that is directed at framing policy approaches; seminars, lectures, and essays that discuss and disseminate information of public concern; involvement of faculty and administrators in community-oriented initiatives; and lifelong learning programs designed to expand access to educational opportunities and educate communities about pressing societal challenges (AASCU Task Force, 2002). This conception, while targeted at state institutions, is transcendent to all institutional types and aptly describes the working definitions of community engagement for the Bonner Foundation and network of programs, one that is made more possible because of an *intensive, multi-year, and developmental approach* for students, staff and faculty, and institutions.

Partnerships That Are Deep

Responding to the new economic and social challenges in the broader society, and addressing these calls to be more locally invested and engaged requires higher education institutions to build partnerships. Partnership is a loaded and challenging term in this work. Often constructed as short-term, course-driven, or project-based, the primary emphasis of campus–community partnerships is often in reality student learning. In this way, "partnership" is loaded with often unspoken and unpacked power relations, and presuppositions about reciprocity, common purpose, and common direction, or lack thereof. The power of the academy—to claim the direction of education, the way to educate students, and be a guarantor of the meaning and quality of that education—may be the main obstacle to the most profound and effective learning experiences our students can have in partnership with communities and community partners. It may also be the most challenging obstacle to partnerships that truly benefit the community. At the core of many common part-nership challenges—communication; clarity of objectives, authority, and responsibility; lack of resources; lack of time, willingness, or capacity to expand, grow, or deepen the partnership; and the like—is the often unexamined power dynamic between the academy and the community. Only when partnerships are self-conscious about this power dynamic can the questions about deeper student *and* community impact be adequately considered.

In the "Democratic Engagement White Paper," Saltmarsh, Hartley, and Clayton propose an aspirational model of democratic community engagement. This model is characterized by reciprocity, an asset-based approach, and academic work done with the public and community con-stituency as cocreators of knowledge and therefore solutions to commu-nity challenges. Such initiatives—whether a community-based research project, a public education forum, or public policy research to understand the most promising solutions to a neighborhood issue—bring to bear the knowledge of involved stakeholders, including community residents, nonprofit partners, students, and faculty. These efforts can involve the creation of community change efforts. An example of this is happening in the New Jersey Bonner network, involving a consortia of institutions and partners. With the help of students and full-time AmeriCorps and VISTA members, meetings of multi-partner groups that focus on solv-ing a problem, such as hunger, childhood obesity, or high school tru-ancy, become part of the institution's ongoing community engagement work. This developmental and system-oriented approach then leads to new possibilities for the developmental, multiyear work of students, staff, faculty, and the institution.

An emphasis on sustained, multiyear partnerships has always been a core feature of the approach to community engagement, supported in practice by the fact that a student can return to the same partner and does, often up to four years. Multiyear placements came early as a core principle for the Foundation. The development of students requires committed long-term, intensive service immersion that spans more than a year. In these longer-term settings, students and partners can explore mutual relationships and discover new ways that student might serve at higher and higher levels of responsibility. In this way, a student who begins as a tutor can, over the course of years, grow to become a program manager, evaluator, or advocate working with the school's teachers, principal, or board of the organization to expand programs, raise funds, or engage parents, or even articulate policies that might address root causes.

Consolidation of partnership best practices took place in 2008. Drawing on the Bonner developmental model, Siena College articulated DEEP—developmental, engaged, educational partnerships—which are focused around sustainability, strategy, infrastructure, and a concerted effort to link to the academic life of the college. The approach applies the same philosophies that the Bonner model utilizes with students and campus centers to the work with nonprofit organizations, schools, and governmental agencies. The College built on the network's wisdom with regard to what makes a strong and impactful partnership, but was less hindered by long-standing but transactional (i.e., event based) partnerships that some programs find themselves wrestling to overcome. Another example of the "from best practice to common practice" philosophy, this notion of "deep partnerships" is now being replicated throughout the Bonner Network, providing a framework for campus center staff to enrich long-range planning with partners, articulate a set of aspirations for long-term engagement that include opportunities for students' highest levels of work, and integrate projects that involve research, policy, and capacity building.

As we collectively looked to understand what might build the capacity of students, partners, and centers, we had discovered that *team-based structures and placements* of students increased both student and partner impact. This "Coalition of Projects" approach (see Cochrane and Schill's chapter in this volume) led to more sustainability. *Site-based trainings*, education provided by the agency or in collaboration with the organization about site-specific issues and skills (such as classroom management), also came into focus as a good expectation of partnerships. Some Bonner

Programs organized students in *site-based teams* in a single organization. Others organized students across sites into issue-focused teams. Whatever the manifestation, the team-based approach knits students (and often faculty and staff advisers) together in a way that magnifies their learning and the impact they have on the issue or agency. Gradually, programs throughout the network have experimented with and offer new understanding of practices for partnership that involve ongoing, value-added, collective activities. Partner meetings offer training, facilitate the discussion of community issues, and deal with urgent resource needs. This "network administration" role moves beyond the more typical community advisory function often reserved for community partners in which they are expected to offer minor input and validate institutional plans. Here, partner agencies are respected as *colleagues* and have access to institutional resources, often joining formal advisory boards and other decision-making bodies.

A Developmental Framework for Partnerships

In November 2010, at the annual fall meeting of Bonner Program administrators from across the 70-plus-institution network, we facilitated a meeting-wide session to tease out stages of partnership development analogous to the student developmental model. Drawing on multiple interactions with campuses and programs over many years, we had begun observing a consistent typology, which was then refined by the network. *Exploratory Partnership* are partnerships in the initial stages of development, with maybe a year of development and a project or relationship initiated between the school and the partner entity. *Emerging Partnerships* are those that have moved into a second iteration of the initial project or relationship and are expanding the scope of the project or relationship. *Established Partnerships* are those that have existed for a few years, are expanding beyond initial collaborations, and have been integrated into the regular operations of the center and its programs. Finally, *Exemplary Partnerships* are those that reflect joint long-term strategic planning between the school and the partners and included multiple partnership collaborations.

Meeting participants cycled through a series of "stations" to generate definitions, practices, and processes at each stage, also addressing practices needed to move a partnership from one level to the next. Table I.2 is a synthesis of the results from more than 150 participants.

While the framework may not be surprising, putting it into practice takes intentionality and focus. When a program, center, and institution adopt and spread a deep approach to campus–community partnerships, it positions the

Table I.2 The Bonner Partner Developmental Model

Exploratory partnerships	Emerging partnerships	Engaged partnerships	Exemplary partnerships
Understand the (developmental) purpose of and have made a three-year commitment to work with the program.	All of the qualities of Exploratory Partners plus:	All of the qualities of Emerging Partners plus:	All of the qualities of Engaged Partners plus:
Have a few first-year Bonner placements and/or an academic community engagement project tied to the center.	A three-year partnership plan that clearly indicates the goals, activities, and evaluation mechanisms for the partnership.	A schedule of ongoing evaluation and semiannual revision of the three-year partnership plan.	Moved from a three-year plan to an ongoing long-term plan.
Have provided all requested documentation/information including mission, program descriptions, nonprofit certification, organizational chart.	The agency has a team (at least three students) with developmentally distinct roles and position descriptions.	The agency has a team (at least three students) with clear student site/issue team leadership roles, regular meetings, and site-specific trainings	An annual report related to the ongoing evaluation of the plan.
Agency and campus have identified a primary point of contact with authority who will manage the relationship.	The center has begun building academic community engagement project opportunities linked to the Bonner team, faculty, or other campus constituencies (i.e., Greek Life, club).	The center has inventoried academic community engagement projects and initiated and supported implementation of at least one ongoing project that involves the Bonner team, a faculty member, and non-Bonner students.	Student team leaders and upper-class students play important roles in academic community engagement projects as well as agency decision making and management (i.e., board presentations, program coordination).
Center staff can clearly articulate the overlaps between the strategic goals of the university and the agency.	Agency point of contact has begun participating in on-campus activities (i.e., training) and center committee work.	Agency point of contact participates in on-campus activities (i.e., training) and identifies own agency as part of the center.	The center provides support and coordination for academic community engagement projects each semester.
Training done by the center for placements (students) and partners	Training is shared by center and agency for students; center provides training/capacity-building opportunities from campus	Training is provided by a partner for students; agency contributes training for center/campus (coeducator)	Agency point of contact and center staff identify and carry out networking opportunities that will benefit their issue work (i.e., policy and advocacy); shared issue-based capacity-building trainings.
			Connected to at least one high-impact practice

institution and its assets as part of that ecosystem of knowledge production and public problem solving that characterizes the approach to democratic community engagement. Moreover, while there may be discrete projects or pockets of civic engagement that are more technocratic occurring between the campus and community, it allows for the development and application of an aspirational vision and practice that is indeed lived out by those who are part of the institution and community.

Part III: Faculty: Exploring New Epistemologies for Academic Community Engagement

The Landscape for Academic Community Engagement

The public mission of higher education has always been present for American colleges and universities (Figure I.3). Since the founding of Harvard College in 1636 and the early Colonial Colleges, often linked to religious denominations, a key mission was to educate citizens for leadership in communities and our democracy. Producing knowledge for the benefit of society has been and remains a primary aim of higher education, present in most mission statements. Public policy, analysis, and funding—such as the 1865 Morrill Land-Grant Act, the 1972 Higher Education Opportunity Act, and the 2006 Spellings Commission Report—have supported and heralded the importance of engagement, whether to ensure a robust economy and democracy or prepare citizens for employment and civic life. The commissioning of a Task Force by the Department of Education that resulted in the 2012 publication of *A Crucible Moment: College Learning and Democracy's Future* is an example of the most recent charge for higher education. Drawing on the input of faculty members, campus administrators, national education leaders, and policy makers, *A Crucible Moment* issues a call to action to higher education to restore education for democratic engagement, promoting civic ethos, civic literacy, civic inquiry, and civic action on campuses. The report documents a decline in students' assessment of whether their campus valued and promoted contributing to the larger community between freshmen and seniors, with only 34.3 percent of seniors agreeing that their campus actively promoted awareness of global social, political, and economic issues (National Task Force, 2012, 5). Yet, civic focus may indeed be part of the solution. David Scobey, arguing that higher education is at a "Copernican Moment," points to the achievements of the academic civic engagement movement and experiments with publicly engaged teaching as suggestions for how higher education could flourish, should we renew a commitment to our civic purposes (Scobey, 2012).

As this volume explores, the work of higher education community engagement has truly ripened over the past 30 years. Supporting administrator and

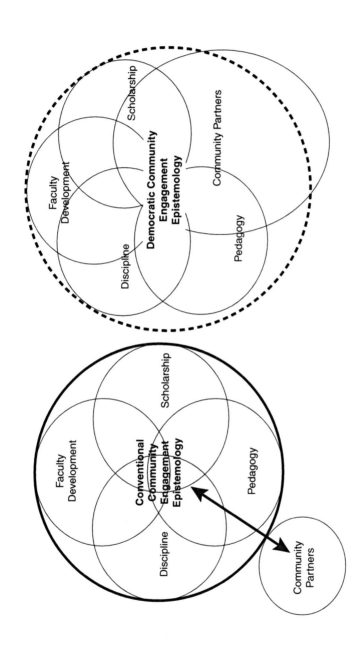

Figure I.3 Faculty development and epistemology.

faculty engagement has long been a focus of the Bonner network, but we are not alone. Campus Compact, which started in 1985 as a pact of seven college presidents, has grown into a national coalition of almost 1,200 college and university presidents and more than 34 state affiliates—representing some 6 million students—committed to fulfilling the civic purposes of higher education. Its 2008 survey of 1,190 campuses found that 94 percent have at least one designated office or center to coordinate community engagement (Campus Compact, 2008). Higher education associations including the American Association of Community Colleges, American Association of State Colleges and Universities, Association of American Colleges and Universities, Council of Independent Colleges, and Council for Undergraduate Research have initiatives dedicated to enhancing civic and personal responsibility and engagement. Even accrediting bodies emphasize a focus. The elective Carnegie Classification for Community Engagement, started in 2006, in 2013 will emphasize depth, pervasiveness, and integration. For the Bonner Program, this growth is also true. What started based on the leadership of a few college presidents from institutions like Berea and Morehouse now involves more than 70 institutions of higher education, private and public, small and large. More than 6,000 students have graduated from the program. Much of the past decades' focus has been building infrastructure for successful, sustained campus–community partnerships. At the core of engagement is a need to bring together individuals (students, faculty, administrators, community partners, and those they serve) to design and carry out projects that achieve outcomes for diverse constituents: (1) enhancing students' learning and application of learning; (2) helping faculty members achieve their teaching aims and convey content; (3) supporting a positive relationship between the institution and its surrounding communities; and (4) achieving a benefit or impact for a community agency or constituent group.

Addressing Perennial Challenges to Faculty Engagement

Today, deepening faculty and institutional engagement in communities must address common barriers: departmental and program silos; risks to faculty member rewards and tenure; and episodic connections with community partners. Unfortunately, some of the institutionalization has resided in traditional boundaries, making it difficult for faculty members to collaborate across departments unless supported by distinct interdisciplinary programs. Another prevalent challenge is the nature of the academic calendar, which often conflicts with the needs of community partners and constituents, which run year round. The 10-week quarter or 15-week semester is often not sufficient for more complex research projects and program implementation. Faculty members, partners, and students often complain that the term ends just when those involved feel more prepared to do effective work.

From the point of view of faculty, effective academic community engagement hence must address these dimensions:

Faculty development: Developing a strong, mutually beneficial partnership with a community agency, school, or constituency takes work. Faculty members must be concerned about how the project fits in with their course or learning objectives. Community partners must be concerned about the nature of the students' or faculty members' work itself, whether it includes direct service, research, or assessment. Legal concerns require that details like Institutional Review Boards (IRBs) be executed, and logistical details like transportation or scheduling requires extra time and attention that may be beyond what a faculty member can give. Here, staff and student leaders play a variety of roles, from knowing the information and research needs of partners to matching them with faculty. Best practices in faculty development (some of which are addressed by Schadewald and Aguilar-San Juan) mirror best practices for student development: cohorts, peer exchange, a dialectical process of learning and doing, reflection, and dialogue.

Pedagogy and teaching methodologies: A key concern for faculty members is pedagogy, defined as the science and art of education. Community engagement and community-based learning has the power and potential to redefine pedagogy. In 1983, Lynton proposed that pedagogy should be rethought: "We must, in a conscious way, develop a much more symbiotic interaction with the world around us. This will require a two-way flow of communication with a wide variety of constituencies, leading to a sharing of responsibility for decisions in many areas which to date we have solely considered our own domain" (Lynton, 1983). This book attempts to highlight some of the ways that pedagogy is changing through community engagement, partnering faculty members with community partners as co-educators and valuing the knowledge produced in both institutional and community contexts.

Discipline: Faculty members generally must connect their approach to the accepted frameworks of their discipline. Each discipline incorporates types of knowledge, expertise, skills, people, projects, communities, problems, challenges, studies, inquiry, approaches, and research areas that are associated with its academic areas of study or areas of professional practice. One achievement of the field has been the development of clear connections between disciplines and community-based learning.

For example, between 1997 and 2005, the American Association of Higher Education published an extensive *Series on Service-Learning in the Disciplines*, a multivolume collection of exemplary practices of service-learning in specific disciplines, such as history, Spanish, Biology, and the like, which serve as guides for faculty. Written by scholars in the discipline and supported by research, course models, annotated bibliographies, and program descriptions, each volume includes theoretical and pedagogical essays.

In the volume *The Engaged Campus*, Butin and Seider make a powerful case for the achievements of service-learning and an important critique: that to mature and move forward, more work must be done to understand community engagement as a discipline itself, including key tenets, readings, and practices. Whether service-learning or community engagement can or should be a discipline in the traditional sense is a contentious debate, as some may argue that a core aim of this work is to rethink discipline and to break down silos. Regardless, the chapters in this volume offer a variety of pathways for integrating community engagement more centrally with curriculum.

Scholarship: For faculty to engage in this work, scholarship must be conceived of more broadly. Beyond peer-reviewed scholarship in disciplinary journals, for example, public scholarship can include research projects for partners, community-wide assessments, civic health index studies, and other forms. This is a call echoed loudly in the field. For example, the catalyst paper "Full Participation: Building the Architecture for Diversity and Public Engagement in Higher Education" by Susan Sturm, Tim Eatman, John Saltmarsh, and Adam Bush points clearly to the interconnection and importance of community engagement with a commitment to access and diversity within all levels of the institution. The failure to support community-engaged scholarship as a valued expression of knowledge production is a barrier to the successful integration of faculty members who successfully teach through engaged learning.

As we propose throughout this volume, to deepen community engagement in higher education, we must rethink pedagogy. A democratic community engagement epistemology will break the barriers among discipline, pedagogy, scholarship, and faculty development. Moreover, expert knowledge will be redefined to include the knowledge of community and students.

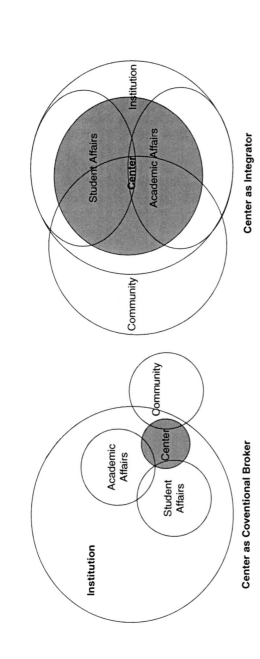

Figure I.4 Recentering the center.

Part IV: Staff and Centers: Integrating the Work of Institutions

In a white paper "Democratic Community Engagement" (2009), Saltmarsh, Hartley, and Clayton address the sense of drift in civic engagement work, raising questions about what is responsible for this stalled momentum. To address this issue, a colloquium of 33 academic leaders gathered in February 2008 at the Kettering Foundation to discuss the barriers and what might be done. This paper, and others like it, suggests a fundamental reorientation of the epistemological foundation of modern American higher education. Such a shift will necessitate a commitment to asset-based understanding, cocreation of knowledge, and viewing the university as part of an ecosystem addressing public problem solving. They note a number of barriers to more democratic engagement, including the lack of a broader public agenda, conflicting and imprecise language, and compartmentalization of the civic engagement movement. Such a shift will also require rethinking the structures through which community engagement is organized, implemented, supported, and valued within institutional contexts. It is the work of a center (or centers) on campus that can facilitate a shift to democratic engagement (Figure I.4). This, too, requires gradual learning. Just as students develop capacity, skills, and leadership through multiyear engagement, those that build and run these programs—staff and faculty—and the infrastructure that they create to do so, must develop and apply the capacity, skills, and leadership required for deeper partnerships and projects.

Hence, a developmental approach to community engagement extends to the center itself and its coordination of students, partners, staff, and faculty. It is through structures—namely centers—that institutions build sustainable partnerships for community engagement, focusing the work of an institution in one or many places, near and far. Yes, individual faculty and some discrete student clubs cultivate and build partnerships as well, but these often suffer because of their short-term nature. For partners, in particular, this experience often has shortcomings, as they begin to develop positions for ongoing volunteers, lists of research projects and information they need, and long-term visions for what a true partnership with the institution may provide. They need and want *consistency, reliability*, and *reciprocity*. Center and their staff—who include faculty, student affairs professionals, and students—shepherd these partnerships, helping partners to negotiate the complexity of working with students and faculty and connecting partners intentionally to more of the assets of the institution. Hence, just as students' development enables more leadership in community contexts, partnerships begin to integrate long-term positions, capacity building, and academic projects; and faculty get connected through multi-semester relationships; institutional collaborations are made richer, more pervasive, deep, and integrated.

An Evolution in Infrastructure

Again, the history here is illustrative. Academic community engagement has been critical to the Bonner vision since 1990. However, to be honest, programs often started with cocurricular focus, often residing in a chaplain's office or student affairs. As the work has evolved, infrastructure and capacity were created along each stage. As Bonner's leadership emphasized student voice, the Foundation developed a reputation for cocurricular focus. This sometimes eclipsed a long history of work with faculty, in particular around community-based research (CBR). With support from Learn and Serve America grants in 1997–2000, 2000–2003, and more recently in 2006–2010 (in partnership with Princeton University), the Foundation received funding to seed CBR on campuses across the network. Mini-grants, faculty training, and peer networking served as catalysts. Partnerships with organizations like the Appalachian-based Just Connections nurtured grassroots organizing work of faculty. Most recently, we addressed the need for more policy and program model analysis through PolicyOptions, an initiative through which faculty at more than 30 institutions have integrated public policy research assignments conducted for the benefit of community partners and constituencies. Faculty teach students how to research and write issue briefs that look at issues—like truancy, childhood obesity, or prisoner reentry. Chapter 7 by Hackett and Donohue describes aspects of this work.

In the past decade, in alignment with work to create civically focused minors, certificates, majors, or academically recognized programs, we saw the repositioning of centers to integrate cocurricular and curricular pathways. By 2008, the architecture of an integrated four-year program was articulated, one that required collaboration across divisions, disciplines, and structures. At the same time, maturing centers often saw the need to incorporate academic leadership and even to shift lines of authority. Principles of good design were captured and published by Hoy and Meisel (2008) in "Civic Engagement at the Center: Building Democracy through Integrated Cocurricular and Curricular Experiences." These principles include:

- Integrated: across divisions with cocurricular and curricular linkages;
- Intensive: coursework and cocurricular activity, requiring student participation over a number of semesters or terms;

- Ongoing: multiyear, developmental (with a progression or sequence), and scaffolded, often with a connection to the core curriculum;
- A connection to public policy and politics: structural and often through courses and internships;
- A focus on poverty, economic inequity, and social inequity: structural, through courses, and through direct experience;
- Global and international perspective: structural, through courses, and through study abroad and international immersions.

Moreover, staff and faculty recognized that students must, in their journeys, be supported to develop knowledge, often in course contexts, which would deepen their abilities to be effective civic-minded professionals. Creating strategies to intentionally educate students about public policy, poverty, international perspective, place, diversity, and relevant issue-based knowledge (i.e., connected to their cocurricular engagement) requires centers with the staff and authority to essentially craft educational pathways. Those involved in these programs, often center staff and faculty, essentially organized pathways through the institution's curriculum, finding or creating a progression through a lead-in, relevant core courses, full-time internships, research methodology and projects, and senior capstones.

Getting to the Core of the Institution

Whether a center falls under student affairs or academic affairs, bridging its work into the life of the college is critical. Indeed, as Welch and Saltmarsh suggest in chapter 13 in this volume, analyzing institutions that have successfully earned the Carnegie Classification, there is evidence that centers propel institution-wide commitment to civic engagement. Moreover, as they evolve, their leadership often develops or claims a background in academic affairs, they operate on hard dollars, and they rely on the support of a critical mass of influential faculty (Welch and Saltmarsh, 2013). Indeed, the language has also evolved, from community service to community-based teaching and learning.

In many ways, the nomenclature and practice of academic community engagement can be said to have its own developmental model. We would describe them, while certainly not attempting to generalize or address every instance, but according to a progression as seen in Table I.3.

When a campus utilizes a robust infrastructure for both cocurricular and curricular programs, it can move toward best practice: the sustained design and application of community engagement characterized by stages 3 and 4, supported by a trained and engaged student body and well-equipped

Table I. 3 Stages of service-learning: Characteristics

	Stage 1	Stage 2	Stage 3	Stage 4
Characteristics of this stage	Connection of an individual course or club with a service project...but driven by course content (not community issue) or club identity	Connection of individual courses or organizations with service project(s), generally carried out by an individual student or small group with some reflection	Course content plus application of content in a individualized experience—enhanced by structured reflection and assessment	Course content designed and taught through experiential application of content to a community need or defined project; includes project work, reflection, and assessment
Examples of this stage	Short-term service requirement tacked onto course. Service club that carries out a one-time or short-term project	20–30 hour service project in a course, with journal requirement. Service organization that operates semester placements (i.e., tutoring program)	Student designs own project, finds partner, and writes a paper that is graded by a faculty member. Students start a new community initiative, seeking out faculty and partner guidance	Course/program designed with community perspective (and need for info); content taught through experiential application and adapted teaching methods. Teams (students, staff, faculty) create or retool programs to address long-term vision
Era (in general)	1980s	1990s	Late 1990s	2000s

and supported community partners. This allows an institution to *redefine engagement to include knowledge and practice*, in the service not only of teaching and learning, but also of real partners with clearly defined community needs. As these changes occur, the teams that drive them to happen and the campus centers they engage can act as integrators for more democratic engagement. More importantly, they redefine the *value* of the college experience, signaling to students (as well as faculty, partners, community, and our democracy) that, in the principle depicted at Highlander so eloquently, *without practice there is no knowledge.*

Part V: Critical Insights and Reflection

In Part V, three outstanding educators and practitioners in the field—Dan Butin, Abby Kiesa, and Tania D. Mitchell—offer their reflections on the chapters in this volume. Each of these authors provides insights and probe at what may be the gaps or next frontiers to deepen civic engagement in higher education. Butin highlights the tensions inherent in this work and the challenges for moving individual illustrations of best practice to truly transform institutions and pedagogies. Kiesa examines the issue of political engagement, an area that we in the field often aim to but struggle to fully integrate and build not only into students' developmental experiences but into the fabric of our institutions' programs. Mitchell looks to the potential for community engagement to address power as well as social justice. All three, we believe, offer important themes and critiques that must be addressed to move civic engagement forward.

Part VI: Conclusion

Finally, in conclusion, we share with you the origins of our network's current work to move engagement forward by intentionally linking engaged learning and high-impact practices with well-designed and intentional high-impact community engagement. While just at the beginning, we believe that the strategies of transforming curriculum, approaches to engagement, and institutional structures and practices can be informed by the thoughtful, steady work of teams of community partners, faculty, students, and administrators working together. We share briefly the seeds of our thinking about high-impact community engagement and how it can be a powerful vehicle for helping our institutions to achieve their missions and maintain their relevance in cultivating and contributing as stewards of place, civic learning, and agents of change.

References

Arum, Richard, and Josipa Roksa. *Academically Adrift: Limited Learning on College Campuses.* Chicago, IL: University of Chicago Press, 2010.

Bradford, H. (2011). 10 States Where Income Inequality Is Growing Fastest. *The Huffington Post.* Retrieved from www.huffingtonpost.com/2012/09/21/income -inequality-states_n_1904321.html

Bringle, Robert G., and Julie A. Hatcher. "Innovative practices in service-learning and curricular engagement." *New directions for higher education*, no. 147 (2009): 37–46.

Brownell, Jayne Elise, and Lynn Ellen Swaner. *Five High-Impact Practices: Research on Learning Outcomes, Completion and Quality.* Washington, DC: Association of American Colleges and Universities, 2010.

Butin, Dan, and Scott Seider. *The Engaged Campus: Certificates, Minors, and Majors as the New Community Engagement.* New York, NY: Palgrave Macmillan, 2012.

Campus Compact. Service Statistics 2008: Highlights and Trends from Campus Compact's Annual Membership Survey. Retrieved from www.compact.org/wp -content/uploads/2009/10/2008-statistics1.pdf

Christensen, Clayton M., and Henry J. Eyring. *The Innovative University: Changing the DNA of Higher Education from the Inside Out.* Jossey-Bass, 2011.

Crutcher, R. A., R. Corrigan, P. O'Brien, and C. G. Schneider. *College Learning for the New Global Century: A Report from the National Leadership Council for Liberal Education and America's Promise.* Washington, DC: American Association of State Colleges and Universities, 2007.

Duderstadt, James J. *A University for the 21st Century.* University of Michigan Press, 2000.

Eckel, Peter, Madeleine F. Green, and Barbara Hill. *On Change V: Riding the Waves of Change: Insights from Transforming Institutions.* Vol. 5. American Council on Education, 2001.

Hatcher, Julie Adele. "The public role of professionals: Developing and evaluating the civic-minded professional scale." PhD diss., Indianapolis: Indiana University, 2008.

Hoy, Ariane, and Wayne Meisel. *Civic engagement at the center: Building democracy through integrated cocurricular and curricular experiences.* Washington, DC: Association of American Colleges and Universities, 2008.

Keen, Cheryl, and Kelly Hall. "Engaging with difference matters: longitudinal student outcomes of co-curricular service-learning programs." *The Journal of Higher Education* 80, no. 1 (2009): 59–79.

Kolb, David A. *Experiential Learning: Experience as the Source of Learning and Development.* Englewood Cliffs, NJ: Prentice Hall, 1984.

Kuh, George D. "The other curriculum: out-of-class experiences associated with student learning and personal development." *The Journal of Higher Education* 66, no. 2 (March/April 1995): 123–155.

Kuh, George D. *High-impact Educational Practices: What They Are, Who Has Access to Them, and Why They Matter.* Washington, DC: AAC&U, 2008.

Laird, T., Rick Shoup, and George D. Kuh. "Measuring Deep Approaches to Learning Using the National Survey of Student Engagement." In annual meeting of the Association for Institutional Research. 2005.

Lynton, Ernest A. "Reexamining the role of the university." *Change* 15, no. 7 (1983): 18–53.

Meisel, W. "The Bonner Scholars Program: A Four Year Community Service Scholarship Program" (2006).

Saltmarsh, John, Matthew Hartley, and Patti Clayton. "Democratic engagement white paper" (2009).

Scobey, David M. "A Copernican Moment: On the Revolutions in Higher Education." In *Transforming Undergraduate Education: Theory That Compels and Practices That Succeed*, ed. Donald W. Harward. Lanham, MD: Rowman and Littlefield, 2012, pp. 37–49.

Spellings Commission. "A Test of Leadership: Charting the Future of US Higher Education (September). A Report of the Commission Appointed by US Secretary of Education Margaret Spellings. THES (2006) The Times Higher Education Supplement World University Rankings" (2006).

Steinberg, K., J. A. Hatcher, and R. G. Bringle. "A North Star: Civic-minded Graduate." *Michigan Journal of Community Service Learning* 18, no. 1 (2011): 19–33.

Sturm, S., T. Eatman, J. Saltmarsh, and A. Bush. "Full Participation: Building the Architecture for Diversity and Public Engagement in Higher Education [White Paper]. New York: Columbia University Law School." Center for Institutional and Social Change (2011).

Sullivan, W. M. *Work and integrity: The crisis and promise of professionalism in America*. New York: Harper Collins, 1995.

Sullivan, W. M. *Work and integrity: The crisis and promise of professionalism in America (2nd Edition)*. San Francisco: Jossey-Bass, 2005.

The National Task Force on Civic Learning and Democratic Engagement. *A Crucible Moment: Civic Learning and Democracy's Future*. Washington, DC: Association of American Colleges & Universities, 2012.

Votruba, J. C., J. I. Bailey, B. W. Bergland, A. Gonzalez, K. S. Haynes, M. A. Howard, J. H. Keiser, R. L. Pattenaude, K. D. Romesburg, and B. L. Siegel. *Stepping Forward as Stewards of Place: A Guide for Leading Public Engagement at State Colleges and Universities*. Washington, DC: American Association of State Colleges and Universities, 2002.

PART I

Students as Civic-Minded Professionals: An Approach for Student Development

CHAPTER 1

Learning through Service: Structures that Promote Student Leadership

Ashley Cochrane and Heather McNew Schill

Introduction

As the civic engagement movement in higher education has matured and evolved, many have advocated for increased opportunities for student leadership and voice. Longo and Gibson (2011) explore models of "new" approaches to leadership development in higher education, approaches that integrate civic engagement activities, practical applications, and student initiatives. Zlotkowski, Longo, and Williams (2006) call for the academic service-learning movement, in particular, to incorporate more opportunities for student direction and influence. These, and other recently published books and journal articles, feature dozens of civic engagement programs at colleges and universities that are providing students with opportunities to serve, learn, and lead. Many of the strongest programs have developed organizational structures that draw upon and make the most of the unique characteristics of their institution, their community, and their student body.

There is no "one-size fits all" answer for how students can most effectively serve, learn, and develop as leaders. Just as each of our institutions varies in geographic setting, cultural priorities, student demographics, size, mission, and history, so our community service and service-learning programs must reflect those differences. We believe that the context in which these programs exist should influence how the programs are structured and implemented.

At the same time there are organizational strategies that have proven effective in a variety of institutions; we contend that awareness of those strategies and a willingness to adapt them to fit the unique aspects of our own institutions will lead to strong programs that effectively integrate student service, learning, and leadership development. In this chapter, we share strategies that have proven successful in developing students as "service-oriented leaders for Appalachia and beyond" at Berea College for many years. The strategies that we explore here include adopting a mission-driven basis for community-engaged work, making connections between curricular and cocurricular service, and utilizing elements of the Coalition of Projects model as an organizational framework. We have found that by implementing these approaches in a way that fits our particular organizational culture, our center provides developmental opportunities that allow students to learn and thrive as they serve and lead. Additionally, these approaches characterize the Bonner Program's model for student development, implemented by more than 60 colleges and universities.

Living the Mission

Most institutions of higher education can identify historical roots of service and mission statements that ground themselves in work for the common good or service to the surrounding community. Connecting our community-based work to the institutional mission has been a way to embody what Kuh et al. (2010) call "living missions." This means that an institution organizes and utilizes resources "in a manner that enables it to realize its aspirations" (27). Centers for community engagement provide students with opportunities to use their skills to achieve the institution's highest goals. In addition, Kuh and others (2008) state that daily use of institution-particular, mission-based language can help students connect to the institution and ultimately succeed in their undergraduate careers.

Berea College's history, mission, student population, and labor program together compose a compelling institutional model. Founded in 1855 by abolitionists, Berea College was the first interracial and coeducational college in the Southern United States. From its beginning, Berea College has had a nonsectarian and unaffiliated Christian perspective and was designed to serve African-American and Appalachian students who would not have otherwise been able to pursue educational opportunities. The College continues to be guided by these founding commitments. Today, each Berea College student receives a full-tuition scholarship and must meet financial need requirements to be admitted. The College's motto, "God has made of one blood all peoples of the earth," is prominently used in Berea College publications, communications, and daily conversations on campus. The College's Eight Great Commitments, which serve as the mission statement of Berea College, are frequently referenced; three of the Commitments explicitly mention service.

Berea College is a mission-focused institution, one that prides itself on its unique history, current vision, and student accomplishments. The roots of the most recent incarnations of service programs are found in the late 1960s, a time influenced by the War on Poverty, the development of the Peace Corps and AmeriCorps VISTA (Volunteers in Service to America) programs, and a national spotlight on poverty in the Appalachian region. In 2000, the Center for Excellence in Learning through Service (CELTS) was founded. It was designed to bring under one umbrella the various community service programs previously housed in several locations, and to establish a formal academic service-learning program. The vision for CELTS grew from the College's strategic plan, which articulates Berea College's commitment to develop "service-oriented leaders for Appalachia and beyond." Today, CELTS's three main program areas are community service, service-learning, and the Bonner Scholars Program.

Berea College's history and mission have provided a language rooted in service, in the Appalachian region, and in student development, which we use in our communication tools and our daily work. For example, the CELTS Shared Values hang in the students' common workspace and appear on students' position descriptions; the Shared Values were written by students and staff of our predecessor program, Students for Appalachia, almost 20 years ago. Using this language ties the present-day work of CELTS to our history and "living mission," and allows us to draw connections with the evolving vocabulary of this field of work in higher education, currently the language of civic engagement, place-based service, and high-impact practices.

Creating Connections

In the Campus Compact publication, *Looking In, Reaching Out*, Barbara Jacoby encourages service-learning practitioners to "make the most of your place in the organization" (Jacoby and Mustascio, 2010, 42) and to build partnerships in their own area, as well as in other areas across campus. This practical advice implies the necessity of understanding an institution's organizational structure and a program's place within it. This understanding can be the basis for building relationships and alliances and for potentially bridging gaps that could otherwise be impediments.

CELTS houses both curricular and cocurricular services and reports to the Office of the Academic Vice President. Our reporting line provides formal and relational connections to the academic program. This, in turn, allows us to build partnerships with faculty, forge connections with the curriculum, and establish understanding, awareness, and acceptance of service-learning as an innovative teaching pedagogy. While based in the academic division, the CELTS staff build relationships with other areas of campus as well, such as student affairs, faith-based programs, and centers focused on diverse student populations. These relationships strengthen our student-focused work by connecting us with colleagues who are well versed in the language, concepts, and practicalities of student development and program implementation. They have also allowed us to work with colleagues to identify ways for more students to have access to community engagement activities and to develop strategies for supporting student academic success.

Within our center, the opportunities for organizational and programmatic links between curricular and cocurricular services allow us to emphasize learning that takes place through all forms of community engagement. For example, the structured reflection activities that we facilitate help students to apply knowledge from their coursework to their community service. At the same time, students tell us that their community experiences provide a context for their academic studies.

Learning through Leading

Coordinating the logistics of mobilizing, supervising, and advising student service and service-learning activities can be all consuming. These challenges include effectively training volunteers, transporting students to community sites, and maintaining sustainable relationships with community partner organizations. In 1995, John Sarvey summarized a set of structural characteristics that he observed as common to many civic engagement programs that were effectively addressing these challenges. He called this set of characteristics the "Coalition of Projects Model."[1] We have found this framework to closely reflect the structure of the community service and service-learning programs coordinated through CELTS. In our case, CELTS is the umbrella organization, and issue-based or population-based, student-led teams are the semiautonomous projects that carry out community-based work. As Sarvey recommends, the CELTS structure also includes "a set of overall student leaders who provide a range of leadership and support functions to all the projects" (1995, 4).

The Coalition of Projects Model consists of ten structural characteristics (Sarvey, 1995):

1. An umbrella organization of multiple programs, where each program is its own identifiable separate program under a larger umbrella;

2. Issue- or neighborhood-focused projects, where students find the issue they are passionate about and volunteer for a particular issue-specific team, not a general or generic service center;

3. Group coordination of volunteers, where student coordinators and volunteers are grouped together as teams, not in individual placements;

4. Cascading leadership structure, where students work their way up from volunteer to managing their own issue-specific team;

5. Coalition-wide support functions for the projects, where student leaders come together to help support each other and share ideas;

6. Systematic training of project leaders, where these students are provided with the skills to help manage their program;

7. Systematic exchange of challenges and best practices among projects, where student leaders come together to learn from each other;

8. Systematic quality improvement process, where students evaluate the state of their program on a regular basis;

9. New project incubation, where a clear process is created for adding more programs;

10. Student office space for the community service program, where each program under the "umbrella" has its own identifiable space, with file cabinets, a telephone, and so on.

Together, these components address many of the universal challenges faced by those creating opportunities for student community engagement. The model provides opportunities for students to focus on a particular social issue and to connect with community organizations and leaders who are experts in addressing that particular issue. It provides a structure for organizing and focusing students in specific roles, and it makes room for students to gradually develop knowledge, skills, and responsibilities as they spend time in the program. The structure allows for continuity from year to year, which leads to strong relationships with community partner organizations that can be developed over time. The model also provides opportunities for students to develop a sense of ownership: students are training and learning from each other, they are helping to identify and address areas of needed improvement, and they have their own space for working and building community with each other and with professional staff. Ultimately, this model allows students to implement the community service and service-learning programming, so that the professional staff can focus on training, advising, oversight, and development of programs.

A cascading leadership development structure is the cornerstone of the way that CELTS student involvement is organized. Our center uses a combination of federal work-study and volunteer positions to implement this

structure, but similar structures are utilized at schools without labor programs: some use work-study positions, some use student volunteers, and
some use a combination of the two. Connecting student leadership positions
with work-study and other funding sources can provide critical support for
the infrastructure that makes this model effective. In our case, the Berea
College Labor Program allows us to leverage a unique resource at our institution, which helps our programs to succeed.

Berea is one of seven federally recognized "work colleges" in the United
States, each of which requires students to make work a meaningful part of
their college experience, and which together make up the Work Colleges
Consortium. At Berea College, every student is required to work at least
ten hours per week in a labor, or work-study, position on campus or in the
community. Students' labor positions provide them with opportunities to
learn practical and job-specific skills; ideally, as students develop experience
in their labor positions, they are able to advance to positions of increasing
responsibility, with many eventually managing other students and programs.
This is the case for students who hold labor positions through CELTS.

During the academic year, CELTS offers eight different community
service programs, focused on a variety of issues and populations, including tutoring and mentoring children and teens, building relationships with
elders, making connections with the Spanish-speaking community, advocating for environmental and sustainability issues, building homes with
Habitat for Humanity, and supporting victims of domestic violence. The
range of issue-specific and/or population-specific programs draws a diverse
mix of students into the work of the center. The student volunteers for each
of these programs are recruited, trained, and supervised by teams of student leaders. The student Program Manager is the leader of each team and
is selected by the CELTS staff after serving as an effective team member
and demonstrating leadership potential; the Program Managers are charged
with the responsibility of training their team members and volunteers, and
with supervising the day-to-day operation of their programs.

Students often begin volunteering as first-year students, spending at least
two hours each week with their issue-specific community service program.
Each spring, students have the opportunity to apply to become a member of
one of the program teams. The current team of students selects the strongest
volunteers—those who have established themselves as responsible and as
having an understanding of the issues addressed by that program—to hold
a labor position with the team.

The program teams usually consist of three to six students at different stages
in their college careers. Here, a student described simultaneously learning from
team members with more experience and training students who have less.

That first year as a full time team member was a new form of learning experience. I realized that all of the older students were graduating, and I was terrified at first, because I didn't think I could run the program. My Program Manager began explaining in detail…all of her decisions so I could understand. [She was] teaching me, but not making it obvious I was going to take over. In the meantime, I taught our new [team members] what I knew because I was still "new" and could relate well to them.

With two years of experience as a Program Manager, the same student reflected on the importance of continuously training new leaders. "I spent my first year [as Program Manager] building my team, training them, recruiting, and focusing on getting them well connected to each other. This year I have been training my replacement, and we've also found who [might come] after her…I [have] worked with both of them on various things such as management and assertiveness, talking to volunteers…self-esteem and scheduling, because those skills being instilled in me are the reasons I've been successful at CELTS."

In the ideal situation, students progress smoothly from volunteer to team member to Program Manager. However, at times, students are asked to take on leadership roles for which they might not feel prepared. There are cases when several experienced students graduate at the same time and the student "next in line" does not possess the skills or capacity to fulfill the expectations of a team leader. Or, the Program Manager position might become vacant unexpectedly, when a student must leave school for family or medical reasons. Within the context of cascading leadership development, students have been training from their first day as volunteers and team members; the foundation of training and the scaffold of the team structure make it possible for student leaders to step up and continue program implementation, with little interruption of service to the community.

Here, one Program Manager described the experience of being in such a situation. "Despite my original reservations about applying because I had so little experience on the team, my labor supervisor encouraged me to apply. Much to my surprise, the position was offered to me. I was so thrilled that my labor supervisors saw my potential and had such respect for me that they would trust me with such an important role…I believe that this opportunity for promotion and development makes a difference in the type of leader produced at CELTS." For strong leaders and programs to emerge from situations like this, CELTS staff members must implement creative decision making. In addition, staff must be prepared to offer additional advising and support for the new leader, and increased involvement in the daily operation of the program.

When the cascading leadership development model is used, program staff can focus on the training and development of student leaders. We and the other staff of CELTS provide developmentally appropriate training and support for student leaders that acknowledge the level of leadership students have achieved. For example, first-year students receive training about our community and the issues we face, as well as essential skills like teamwork, time management, and meeting facilitation. Trainings for program managers focus on the management aspects of their work such as supervising a team, creating a budget, and designing a strategic plan. We also provide general trainings for all our students on a weekly basis. These trainings focus on issues such as environmental racism, skills such as professional communication, and reflection practices such as program evaluation or vocational planning. Often upper-level students help to lead these sessions and provide their peers with support and advice.

As we engage in our daily work of training and advising students, we are also able to focus on connecting them with local, regional, and national resources related to their specific interests. These connections beyond our center lead students to bring new ideas back to us, which helps to influence the development of the center. In the section that follows, we highlight two illustrations of student leaders shaping the work of the center. While we do spend time working with students who do not meet work expectations, even in these situations, we empower student supervisors to hold their peers accountable, with staff providing coaching or intervening as appropriate. We strive to work with students as emerging colleagues because, truly, that is what they are. Our proudest moments occur when graduates become our colleagues as local community partners, student affairs professionals or faculty at other institutions, or professionals who provide resources in fields related to our work.

Building Bridges on Campus and in the Community

A Spanish professor, who has historically used his own Spanish language skills to assist individuals and communities, began implementing a service-learning component in one of his advanced Spanish courses. He understood the service-learning component of his course as a way to educate his students about the practical applications of their Spanish skills, and as a way to provide needed services in our community, which had a growing Spanish-speaking population. Two of the students who took his course were also leaders in CELTS. They experienced some challenges in implementing the service-learning assignment, but they saw the challenges as an opportunity. One of these student leaders recalled the impetus for their new idea. "Unfortunately, there were barriers to many of the service-learning projects, including transportation, communication, and sustainability...[which] ended up causing a lot of confusion with our community partners and our clients. These projects were needed in our community, yet, it was difficult to accomplish them...I know that if I had not been involved with CELTS, I would have been extremely discouraged and would have given up. I knew, however, how to create a successful and sustainable service project, and...I realized that these barriers could be overcome."

The two student leaders initiated meetings with the professor, CELTS staff members, and other interested students, during which they introduced and further developed their idea that the Spanish service-learning course and CELTS could strengthen each other. They saw the needs of the Spanish-speaking community as a pressing issue that CELTS was not—but should be—addressing, and they saw CELTS as a vehicle to provide needed infrastructure to the course. They also saw that the Spanish professor and his students could provide the language skills that would make it possible for CELTS to get involved in this work.

The groundwork laid by the students led to the formation of a pilot partnership. With advice from the professor and a CELTS staff member, the students built relationships with community partner organizations, helped to plan the service-learning assignments, and coordinated transportation for the students to get to their sites. The partnership worked. As the program established a record of successful implementation, we were able to make the case for additional labor positions; thus, the Hispanic Outreach Project (HOP) began operating as a team, with a Program Manager, within the cascading leadership development structure.

The same student recalled some of the factors that prepared her for this leadership role. "Through my experience in the Bonner Scholars Program, I realized early on that students could make a difference, empower communities, and had a voice. The CELTS program taught us how to find and advocate for causes and resources so that we are able to achieve change...We were able to make a good case for why HOP fit with CELTS and reasons for CELTS to support us, thanks to the training that CELTS gave us initially!"

Extending the Model

During a particularly challenging semester, with much staff and student energy focused on managing team conflicts and other student issues, members of the CELTS staff found ourselves consulting regularly with the three students who held the most senior leadership positions in each of CELTS's main areas of programming. At the same time, these three leaders found that many of the other students in CELTS were approaching them with questions, concerns, and suggestions. Eventually, these students proposed the creation of a formal role for their positions. Their proposal reflected their understanding of the organizational framework of the cascading leadership development model. The staff of CELTS embraced the idea.

One of the students who initiated the idea recalled what prepared her for this new role. "[The other two student leaders] inspired me to be better and to work harder ... [We] shared a cubicle area, and many of our ideas and projects were enhanced by the ideas of the other ... We all knew the importance of a team and how to work through the different stages of a team."

This group of leaders is now called the CELTS Student Leadership Team. They serve as resources for the rest of the CELTS student staff, by consulting with program managers about program and supervisory challenges, managing the smooth operation of the office, and consulting with the professional staff about center-wide morale, student needs, and training programs. They also plan and implement a series of community-wide service opportunities.

It took a set of challenging circumstances, and a set of student leaders who were well prepared for their roles, to initiate this change. As a result of this student-led initiative, the CELTS organizational structure has been strengthened.

Conclusion

In recent years, Kuh (2008) and others have identified high-impact practices that are particularly effective at helping students to succeed in college. Service-learning and community-based learning are two of those practices, and we have observed their impact in the lives of our students. A student telling us that he is still in college because he became a volunteer in his first semester, or a student telling us that she stayed in school after a personal trauma because of the support she received through CELTS, suggests that the structures we have in place to support students are working. The graduates telling us that they use the skills they developed in CELTS in their current careers, or the ones telling us that their work in CELTS helped them to discern meaningful career paths, suggests that the skills students develop have a lasting impact.

Recent data compiled by CELTS staff and Berea College's Office of Institutional Research and Assessment also reflect a correlation between participation in service and service-learning activities and completion of college. The data show that in each area measured, students who engaged with CELTS programming were significantly more likely to graduate in five years, when compared to their peers who were not involved with service or service-learning activities. These data are consistent with research conducted at other institutions and on a national scale, and they verify what CELTS staff observe daily through our work with students.

We do not suggest that the strategies we have found to be effective will lead to civic engagement programming without challenges or logistical stumbling blocks. In fact, as we have worked on this chapter, we have been pulled away from our writing by missing vehicle keys, absent students, team conflicts, communication glitches, and students dealing with personal crises. At the same time, student leaders were recruiting and training volunteers, collaborating with community partners, and holding each other accountable. They were mentoring children, strategizing with teachers, constructing sustainable, low-income housing, building relationships with elders, learning to become English-language tutors, advocating for fair trade practices on campus, cleaning up our community, and stocking the shelves of our local food bank.

Our daily work reminds us that the organizational structures we have in place are essential, but alone, they are not sufficient. Implementing community engagement programming also takes compassion, creative problem solving, and the willingness to set aside a well-organized plan to adapt to the realities our students and our community partners are facing. As Kolb (1984, 2006) and others have described, the work of our students is a continuous cycle of doing, observing, thinking, planning, and doing again. Our job is to facilitate their engagement in this learning process. The structures we have implemented in CELTS help us to do this more effectively, and allow us to engage in the same learning cycle, alongside our students. As the service-learning adage reminds us, we are all teachers, and we are all learners. When effective structures are in place, we are better able to engage ourselves and our students in the teaching and learning process.

Note

1. This model was also championed during the 1990s through the national organizing by the Campus Outreach Opportunity League (COOL), an organization with connections to the Bonner network and its model, given its 1985 founding by Wayne Meisel and Bobby Hackett, Bonner Foundation's historic and current leadership.

References

Jacoby, Barbara, and Pamela Mutascio, eds. Looking in Reaching Out: A Reflective Guide for Community Service-Learning Professionals. Boston, MA: Campus Compact, 2010.

Kolb, David A. *Experiential Learning: Experience as the Source of Learning and Development.* Englewood Cliffs, NJ: Prentice Hall, 1984.

Kolb, David A. *Experiential Learning: Experience as the Source of Learning and Development.* Englewood Cliffs, NJ: Prentice Hall, 2006.

Kuh, George D. *High-impact Educational Practices: What They Are, Who Has Access to Them, and Why They Matter.* Washington, DC: AAC&U, 2008.

Kuh, George D., Jillian Kinzie, John H. Schuh, and Elizabeth J. Whitt. *Student Success in College: Creating Conditions that Matter.* San Francisco: Jossey-Bass, 2010.

Longo, Nicholas V., and Cynthia M. Gibson. *From Command to Community: A New Approach to Leadership Education in Colleges and Universities.* Somerville: Tufts University, 2011.

Sarvey, John, and Heather McNew Schill. *How program/organizational structure shapes the performance and sustainability of student-led co-curricular community service programs.* Poster session presented at the annual meeting of the International Association of Research on Service-Learning and Community Engagement, Baltimore, MD, 2012.

Sarvey, John. *Building it up: a one-day workshop on building and strengthening campus-based community service programs.* Paper presented at the annual conference of the Campus Outreach Opportunity League (COOL), Arizona State University, Tempe, AZ, 1995.

Zlotkowski, Edward A., Nicholas V. Longo, and James R. Williams, eds. *Students as Colleagues: Expanding the Circle of Service-Learning Leadership.* Campus Compact, 2006.

CHAPTER 2

Student Development in Theory and Practice

Nicole Saylor, Patrick Gruber, and Michelle Nix

Introduction

At the root of much of our institutions' commitments to engaging students in their communities—through volunteering, service-learning, community-based research, internships, and other forms—is an implicit understanding as well as evidence of the power of this engagement for students' learning. High-quality community engagement is responsive to students' intellectual as well as the affective and behavioral development while also effective at equipping students to understand and be responsive to needs in the larger community. Hence, providing opportunities for students to emerge as leaders, alongside college faculty and staff, empowers them to move beyond self-focused education models into community engagement. Such opportunities likewise develop students so that they can transform from consumers of information to participants and contributors of knowledge and skills to the larger community, as part of the educational as well as community change process. This chapter will contribute to the emerging dialogue about creating developmentally sensitive structures for college student engagement within community contexts. By providing a review of psychological theory and research, the authors aim to support practitioners of community-engaged learning to be better able to support students in embracing, developing, and sustaining an identity that places a high value on community engagement as a student and often translates into engagement in the years beyond.

The examples herein demonstrate student leadership success stories within the programs at Carson-Newman University and with community partner sites that have been successful at engaging students as coleaders with reflection on how such opportunities are developmentally sensitive and appropriate to student needs. Each example highlights how student leadership was instrumental in either campus or community transformation. The proposed models are intended to strengthen, expand, and refine the other strategies and models for engaged learning and high-impact practices rather than supplant them. This emerging practice particularly addresses students' reasonable expectations that their educational experiences address distinct developmental needs, providing support that scaffolds their learning.

The Emerging Adult

The traditional college student is an emerging adult, experiencing a life stage that both builds the foundation for his or her educational and occupational course, as well as creates the foundation of the student's worldview, relationships, and identity for adult life. Through a careful evaluation of current psychological theory and research, community-engaged academic programs and institutions can create an educational environment that achieves the dual aims of meaningful student development and effective community engagement while furthering the aims and mission of the academic institution.

Arnett (2000, 470; 2011, 25–38) proposes the concept of emerging adulthood as a unique developmental period from the late teens to early twenties. Drawing on the work of Erikson, Levinson, and Keniston and their concepts of adolescence, novice adult, and youth, respectively, Arnett sets forth emerging adulthood as a developmental stage that is particularly applicable to 18–25 year olds in Western culture. Conditions that particularly cultivate emerging adulthood are: postponing the entry into adult roles and responsibilities such as marriage and vocation until well past the late teens, belonging in higher class or socioeconomic conditions, and the presence of a wide range of educational and occupational opportunities. These conditions are particularly true for traditional college students from middle- and upper-class socioeconomic backgrounds, who attend college directly out of high school with no previous substantive employment.

However, students from exceptional backgrounds (e.g., students of color, first generation, low income, etc.), or who have had to "become adults" before college due to family and income circumstances, still experience the developmental pressures of emerging adulthood. These are the students who often comprise Bonner Scholar and Leader Programs. The structures of colleges and universities are constructed to support the majority experience, and thus create an environment that further sustains the delay of adulthood, the expectation of social mobility into the upper classes, and vocational exploration. Students from less conventional experiences often have lower rates of college completion. Nontraditional students can benefit from more support in navigating these dominant culture expectations of emerging adulthood that may contradict their real-life experience.

In the subsequent years since the conceptualization of emerging adulthood as a developmental stage, research continues to affirm that such a trajectory seems accurate on a number of factors for 18–25 year olds in Western culture, specifically in the United States (Arnett, 2011, 255–275). Three primary characteristics distinguish the emerging adulthood period: an intense period of identity development, lack of normative demographics, and the subjective experience of feeling as if one exists somewhere between being fully adolescent and fully adult. By addressing each of these areas when developing community engagement practices at colleges and universities, faculty, staff, and community partners can create transformative experiences for students that also meet the goals and aims of the institution and the community.

Demographic Cohesion and Norming

The lack of a "normative" experience for ages 18–25 years is one key component of emerging adulthood, as is the subjective experience of feeling as if one exists somewhere between being fully adolescent and fully adult. Emerging adults have variable experiences; residential status (where and with whom one lives) and school status are two key components of demographic diversity. While one individual lives with his family of origin attending community college in the same town, another may be enrolled in a four-year institution hundreds (or thousands) of miles from her home, while a third works full time and attends night classes in between caring for his child and partner. The only consistency of the population is inconsistency and lack of a shared normative experience based upon age and life stage (Arnett, 2011, 265; Arnett and Tanner, 2006, 25–37).

Therefore, the community engagement center should endeavor to create programs that provide cohort cohesiveness that extends beyond the life situation of each individual student. Doing so creates a shared demographic experience that is lacking for the emerging adult in other domains. Kuh's (2008, 9–13) *High-Impact Educational Practices* already supports the utilization of academic activities that create a group dynamic, including first-year seminars, learning communities, collaborative group projects, and common intellectual experiences. The community engagement center can combine many of Kuh's (2008, 9–13) practices into a successful scholarship or service program, as modeled in the Bonner Program and others like it. Creating cohorts of students that have key experiences together helps create this demographic identity. For example, Bonner Scholars matriculate into a class-based cohort, with a week-long orientation, regular meetings during the semester, a first-year service trip, shared course sequence, annual retreats, and annual developmental markers such as a structured immersion in the sophomore year in partnership with another program and campus, a leadership role in the junior year, and a senior capstone project.

Within a community engagement program, or as a stand-alone, the college or university can also create similar experiences by placing teams of students at a particular community site. Individual students work together on a single project, or may have differing roles based on site needs. Regardless, the students come together in regular meetings to discuss and address site-wide issues. Such teams also provide opportunities for students at different levels to work together and to provide clear leadership pathways for students.

At Carson-Newman, the Bonner Center has endeavored to address the demographic variability of the emerging adult population by establishing multiyear community engagement partnerships and positions where students work in teams and have clear developmental pathways that provide a structure through which students can attain civic and other learning outcomes. By creating a demographic commonality and sense of belonging to a group committed to a cause, students experience a shared objective that draws them together across their differences.

One of the ongoing challenges is engaging commuter students in program activities. The intentional community formed through the Bonner experience is crucial to student development, and, while engaged in their community of origin, commuter students can sometimes view the campus community solely as the place they go to class. One student, Emma, excelled through her freshman year, serving as a member of a Bonner site team at a local after-school program. As she transitioned into her sophomore year, she requested transfer to a community site closer to home. However, this site was not host to a Bonner site team; Emma would be working in isolation.

After meeting with Emma, she and program staff mutually decided that she would stay with the after-school program for another year. She was even offered a leadership position in that program. Continuing with the after-school program, Emma became integral to its success and deeply invested in the youth. She also demonstrated increased participation in on-campus events, eventually deciding to move onto campus for her junior year. She made this transition despite several challenging family changes and financial challenges that emerged during the summer term between her sophomore and junior years. Both program staff as well as the student credit the experience on the site team, working closely with peers to address a community need, with drawing in and allowing her to invest fully in the community and the scholarship program.

Emma's example of working in the BOOST after-school program at Carson-Newman is an exemplar for how multiyear, developmental placements can create a cohort experience. Emma's time as a tutor in her first year focused on direct program provision with increased responsibility in subsequent years by taking on roles such as planning, writing curriculum, or coordinating assessment, creating a clear path for Emma joining a cohort, and as will be highlighted later, in discussing the development of leadership identity.

Emma and other advanced students became site leaders, responsible for oversight of onsite volunteers, opening and closing of the site, and training other tutors. The most developed students could move into higher leadership roles such as program coordinator, with responsibility for scheduling, coordinating with community partners, communicating with parents, and training volunteers. Teams are comprised of students who come to the after-school program from many streams: students in the Bonner Program, Federal Work Study placements, and general campus volunteers. Anyone can advance, regardless of which volunteer stream he or she derives from, and the identity of the cohort is based upon the site.

While Kuh and others propose that increasing student engagement is the mechanism that leads to greater retention, perhaps it is actually the opportunities for cohort formation and norming that contribute to better outcomes. Research on service-learning supports this assertion. Young adults who participate in service-learning are more politically and socially connected to their communities, both as leaders and role models, and are often more active members of society. Students who engage in service learning have frequently been demonstrated to show increases in personal and social responsibility and altruistic motivation. Research also indicates that students participating in service-learning have a stronger connection to the college or university as evidenced by strong relationships with faculty (and that such a connection contributes to a greater likelihood of graduation. All of these indicators relate back to a sense of belonging and being a part of the larger institution [Seifer, 2002]).

The Links of Engagement to Student Success

Psychological research also supports the fact that student engagement may be a key to retention. Broadly speaking, the field of psychology has found three key protective factors to coping with life changes: a sense of efficacy, a sense of meaning and purpose, and a sense of social support. By creating cohort-based site teams working for the community good, with opportunities for leadership and success, the center can address all three of these needs. When a student is part of a community to which he or she is committed, he or she has obligations and expectations from that group. The student cannot simply exit from the team experience and go unnoticed, promoting a sense of belonging and cohesiveness. This may increase their likelihood to remain engaged and connected to the subgroup at the college or university, a claim ripe for empirical research.

The creation of the demographic identity can be further strengthened by approaches that integrate cocurricular and curricular service. To the student, the line between classroom or academic affair activities and student development activities is permeable if not invisible. The student's sense of place is firmly rooted in the institution and the larger community, not in the academic department or student organization. Such an approach allows the center to create opportunities for students across domains. For example, a student may be a tutor and later a program team leader at an after-school program. That same student can organize a campus organization in which he or she is involved to host a fund-raising fun run for the after-school program, and also support his or her academic honor society to undertake a book drive and for members to volunteer to read to children for the after-school program one day a week. To the student, identity is firmly rooted in the community, at a particular site, and perhaps with a specific community-identified need or population as well as with the education institution.

We have found that a center can create programs that link to high-impact practices such as internships, writing projects, undergraduate research, and capstones. The same student may serve his or her teacher education practicum at the after-school site, focus on the site's programs when undertaking course papers and research, and formulate a senior capstone project that serves the site in a meaningful way. Thus, a student's demographic identity becomes a member and leader of the site, and its mission becomes the student's mission, creating stability and identity amid a sea of other fluctuating factors.

The Development of Leadership Identity

The varying pace at which diverse students grow and develop in the context of their community engagement work contributes to the lack of developmental markers that distinguish a student as an emerging adult. By working in multiyear teams, students are also provided with developmental trajectories that support investment in the group and development of a leadership identity. With clear positions for growth, a student can progress from volunteer to project manager to team leader, allowing students to increase responsibilities and personal expectations. In addition to providing a formative experience for students, multiyear, multilevel team placements also provide greater likelihood that community partners can achieve their aims through the cumulative value-added experience of having returning students over several academic years taking on increased responsibilities and progressing as adult leaders. Also, the site, its work, and the community–institution relationship are left less vulnerable to the impact of one unsuccessful student placement.

Designing programs that create a sense of demographic cohesiveness additionally contributes to creation of incremental leadership roles that develop students into coeducators and colleagues. Research indicates that the characteristics that matter most to emerging adults in their sense of attaining adulthood are "not demographic transitions but individualistic qualities of character" (Arnett, 1998, 300–305). Specifically, the two top criteria for the transition to adulthood in a variety of studies have been accepting responsibility for one's self and making independent decisions (Arnett, 1997, 7–15; Greene et al., 1992, 364–370).

By participating in a multiyear team working with a particular community agency, described earlier, students experience a sense of belonging and commitment with their team. This affords the student the opportunity to take on increasing responsibilities and innovations within a familiar context. This results in the student discovering that he or she has become capable of accepting responsibility for his or her work and making independent decisions to carry out those responsibilities. However, because the progression of such development has been incremental and within a relational context of student development, the arrival of the adult identity is rather surreptitious for the student, suddenly secure in the role of leader and adult.

Carson-Newman has endeavored to create incremental leadership opportunities for students by providing avenues for student voice at their community sites and within the programs of the center. This may mean identifying students who have leadership skills and abilities, but have not yet embraced a leadership identity, and therefore are hesitant to step forward and take on a leadership role. One example is Abigail, who was surprised when the staff invited her to the Bonner Center's Winter Staff Retreat. Over the past two and a half years, Abigail had served as a member of the Boys and Girls Club site team. The staff reviewed Abigail's history at the Club, and how she saw the program developing. Abigail had a number of substantive ideas for expansion, but she did not feel she had the organizational authority to put those projects into action.

The staff then broached the idea of instituting a formal site team leader position at the Club, who would be responsible for schedules, budgets, new project design, and volunteer management. Abigail jumped at the chance. She instituted a college week of service at the club, mobilizing student groups and community members to become engaged at the Club. Behind the scenes, it is clear that having the student team leader facilitates greater communication and better quality engagement. Abigail was waiting for the invitation to become a leader. Such is the value of having a developmental model and teams with continually evolving leadership roles. By encouraging Abigail to take the next logical step at her site, the Bonner Center gained a key ally, strengthening our relationship with an existing community partner; meanwhile, Abigail emerged as a strong leader and community organizer.

Identity Formation and Its Links to Community Engagement

The third, and possibly most predominant task of the emerging adult, is forming an identity via the exploration of varied opportunities and progressing toward making decisions with lifelong impact. Arnett (2011, 47) identifies work experiences and worldviews as two key areas where identity formation is focused for the emerging adult. Emerging adulthood is the time for exploring unusual work and educational possibilities. For this reason, short-term volunteer jobs in programs such as those supported by AmeriCorps and Peace Corps are more popular with emerging adults than with persons in any other age group. Emerging adults may also travel to a different part of the country or the world on their own for a limited period, often in the context of a limited-term work or educational experience. This too can be part of identity explorations, expanding their range of personal experiences prior to making the more enduring choices of adulthood.

The process of identity formation also involves questioning and at times abandoning beliefs. As Arnett notes, emerging adults often undertake this exploration without the support of others and are thus at risk of deconstructing former beliefs without building new ones. Here, community engagement programs engage students with faculty, staff, community members, and peers and can provide an environment to scaffold the emergence of new work experiences and worldviews in students. By balancing the doing of community engagement with the being and thinking of reflection, emerging adults experience an environment that promotes and encourages both breaking down and building up of identity and changed worldviews.

Best practices within engagement call for integrating community voice into institutional planning and decision making. Community listening projects, where the perspectives and knowledge of community partners and residents are intentionally gathered, for example, can be a step in the design and integration of assessment and community impact measurement. Here, again, is an opportunity for students to observe and participate in practices that encourage identity development in the context of others, because they give a student the opportunity to reflect on relationships and evaluate their own roles and commitments. Such decision making can extend to evaluating and making service placement decisions that mesh with the developmental needs of students. Opening the avenues for the institution and the community to have mutual dialogue that is transformative is a practice that must be carried into the direct experience of students. Inculcating the attributes of humility, empathy, openness, and critical reflection requires that students experience honest, supportive feedback from those with whom they work, including community members. Direct feedback addresses the developmental needs of students. Moreover, it provides students with a chance to see humility demonstrated by leaders, faculty, staff, community partners, and their institutions as they share and respond to feedback.

Creating teams with multiyear placements also constructs a relational environment that promotes emotional safety. Under such conditions, students can tolerate higher levels of personal feedback, both positive and negative, as an opportunity for growth, affording the opportunity for community members to integrate their voice and wisdom into the student's development. Students are able to explore a wider range of positions, roles, and unusual occupational experiences within the same site. With flexibility to experiment with a variety of positions but remain in the same team with strong supervisory connections, students' transformation is supported through longer-term projects and relationships. Students also have the opportunity for failure and subsequent success. Students who fail to meet guidelines or expectations (their own or others') in a given semester or year have the opportunity to recalibrate, learn, and try again, and are often stronger for it.

At Carson-Newman, the opportunity to "fail" and try again is a model and culture that we seek to inculcate in our programs and one that we establish with our community partners who work so closely with our students as coeducators. One student example is Sabina, an international student, who was struggling in her junior year. She was a highly capable student who seemed overwhelmed by the many roles that she juggled. She sometimes came across as scattered, disinterested, and unmotivated. Both her community service site as well as her on-campus service placement had reported concerns about her lack of follow through and distracted presence that seemed unchanged despite many conversations with site leaders. The center staff members were aware of the advanced level of work of which Sabina was capable, as she had completed an extremely successful program in her home country the previous summer. She seemed unable to achieve that same level during the academic year.

After hearing similar feedback from multiple sources, the program coordinator had a meeting with Sabina. After expressing concern and care, he also communicated disappointment and gave a disciplinary strike in the program as the result of failing to meet community partner expectations. A tearful Sabina left the office that day, and while her commitment increased, she seemed hurt and distant as a result of the interaction. It was one of a handful of meetings for the program coordinator that day. He came into my office to reflect on how he feared his job was to make students cry and to discuss the difficulties of giving constructive, caring feedback to students.

However, Sabina took that experience with her when she was accepted for an internship with an international nonprofit and national foundation the following summer. During her summer internship, she asked for feedback and input on her experience the previous year with our staff. Through Sabina's openness and seeking of feedback during her summer experience, she returned after a successful summer to an extremely successful senior year. Sabina became more invested and present at her community partner sites, learned how to overcome cultural obstacles and miscommunications, and reestablished strong mutually respectful relationships with program staff. She established new professional habits, and was able on many occasions to discuss her previous negative experience and understand how a wide range of factors both individual and systemic had contributed to the situation.

Secondarily, the community partner site where Sabina was placed often refers back to the event as one of the key turning points when they developed a relationship of trust with the Bonner Center. The Center staff's willingness to take community partner concerns seriously, to respond to them with firm but caring feedback to students, and to work together for the good of both student and community partner, cemented a bond of trust that continues today.

When all of the components come together, the result is a dynamic working relationship that adds value for the student, the community partner, and the center. At Carson-Newman one of the strongest and most productive community partnerships that has been formative for students is a partnership with the Jefferson County Juvenile Court (JCJC). In efforts to address truancy, a local youth service officer saw the need to establish a new program that addressed the family, personal, school, and economic factors that lead to truancy. However, as a JCJC employee, the Youth Services Officer (YSO) identified the need to enlist college students to work as mentors for the teens to provide near peers for a more effective intervention and to provide a younger perspective on the issues. After approaching Carson-Newman University, the YSO learned about the ability to become a community partner with the Bonner Center, which subsequently placed six students with the JCJC to develop this new program known as *Journey*.

The YSO included the students in the process to brainstorm and develop the curriculum and program, which ultimately included topics such as self-esteem, stereotyping, and drug use. The students were instrumental in developing the curriculum, and provided input to have engaging lessons and materials. The student leaders quickly became the apparent most effective instructors, with the YSO acting as a consultant. Each college student was assigned a small group of teens to mentor as well as given a selection of topics to lead throughout the series of life-skills classes. The students were able to engage the youth in the program far exceeding that of adults or court personnel.

After several initial classes, the college student leaders began to have insight into the deeper, complex issues that the youth enrolled in the Journey program were experiencing. Several students took on creative leadership roles, with one mentor developing a class entitled "Telling Our Story." At this class, the college student leaders shared their own struggles and challenges, including issues with college access, personal experiences with divorced parents, eating disorders, prior drug use, bullying, moving to new places, and so on. The leaders were open and appropriately honest, and allowed the youth to ask questions.

For the college student leaders, this experience was the first time that they had reflected on how they persevered through struggles. The experience of leading and owning the leader identity, while reflecting on their developmental process, helped many of the college students involved to incorporate modifiers such as "strong," "perseverant," and "resilient" into their self-descriptions. The college students also identified areas for personal growth through the experience.

One particular leader, Mia, struggled with being assertive. She was assigned a participant who refused to complete assignments and engage with the program. Initially, Mia asked that the youth be reassigned to another leader. After discussion, the leader realized she was partly responsible for enabling the teen to not cooperate by not setting clear expectations and not following through with consequences when assignments were incomplete. Mia was able to explain to this participant that she was doing her an injustice by not making her stand on her own two feet. The leader began to set clear expectations, and she saw small victories along the way, such as increased participation in activities. Mia kept her ground and eventually saw success in the relationship. These near-peer experiences helped Mia to develop a leadership identity, taking responsibility for her actions and role, and responding accordingly.

The leaders developed a commitment to the teens and the program, with all of the initial leaders remaining with the Journey program until college graduation. The initial cohort also trained new leaders to be successful and continue the program. The leaders developed a strong, cohesive group identity, and were able to give feedback to one another and work collaboratively to plan activities, address difficult topics, and to effectively mentor the youth participants. Again, this type of learning and application, as it occurs over multiple semesters and even years with the same group of peers, offers development that may even not be possible in a typical semester-bound class.

Positive Outcomes for the Partner and Institution

Operating such a program need not be expensive. For the first three years, the program has no budget, with the leaders utilizing creativity and resources through the college to apply for small community grants of less than US$500 to provide a few supplies and snacks for the class. Through the support of the Bonner Center, JCJC applied for and received a grant to finance an AmeriCorps VISTA staff member, as well as to add outdoor excursions to the program curriculum at the time of this writing.

Through this relationship, the JCJC and the founding YSO have been able to have a staffed program that is in its fourth year now. Area youth are provided with new resources for escaping the cycles of truancy and poverty that ensnare so many in the surrounding community. The student leaders thrive as a result of their experiences of utilizing their education to make an impact on the life of another. At the program's most recent graduation, a youth shared his experience that a leader inspired him to apply to a local community college, and that he had been accepted. After graduation, the leader shared with me how proud he was now and at that moment. The leader felt that he was changed into a better person.

As is evident from the Bonner Center's collaboration with JCJC, greater understanding of the developmental needs of the emerging adult is an essential component to creating community engagement programs that are of benefit to the student while also inculcating understanding and commitment to the community partner's larger needs. By creating multiyear teams focused on specific issues or partner sites, students are able to experience demographic cohesion across difference with their peers as well as create norms that guide pathways into adulthood for college and university students. By creating a leadership identity, and providing a supportive relational environment that cultivates identity development, students remain engaged and committed, with the secondary gains of professional skills and competence.

The results are beneficial to the center and institution, which achieves goals of developing students who are committed to service and community beyond college graduation, and who have the skills to do such work with competence. Community partner sites are more satisfied and benefit from committed multiyear volunteers who grow in competence each year and who think holistically about the community, the work of the organization, and how to contribute more deeply to that work. Finally, students are able to develop in a setting that meets their unique needs, multiplying the positive effects of the educational experience.

References

Arnett, Jeffrey Jensen. "Emerging Adulthood(s): The Cultural Psychology of a New Life Stage." In *Bridging Cultural and Developmental Approaches to Psychology: New Syntheses in Theory, Research, and Policy*, pp. 255–275. New York, NY: Oxford University Press, 2011. PsycINFO, EBSCOhost (accessed January 14, 2013).

———. "Emerging adulthood: a theory of development from the late teens through the twenties." *American Psychologist* 55, no. 5 (2000): 469–480. PsycINFO, EBSCOhost (accessed January 14, 2013).

———. "Learning to stand alone: the contemporary American transition to adulthood in cultural and historical context." *Human Development* 41, no. 5–6 (1998): 295–315. PsycINFO, EBSCOhost (accessed January 14, 2013).

Arnett, Jeffrey Jensen, and Jennifer Lynn Tanner. *Emerging Adults in America: Coming of Age in the 21st Century*. Washington, DC: American Psychological Association, 2006. PsycINFO, EBSCOhost (accessed January 14, 2013).

Greene, A. L., Susan M. Wheatley, and John F. Aldava. "Stages on life's way: adolescents' implicit theories of the life course." *Journal of Adolescent Research* 7, no. 3 (1992): 364–381.

Kuh, G. D. *High-Impact Educational Practices: What They Are, Who Has Access to Them, and Why They Matter*. Washington, DC: AAC&U, 2008.

Seifer, Sarena D. (2005). "The Evidence Base for Service in Higher Education. Community-Campus Partnerships for Health" (accessed January 14, 2013).

CHAPTER 3

Engaging Faith: Spiritual Exploration as a Critical Component

Wayne Meisel

A Story of Faith

My lens is shaped, deeply, by the perspective of faith. As the former president of the Bonner Foundation, where between 1990 and 2010, I worked with Robert Hackett (the Foundation's current president) to guide the creation of the Bonner Scholars and Leaders Program model, partnerships with more than 60 colleges and universities, and to carry out, as well, the wishes of Mr and Mrs Bonner. Being a preacher's kid, no doubt, influenced this story. I met Mr and Mrs Bonner as a child through my father's church. It was in that faith community where those relationships were established, but also where we trace the early vision, energy, and commitment to much of what is now the Bonner Program and to one of its six common commitments, *spiritual exploration.*

The importance of spiritual exploration is also affirmed by studies in higher education more broadly. In 2003, the Higher Education Research Institute began a major, multiyear research project to examine the spiritual development of undergraduate students during their college years. With funding from the John Templeton Foundation, the study aimed to enhance higher education's understanding of the role that spirituality plays in students' lives and to identify strategies that institutions can use to enhance students' spiritual development (Astin et al., 2005). The report "A National Study of College Students' Search for Meaning and Purpose" (2005) reflected surveys of 112,232 students attending a national sample of 236 colleges and universities. Students' responses to six-page survey questionnaire addressed questions about their backgrounds, educational and occupational aspirations, and values and beliefs with respect to spiritual and religious matters. In fact, "The study revealed that today's college students have very high levels of spiritual interest and involvement. Many are actively engaged in a spiritual quest and are exploring the meaning and purpose of life. They also display high levels of religious commitment and involvement" (Astin et al., 2005). Co-Principal Investigators, Alexander Astin and Helen Astin, wrote:

> The project is based in part on the realization that the relative amount of attention that colleges and universities devote to the "exterior" and "interior" aspects of students' development has gotten out of balance...we have increasingly come to neglect the student's inner development—the sphere of values and beliefs, emotional maturity, spirituality, and self-understanding.

Indeed, the realization that college students nationally share an interest in exploring their faith perspectives is one that resonates.

This chapter explores how that theme has played out in the network of campuses involved in the Bonner Program, especially between 1990 and 2010. The work that we are examining, describing, evaluating, and celebrating has at its core a small group of people who drew on their faith to build a program designed to create opportunity while also fighting injustice. Telling this story offers an opportunity to look deeply into the way faith can and does play an active role in the service world. Just so that there is no mistake, this is not merely a Christian story. It is true that Mr and Mrs Bonner were Christian and their faith was very important in their lives. However, they did not start the Bonner Program as a force to convert people to Christianity or proclaim their faith at the expense of disclaiming others. From my perspective, their faith motivated action. It was born out of a faith of "radical welcoming" not just to include, but to involve and integrate.

The Legacy of Mrs Bonner

Nowhere was this more prevalent than at Mrs Bonner's memorial service in 2003. On that day, close to 1,000 people gathered at the Princeton University Chapel not to mourn a loss, but to celebrate a life. The only thing firmer than Mrs Bonner's handshake was her faith. It was as strong as it was simple and founded on daily scripture reading, morning and evening prayers, and regular attendance at church. People of different faiths encountered her and

felt her support. During her memorial service, Lan To, a Bonner graduate, opened her remarks with the ringing of the bell, as is the tradition in
her Buddhist background. She explained that the bell was "a calling...and
Mrs. Bonner is like that bell. Mrs. Bonner was our Bodhisattva that stood
before us to say: 'You can do it.' " She went on to say that her service experience called her to explore her Buddhism and the faith traditions of others.

Mrs Bonner's faith touched others. Mal Hajdini, a Muslim from Kosovo,
described how Mrs Bonner was not concerned with religious difference.
"Mrs. Bonner taught me the truth about God's love and commitment and the
truth that Muslims and Christians are brothers and sisters," she said. Abhishek
Singh, a student at Concord College and a Hindu born in India, talked of his
faith by describing that "completion is pristine and a pure state. Most of us
strive for completion, but only some of us realize it. I encountered one such
soul: Mrs. Bonner. She touched my life in a way which provided me the education I need to realize my potential." Linda Meisel, the head of Jewish Family
and Children's Services in the Princeton, NJ, community, spoke about how
Mrs Bonner recognized and honored the core values of Judaism. Mrs Bonner
provided the initial funding for the Kosher Food pantry, understanding that
for some Jews, being kosher was a strong and vital link to faith.

The lifting up of faith, not the downplaying of it, has given the Bonner
Program strength and perseverance. Mrs Bonner may have been a focal
point but it was what she embodied and how we related to one another that
gave definition and hope moving forward. Faith strengthened our resolve to
serve; it did not isolate or seek to diminish or distinguish one group from
another. Instead, as described by these individuals who were so intimately
impacted by their experiences in the Bonner Program, personal faith was
often strengthened and shared.

The Founding Fathers and Mothers of the Bonner Program

Starting the Bonner Program was not a simple process. There were many
questions. Which schools would be interested? Which institutions would
be a good fit? Which campuses and their leaders would be inspiring and
inspired? The Bonner Program took three years to launch. The first year
was a pilot year with Berea College, the second involved schools located
in the Appalachian region, and the third year included institutions in the
midwest and southeast that had distinguished themselves by demonstrating
a commitment to academic excellence, community engagement, and access
to low-income students.

All but one of these institutions were private schools. Moreover, all of
them had some type of relationship with a church or a denomination, or

a founder whose faith conviction led them to establish the church. Robert Fife, the founder of Berea College, also founded Union Church near campus. Charles Finney, the leader of the Second Great awakening, left Rochester, New York, to become the president of Oberlin College. The Atlanta Baptist Female Seminary was established in the basement of Friendship Baptist Church in Atlanta, Georgia, by Harriet Giles and Sophia Packard, and was later renamed Spelman College. Schools were selected not because of their religious affiliations or school mottos, but rather because of the shared vision with the Bonners.

The first call we would place to potential schools was to the college and university presidents, who then gathered around the table at the Boone Tavern in Berea, Kentucky. These discussions, led by then Berea President John Stephenson, were followed up by gatherings of other campus staff and students to envision and build the Bonner Program at their own institution. Unlike today, few schools had campus service programs, let alone center directors, to lead this effort. Instead, the presidents turned to faculty and student life administrators and most of all, chaplains. In the early 1990s, most of the service activities at schools around the country were being run out of chaplains' offices. And so many of the founding directors on participating campuses were clergy or those who were very public about their faith commitments and the integrity of their spiritual journey.

Two things were impressive. One was the number of founding directors who were religiously trained and ordained in different denominations. The other unique characteristic of those initial meetings was that there was little, if any, "religious speak." I do not remember people quoting scripture or even speaking the name "Jesus." Instead, the people in the room drew on their faith and spirituality in founding the Bonner Program without having to talk much about it. It was the best example of *walking the talk.*

The Great Divorce between Faith and Service

Although most Bonner Programs were originally housed in the chaplain's office, it was not long before there was a mass movement of service programs away from religious life and toward student life. One challenge was that the chaplain's office did not have the capacity to oversee a large, campus-wide program that in many cases had more student participants than any other program other than the football team. Additionally, there were some chaplains who felt that the focus on service kept them away from other duties, in particular pastoral care and counseling.

However, a real reason for the movement, in my view, was the fact that there was a strong push to secularize the service world at the college level.

More and more people were categorizing faith-based service as narrow minded and limited and schools could not be strongly tied to a religious identity and have a broad service reach. As more and more funding became available for service work, particularly through Federal programs like AmeriCorps, the split went from being a choice to a perceived requirement. Resulting from the need to separate Federal funding from religious proselytizing, the growing list of "prohibited activities" had the effect of pushing out any faith language in conversations, reflections, and journaling. The separation has grown even wider as schools continue to move their service-learning programs and civic engagement centers onto the academic side of campus culture, which in many cases is even less friendly and less tolerant of faith conversations. While understandable from policy and legal perspectives, this separation may be masking part of the story of students' interest and development.

Faith as a Common Commitment for the Bonner Experience

The faith and service connection into the Bonner Program was finally made and given voice when the Bonner Common Commitments, a set of values identified as core to the program, were created and *spiritual exploration* was identified as a core tenet of the Bonner experience.

Our strategy in developing the Bonner Program was to let the program unfold and bring the diversity of experience from each of the schools together to create homegrown expressions with a national connection. But when the program celebrated its tenth anniversary at Berry College in 2000, we knew it was time to give some definition to what we had done, who we were, and where we were headed. In order to do this, a series of three large gatherings were held to discuss these very questions. First was a gathering of all program directors and coordinators. The second was a meeting of student leaders and the third a mixture of the two along with national leaders in the field of service who had some type of relationship with or strong interest in the Bonner Program. For the purpose of this chapter, it is important to note that one of the six themes that appeared in each conversation was *spiritual exploration*, which was defined as "exploring personal beliefs and values while respecting the beliefs of others."

To many, it was a huge surprise that spiritual exploration surfaced. However, for others, it was an obvious reclaiming and explanation of where the motivation for much of these activities came from. As the list became more public, the Foundation received calls expressing caution and even urgency, expressing "Bonner should not go there! You don't want to get into that religious mess!" They warned that if we used the term "spiritual," it would prevent us from partnering with state schools or secular institutions.

Those who stated these concerns were correct at one level. Since the time when we embraced the Common Commitments, including *spiritual exploration*, I have had conversations with potential institutional partners who said that this was "troubling to them." In turn, I admitted that it had been troubling to me at times as well, but that it represented a fact about what is important to people and how they define and engage in the world.

Case Study: Rhodes College

Rather than moving the Bonner Program out of the chaplain's office like so many other schools, Rhodes College decided to use it as a cornerstone to reclaim tradition and proclaim a commitment to be an intentional interfaith community. The school describes it this way: "Our emphasis on community service and spiritual growth springs from our historic affiliation with the Presbyterian Church. While our students come from many faith traditions, they share a passion for making this world a better place for all" (Flaum, 2012).

The Bonner Center for Faith & Service supports Christian, Jewish, and Muslim student groups, as well as other religious and cultural groups on campus. While living and growing in one's own particular faith, students are called to live with respect for a diverse community of many beliefs and practices. Common commitments to servant leadership, social justice, and compassion for others often link students of different religious backgrounds in service, learning, and ecumenical ministries. The college's Presbyterian history teaches the value of the life of faith and spiritual integrity, as well as the life of the mind; to respect religious freedom and diversity; and to serve God by serving our neighbors, seeking peace and justice in all of God's creation.

Walt Tennyson came to Rhodes after serving as the senior minister at Broadway Presbyterian Church in New York City. One symbol of that community of faith is that the church billboard, rather than posting next Sunday's sermon title and worship times, lists the menu of the day for the soup kitchen. Tennyson left to lead the charge in maintaining the connection between faith and service at Rhodes. In a recent article, he states, "I think it is true there is something—a God-sized hole—in people. People are desperate for meaning. They are aware the world they are living in is in crisis." Students want to make sense of and repair it "and our office is where they get connected to that world."

Tennyson describes the religious culture at Rhodes as "hugely dynamic," from students who remain closely tied to the religious tradition in which they grew up to those who keep a deliberate distance from an organized religion. A common denominator among many of the students, however, is a desire to connect with the broader world—people of other countries, religions, and experiences. He claims that there is "real enthusiasm" among college students for interfaith experiences. "Our students really enjoy experiencing other peoples' religious beliefs and traditions and services," Tennyson said. "Probably the most dynamic religious role I have is leading our interfaith group on campus."

Students who may not be churchgoers volunteer with Streets, an evangelical ministry that serves children in one of the poorest zip codes in the country. Rhodes students teach pottery, painting, and other artistic skills in the "More than Art" program at Idlewild Presbyterian Church, which provides creative opportunities to disadvantaged people. The same church runs More than a Meal where students work with Idlewild "to build relationships between the church community and people from the nearby neighborhood for whom affordable shelter can pose a challenge."

A recent profile of Noor Eltayech, a Bonner Scholar, tells the story of how a school affiliation with the Christian faith can be a source of strength, affirmation, and light to someone of a different faith. Coming to Rhodes seemed like a natural fit for Noor. Her love of community service dovetailed perfectly with her Muslim faith when she was offered a job in the Bonner Interfaith office her first year. "I came to Rhodes and I'd always done community service in high school, but I expanded religiously when I came to Rhodes," she says. After her first year, she applied to the Bonner Program and became a Bonner Interfaith Coordinator. Although she grew up with religion as an important part of her life, her new job was not easy at first. "I view religion as something very personal," she says, "and I don't like talking about it or doing anything to disrupt anyone's peace. It was something that I had to get used to, because it was definitely out of my comfort zone." Her discomfort faded fast as the college chaplain, Walt Tennyson, sent her to workshops to learn how to talk to people about religion and be a leader to people of other faiths. "I think it's really helped me develop skills to understand what I believe in and what others believe and how to bridge the gaps," she says. As part of a religious minority on campus, Noor says that being Muslim has not been an issue.

The Bonner Student Impact Survey

After ten years of "doing" and at the urging of Bob Bottoms, then president of DePauw University, the Foundation reached out to Jim and Cheryl Keen to help us design and administer a survey of the students in the program and evaluate the results. The Bonner Student Impact Surveys suggested that faith was not just a motivator but also a source of fulfillment for the engaged student. For example, in 2003, Cheryl Keen reported to the Bonner Network the results of the outgoing senior surveys, which involved students across 25 institutions that participated in the Bonner Scholar Program. Among those students, 62 percent identified themselves as "religiously affiliated," an increase from 50 percent in 2002 and 56 percent in 2001. Morever, 23 percent of the students said that they were "spiritual but not affiliated." Additionally, 4 percent of the students indicated that their affiliation had changed during college, and 7 percent of the students said they were not religious (C. Keen and J. Keen, 2003). Moreover, dialogue about spiritual beliefs that was one of the types of dialogues across issues of difference and diversity was suggested as important to students. Measuring growth between freshmen and seniors, Keen and Hall (2009) reported that "the strongest positive difference between the same freshmen and seniors was the importance of the BSP as an opportunity for dialogue." Moreover, they noted:

> Moderate academic differences between freshmen and seniors, represented by increased time spent studying ($\_ = 0.333$, $\div 2 = 144.538$, $p < 0.000$), were also not muted by the requirements of a service scholarship, nor the increased time spent in athletics or exercise ($\_ = 0.294$, $\div 2 = 114.328$, $p < 0.000$). Weak but significant variables included hours spent using the internet; importance of the BSP for developing new skills, leadership development, enhancement of resume, developing an international perspective, *furthering faith development, exploring faith development*, influencing the political structure, engaging different dimensions of diversity, developing a philosophy of life, and opportunity to work with people; and *hours spent in faith development*, social life, and jobs. (Keen and Hall, 2009)

What was going on? We expected that students from religiously affiliated schools would have a strong response, but we were shocked, in some ways, that students in all types of institution expressed these sentiments. As Cheryl Keen reported, clusters of colleges—faith-based, elite, racially and economically diverse, urban, and those who sent Bonners on international service projects more—were created and evaluated against the clustered dependent variable of desired outcomes. Seniors from faith-based institutions did not have a significantly different experience with the program than the students from the remaining group of colleges. Rather, students from faith-based institutions had a significantly similar experience to those from economically and racially diverse campuses (Keen, 2013).

Closer analysis was prompted. The analysis led to the realization that the Bonner Program's model would need to allow for the connection between faith and service. The response was not to establish Bible study or to make chapel mandatory. Instead, as foundation and program staff and leadership, we could encourage students, faculty, administrators, and community leaders to ask questions, share stories, and lift up examples of where faith and service came to life. Reflections and dialogue about spiritual exploration, which are designed and conducted in inclusive, interfaith ways and often connected with exploration of values, vocation, and long-term interests, are a part of the program, customized by the unique context of each institution and its programs. By identifying and engaging in the connection between faith and service, I believed, we could be more responsive to the students that we were there to serve, nurture, and develop. In the end, we recognized a deep yearning on the part of the students to explore, to discern, to experiment, to learn, to engage, and to move down the path of spiritual exploration.

If we genuinely care for the students whom we work with, we will take the time not just to share our own spiritual journey but create a safe space for them to share their stories and move along on their own journey without fearing retribution or humiliation. And beyond nurturing the inquiry of our students, it is important to take the time to understand, respect, and engage our community partners and their members in developing their understanding of their faith. Many of our programs and those who lead them and show up time and again are born out of the faithful witness of communities of faith that care about issues of social justice and community service.

References

Astin, Alexander W., Helen S. Astin, J. A. Lindholm, A. N. Bryant, K. Szelényi, and S. Calderone. *The Spiritual Life of College Students: A National Study of College Students' Search for Meaning and Purpose.* Los Angeles, CA: UCLA Higher Education Research Institute, 2005.

Flaum, Jackie. "Learning through Real-World Service." *Rhodes College Magazine,* Winter 2012.

Keen, Cheryl, and Jim Keen. Memorandum on Graduating Senior Survey Spring 2003.

Keen, Cheryl, and Kelly Hall. "Engaging with difference matters: longitudinal student outcomes of co-curricular service-learning programs." *The Journal of Higher Education* 80, no. 1 (January/February 2009).

Keen, Cheryl. Personal communication, 2013.

"Religious Life & Community Service." Rhodes College. Web: February 6, 2013.

Scanlon, Leslie. "Young adults do connect with church—but often far beyond the church walls." *The Presbyterian Outlook,* October 15, 2012.

CHAPTER 4

An Untapped Reservoir for Student Community Engagement: What We Are Learning from the NASCE

Mathew Johnson, Don Levy, Pete Cichetti, and Craig Zinkiewicz

Introduction

Despite the growing importance of community engagement in American higher education and the academic interest in its impact on students, little effort has been made to clearly quantify volume, frequency, or depth of community engagement activities on individual campuses or among significant numbers of college students. In order to address the need for an objective assessment tool that can measure the aggregate amount, frequency, and depth of community engagement across an institution, the authors developed the National Assessment of Service and Community Engagement (NASCE). At the most basic level, NASCE seeks to determine the extent to which students at institutions of higher education are engaged in their communities. The NASCE is the first tool that uses student-reported experience to quantitatively measure community engagement among individual students and the institutions in which they are nested. Now implemented on 36 colleges and universities, its results are suggesting key insights about what might propel community engagement to higher levels on college campuses. Campuses in two key national networks—the Bonner and Campus Compact networks—have been among early adopters of this assessment instrument, integrating its lessons into long-range planning for community engagement.[1]

This chapter introduces the NASCE and provides quantitative data on community engagement and service among college students through the unique Percent of the Possible (POP – the quantification of service simultaneously considering participation, frequency and depth) Score and Capacity Contribution prisms by nine need areas. This chapter also demonstrates the utility of the NASCE as an assessment and planning tool that allows colleges and universities to accurately identify their current contribution to the community and take steps to improve their overall level of community engagement. The NASCE looks at the sample from five different study aspects including: (1) measuring the community engagement and service performed by students before enrolling in, and while at college; (2) measuring and reporting the engagement and service across nine areas of human need; (3) expressing engagement and service performed as a percent of the possible service an institution can offer; (4) providing colleges with a measurement of their capacity contribution; and (5) providing a tool that can be used to pinpoint strengths and weaknesses for use in institutional planning.

Method

The NASCE is delivered online to students of participating college campuses. An e-mail invitation is sent to the entire student body that includes a link to the survey. Students are encouraged to participate within the invitation (the value of the project to the institution is highlighted) and participating institutions are coached in a variety of techniques that increase response rates. Response rates across the 36 participating schools range from 2 percent to 41 percent. While sample distribution by year in school has been representative, we find that women are more likely than men to respond to the survey. Additionally, qualitative supplementary research shows that the NASCE tends to slightly overstate service; engaged students are more likely to complete the instrument. The selection bias does not undermine the merit of the methodology in this case as the NASCE reports surprisingly low levels of student participation in community engagement. Therefore, the data collected and findings are highly instructive and a valid measure of community engagement of students if still subject to minor sampling error.

The Sample Demographics

To date, the NASCE has interviewed 19,078 students from 36 colleges and universities of varying sizes and affiliations. The colleges and universities range in size from 800 to 21,000 students and span ten states in the United States. The institutions differ in characteristics such as religious affiliation, public or private, and size. Of these, 25 institutions are private, 11 public; 9 religiously affiliated, 27 with secular beliefs; 6 are large schools with 10,000 or more students, 6 are medium-sized schools with between 5,000 and 10,000 students, and 24 are small schools with less than 5,000 students.

Of the 19,078 students, 30 percent of the respondents are male, 70 percent are female, 72 percent Caucasian, 9 percent African American, 8 percent Asian, 4 percent Hispanic or Latino, and 4 percent multiracial. The average age of respondents is 22 years and their average college grade point average (GPA) is 3.25. All of the colleges and universities in this data set are four-year institutions and the breakdown of class year is: 26 percent seniors, 24 percent juniors, 24 percent sophomores, and 26 percent freshman.

NASCE Contribution #1: Doing Service "Before" and "While at"

The NASCE uniquely measures students' community engagement before and while at college by quantifying their community service. Strikingly, the overall measurement of community engagement, by the question, *"Prior to coming to XYZ College, did you engage in community service of any kind?,"* is far greater in high school or prior to attending college than while at college. Across the sample, 85 percent said that they engaged in service in high school but only 46 percent said that they performed service while in college. Keep in mind that the NASCE indicates that community service *"includes any activity in which you participate with the goal of providing, generating and/or sustaining help for individuals and groups who have unmet legitimate human needs in areas like shelter, health, nutrition, education, and opportunity."* NASCE asks respondents to *"keep all the types of service in which they engage in mind as they answer"* all the questions.

The NASCE casts a wide and inviting net. Any type of service a student may have participated in whether individually, in a class, or through a club or organization (inside and outside school) counts as service and is measured as a component of community engagement. Some students may not perceive their contribution as community service and therefore will not report participating in service, or students may perceive certain contributions as community engagement that is not taken into consideration, such as voting. These student perceptions may ultimately lead to slightly skewed data. Certainly, some respondents may forget a project on which they worked or say that they did service that they did not however, the NASCE clearly tells respondents what the survey is about and repeatedly asks them to describe any and all ways that they have participated in community service (engagement).

After working through the questions probing service across nine different potential areas of engagement in high school, respondents transition to thinking about their life at college. Out of the sample of 19,078 students, the reported rate of community service drops 39 percentage points from high school to college. Among the colleges themselves, the average college has students with a "*before*" rate of service of 86.6 percent and a "*while at XYZ*" rate of 51.7 percent, only slightly different, albeit greater, than the sample as a whole.[2]

Despite the similarity of the means of the sample of students and sample of colleges, significant variation in the "*before*" rates, "*while at*" rates, and consequent drop scores does exist. For example, the highest performing school, defined by rate of service "*while at*" college had a "*before*" rate of 96 percent and the smallest drop rate of 9 percent yielding a "*while at*" rate of nearly 87 percent. Another small elite liberal arts college had a "*before*" rate of 95 percent and a drop rate of 58 percent. The NASCE reveals an overall pattern of decline in community engagement (service) from high school to college as well as expresses the difference between individuals' rates of service among the participating institutions.

This first measure in the NASCE provides schools with (1) an overall assessment of the global service performed by their students; (2) a quick understanding of the change that occurs from high school to college; and (3) an early indication of the contribution, or lack thereof, being made by the institution to the generation of service and community engagement. Most students say that they engaged in service in high school, but nearly half (45%) stop while in college. It is a reasonable argument that students are more engaged in service prior to college in an attempt to pad their resume; however, other reasons may exist. Whether it be that the structure for service is more in place in high school or the act of living at home with family providing the framework for service, the NASCE invites colleges and scholars to more systematically probe the data, the experience of students, and the structures that colleges offer so as to understand this significant fall off in the rate of community engagement among students.

NASCE Contribution #2: Measuring Nine Areas of Service

In addition to ascertaining whether students have been involved in community engagement at all, the NASCE also asks all respondents who indicate that they do participate in service to say: (1) if any of that service is done in each of nine areas, (2) how often and (3) at which of the three distinct levels of commitment. This sequence of questions is replicated for "*before*" and "*while at*" behavior.

- Respondents who do perform community service either *"before"* or *"while at"* are then asked to indicate in which types of service they participate: Addressing homelessness or housing (e.g., Habitat for Humanity);
- Addressing hunger and nutrition issues (e.g., working at a soup kitchen or on a food drive);
- Economic opportunity and access (e.g., financial literacy, business development, or international development);
- Elder care (e.g., adopt a grandparent);
- Environmental efforts (e.g., local cleanup);
- Promoting public awareness or civic participation (e.g., working on voter awareness, tolerance, or issues of safety)
- Religious or spiritual service (e.g., teaching a Sunday school class);
- Working to promote health or fitness (e.g., donating blood, visiting the sick, or raising money to combat a disease);
- Youth services (e.g., tutoring, coaching, or working on a toy drive).

These issue areas were generated through focus groups with students during the developmental and pilot phase of the NASCE. Respondents who indicate serving in any one area are then asked to describe the frequency with which they engage in that activity: *"once or twice a year," "several times during the year," "about once a month," "several times a month," "about once a week,"* or *"more than once a week."* Finally, for each activity in which respondents indicate they participate, respondents are asked to indicate their depth of involvement by choosing among (note: respondents can indicate more than one level of involvement): (1) *"participate at an event or short-term drive"* (2) *"involved on a regular basis for a period of time"* or (3) *"deeply involved in a project or cause and dedicated to it."*

The NASCE moves from one measure that offers no specificity and no intensity to a rank order of service by area and to two measures of intensity for each student. Schools can know the percentage of students working in each of the nine areas as well as the relative intensity with which students are engaged in each area. Schools can use the NASCE to more strategically target specific need areas for improvement by gaining awareness about where and to what extent they are of service to their community. Finally, participating schools now can say with a far higher degree of reliability what percentage of students is involved and how involved they are.

Table 4.1 shows that, across the entire sample, the greatest percentage of students are involved in activities that focus on *Youth* (25%) followed by *Health* (24%), the *Environment* (20%), *Hunger* (18%), *Civic Awareness* (15%), *Homelessness* (14%), *Religion* (7%), *Elder Care* (7%), and *Economic*

Table 4.1 Percentage of student participation, frequency, and depth by area across entire sample

Service Area	Percent of engaged students	Of those that engage, percent engaging:		
		Once a year	Several times a year or more	Deeply
Youth	25	15	85	40
Health	24	27	73	22
Environment	20	36	64	16
Hunger	18	33	67	17
Civic	15	22	78	32
Homelessness	14	37	63	20
Religion	7	9	91	52
Elder	7	31	69	24
Economic	4	21	79	35

Opportunity (4%). Many students—ranging from a low of 9 percent in religion to a high of 37 percent in the *Homelessness*—engaged in any area, may only serve once or twice a year—perhaps at a drive, event, or fundraiser. On the other hand, in some areas of service, nearly all or above 80 percent of students do so several times a year or more often: This includes areas such as *Religion* and *Youth Services*. The "Deeply" column refers to those students who participate in addressing that area of need at the highest level of depth, indicating that they are committed to the cause and dedicated to it. That is, when given the choice between one-shot engagement, regular involvement for a period of time, or deep commitment, 40 percent of those addressing *Youth Services* claim to be deeply committed to serving that need area. Thus, of the total number of students across the entire sample that work toward addressing *Youth Services*, 40 percent are involved at the highest level of depth. At the same time, only 16 percent of the 20 percent of the sample that participates in service addressing *Environmental Concerns* is deeply engaged in that area. The NASCE then combines the responses in these nine areas to compute the unique *Percent of the Possible—POP Scores*.

NASCE Contribution #3: The Percent of the Possible—POP Scores: A Measure of Community Engagement

The NASCE combines (1) the rate at which each respondent serves in every category, (2) the frequency with which they are engaged, and (3) their self-described level of depth, to compute a raw individual score and then the percent of the possible score (raw and normalized) for each school overall and in each service area. In doing so, schools can understand the collective degree of overall service they offer to their community and the manner in which that service is dispersed across their student population, by issue area, and intensity.

POP Scores are computed in the NASCE for individuals both prior to college and while at college. Respondents who indicated that they did not participate in community engagement and service of any kind prior to college—15 percent of the entire sample—or while at college—54 percent of the entire sample, do not contribute to elevating the *POP Score*. By definition, their contribution is nonexistent. Surely, some error exists here. Those students who say that they did no service in high school or that they do no service today may very well have done something but conceptually in our analysis, they count as a zero, that is, they do no service and they are not engaged in their community.

The *POP* score is a percentage of what is possible. The ultimate or the possible would be an institution in which 100 percent of students not only answered yes to the global question (they are engaged) but they also said that they perform service frequently and deeply. For example, a student in this abstract scenario will have participated in service addressing hunger needs as often as weekly as well as with deep involvement (involved in a project and dedicated to its cause). Rather than thinking of service as a chore or time commitment, these students are drawn to serve by the issue or problem and work toward its resolution. The abstract continuum then extends from zero—no one does any service at any rate or at any depth—to total or 100 percent—everyone does frequent service at meaningful depth in every area.

Institutions do however have students—54 percent in college and 15 percent prior to college—who *do no service*. The other half of students may participate once in a while at an event or drive as a participant in one or a couple of areas. For example, over the course of a year, a student may take part in one Saturday morning environmental cleanup and then months later see a sign for a food drive and drop by with some cans of soups. Surely, that student has served but his or her contribution is quite modest. In terms of the NASCE, yes, they served, in two areas, but in each area, only once and at the least significant level of depth. Another student may also have had similar one-shot opportunities with environment and hunger but also got involved in a tutoring program weekly. This student is active in three areas, two in the least contributory sense and one in the more frequent and more deeply committed sense.

The NASCE accommodates the measurement of these and many other types of students by assigning values to those students who perform service in each area:

1. Engagement. In any of the nine areas—Yes (1), No (0)
2. Frequency. Once or twice a year (1), several times a year or once a month (2), several times a month (3), weekly or more (4)
3. Depth. An event or drive, one-shot (1), regular basis for a period of time or a service trip (2), deeply involved and dedicated to a project or cause (3).

Each respondent's value for engagement, frequency, and depth are multiplied to find the total units of service produced in each of the nine areas and then summed across those nine areas to find that respondent's total units of service altogether.

While students who do no service of any kind score 0 points, students similar to the first example mentioned earlier would score by virtue of being engaged in two areas, once or twice a year, at events, a total of 2 points ((1 × 1 = 1) + (1 × 1 = 1)). The second student would score 6 points ((1 × 1 × 1) + (1 × 1 × 1) + (1 × 2 × 2)) having engaged in two one-shot activities but also been frequently involved on a continuing basis in the tutoring program. The third student would score 2 points for his or her one-shot engagements and an additional 12 points (1 × 4 × 3) for his or her frequent and deep involvement in the elder program. By virtue of the multiplier effect, the maximum units of service a single student can produce is 108 (a raw score of 12 multiplied by 9 areas of service).

While it may not be exact, the student who was involved in one area, one time at a drive (1 point/unit of service) obviously generates far less service than the student who is continuously involved several times a month (6 points/units of service). However, that student is still less engaged than the student who is fully devoted and actively involved (12 points/units of service).

The NASCE moves from developing each individual's units of service in each of the nine areas (0–12) to computing the *POP Score* by first expressing the sum of the individuals' units of service scores as a "percent of the possible." Again, the possible is that degree of service that would be expressed if 100 percent of students were "12"s, that is, all were frequently involved at a significant depth.[3]

The raw POP score for each area is expressed as:

(Service * Frequency * max(Depth))/12 (12 being the maximum possible units of service)

And the institutional raw *POP Score* is computed where n = the number of areas:

$$\Sigma \text{ (Service * Frequency * max(Depth))}/n * 12$$

Table 4.2 displays the high school and college mean service that is the total units of service expressed by the entire student population of 19,078 (Economic was only asked of 16,279) as a mean, the computed raw score for each area, the *POP Score* for the sample both while in high school and now in college, and finally the total service expression as a mean, a raw score, and a *POP Score* both in high school and in college.

In order to understand the chart in table 4.2 and prior to a discussion of the results, follow the quantitative expression first across one area and then across the total sample (shown as the total of nine areas). The high school mean service is the average across the entire sample of 19,078; an identical computation is done for individual schools, of units of service, that is, engagement (0,1) times frequency (1–4) times depth (1–3). The mean service of youth, in this case 3.41, is the average expression of service of the total sample. Another way of looking at it would be to multiply the mean (3.41) by the total sample to compute total units of service (65,056). The mean service is divided by 12, the maximum service expression of any individual, to find the raw *POP Score*, in this case 0.28 or about one quarter of the possible.

Table 4.2 Sample-wide service: Mean, raw score, POP scores – By area and overall

Service area	N	High school			College		
		Mean units of service	Raw POP score	POP score	Mean units of service	Raw POP score	POP score
Youth	19,078	3.41	0.28	84	1.74	0.13	39
Health	19,078	1.50	0.12	36	0.95	0.07	22
Civic	19,078	0.83	0.07	20	0.75	0.06	18
Environment	19,078	1.31	0.11	33	0.71	0.05	16
Hunger	19,078	1.23	0.10	31	0.67	0.05	16
Homelessness	19,078	0.67	0.06	17	0.55	0.04	13
Religious	19,078	1.86	0.15	46	0.55	0.04	12
Elder	19,078	0.79	0.07	20	0.32	0.02	7
Economic	19,078	0.28	0.02	8	0.24	0.02	7
Total of 9 areas	**19,078**	**11.72**	**0.11**	**33**	**6.34**	**0.06**	**17**

Because it is difficult to discuss small numbers, and due to the finding that the overall sample and individual colleges yield raw percent of the possible numbers that are quite small, a normalization process is used to express the final *POP Score* in larger, more accessible numbers. We argue that a raw score of 0.33, that is, a mean score of 4 divided by a possible of 12 would be demonstrative of an engaged campus and therefore use that definition of engagement as the basis of the POP normalization. On average, all students would score 4. While it is unrealistic to expect to have no "0"s, an average of 4 of 12 could be framed as the mean of students engaged in the area, at least once a month, with a moderate depth. A NASCE raw score is normalized to a *POP Score* of 100. A score of 100 in any one area or across the entire institution would be a worthwhile, meaningful but aggressive goal. Quantitatively, that normalization entails multiplying the Youth raw score by 303.03 in order to arrive at the POP score of 84 for the area of Youth across the entire sample while in high school.

The Drop of Service from High School to College

Immediately, we find that the *POP Score* for *Youth Services* (39), although being the highest single area among our sample while in college, is less than half the *Youth POP* while in high school (*POP score* = 84). We also see that the expression of service as stated by the *POP* drops across our sample in each of the nine measured areas. Not surprisingly, the total service here discussed as 9 areas falls from a POP of 33 in high school to 17 while in college. The mean score in high school 11.72 of a possible 108 falls to 6.34 of a possible 108 while in college. The potential 108 represents the possible raw score of 12 for each area, multiplied by 9 areas of service.

Individual institutions' POP scores vary significantly. For example, while the overall sample POP for Youth is 39, the average across the sample of schools is 54 and the range among the sampled schools is 5–151. The amount and depth of service performed by students at different schools vary greatly. On an institutional level, the overall POP scores also vary tremendously. Of the 36 schools in the sample, the institutional POP scores ranged from 3 to 52. The NASCE stipulates a POP score of 100 as the goal and identifies the following scores accordingly: scores below 20 as low, at least 20 but below 40 as moderate, at least 40 but below 60 as high, and 60 or greater as impressive.

By identifying scores using the *POP*, we now see (1) a single score that expresses service in each of the nine areas of service, (2) a total score of service performed by a sample of students from an institution, (3) a total score by area and overall for a large sample of college students, and (4) an expression of service by area and overall.

NASCE Contribution #4: The Capacity Contribution: An Institution's Contribution to the Community

Colleges possess and can mobilize a significant capacity to serve their community; many would argue that it is their duty. The NASCE provides schools with a quantitative and graphic measure of that capacity contribution to the community. Some colleges assert that as many as 95 percent of students perform meaningful community service that has a dramatic positive effect on the local community. The NASCE shows that less than 50 percent of students in general, more at some institutions, less at others, do any service. Using *POP*, NASCE shows that in many areas, little service is done and few students are deeply engaged. This suggests that, rather than being at a ceiling, community engagement in college still has enormous potential to increase.

Schools can use the NASCE to see how much capacity they are expressing and how they plan to enhance that contribution. A capacity contribution graph for the total sample of 19,078 is shown in Figure 4.1. Each institution that participates in the NASCE receives a capacity contribution graph overall and for each area surveyed. The Y-axis is the expression of service both in terms of *POP* and also stated as units of service. The X-axis represents the percentage of all respondents or students who collectively generate that service or express that capacity. Among the sample, the capacity contribution area begins at 46 percent in college. The X-axis is stated in terms of least amount of service to greatest amount of service. The red line in Figure 4.1 represents the total units of service generated by the overall sample of 19,078 students.

Figure 4.2 shows the work done for one area, Youth services, for the entire sample. Individual school curves would vary based on how many students participate in *Youth Services*, at what frequency, and at what depth.

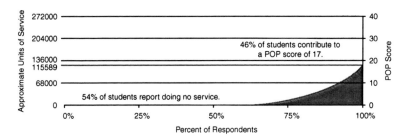

Figure 4.1 Capacity contribution: Institutional. Fifty-four percent of students report doing no service. Forty-six percent of students contribute to a POP score of 17.

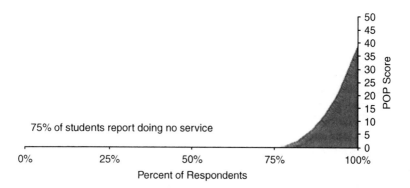

Figure 4.2 Twenty-five percent of students contribute to a POP score of 39. Ten percent of students account for 67 percent of the Youth POP score.

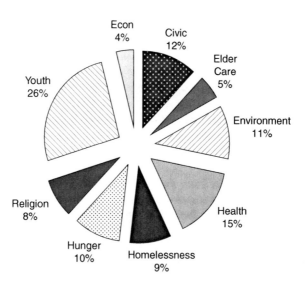

Figure 4.3 Total service by needs area.

Here we see that while a POP of 39, which falls just into the range we label high, is only generated by the participation of 25 percent of students. When frequency and depth are considered, 67 percent of the POP or units of service are generated by only 10 percent of the students.

Given that *Youth Services* is, across the entire sample, the area in which service is greatest and is consequently the area with the greatest individual

POP Score as well as the largest contributor to overall units of service, the capacity contribution graphs of each of the other eight areas are less impressive. Figure 4.3 shows the percentage of the overall service by area across the entire sample. A small percentage of students contribute to the overall *POP score* in most of the nine areas of service. Ultimately, schools can use this tool to understand how service expression is measured, how great their expression of capacity is, and to plan strategies to enhance their capacity contribution.

NASCE Contribution #5: Institutional Implementation Strategies

The NASCE provides to participating institutions a measurement of how many students are engaged and to what extent across nine areas of service. The NASCE gives institutions an invaluable strategic planning tool through its use of advanced data collection in the unique *POP* score system and the foundational "units of service" or *Capacity Contribution* graphs.

Assume first of all that an institution received the overall *Capacity Contribution* graph pictured in Figure 4.1 (note that the units of service would be less given a smaller number of students while the *POP* as a *percent of the possible* would be the same). In this case, the institution, call it XYZ University, is performing at the same rate as the sample of 19,078. Given the validity and reliability of the NASCE, institutions can take any of the following steps.

1. Seeing that their students expressed service at a greater rate in high school, that is, 85 percent did service then and only 46 percent did now, they could move to increase the number of engaged students so as to pull the college curve to the left so as to strive to at least replicate the starting point of the high school curve. No doubt simply having more students engaged, all other things remaining unchanged would increase the overall units of service and institutional *POP* thereby increasing *Capacity Contribution*. For many institutions, the strategy of increasing overall student participation, even through large-scale one-time, short-term, or occasional activities, such as service clubs, is a viable strategy. Many campuses have built an infrastructure for this type of engagement, which, when done well, can lead to sustained engagement.

2. Knowing that the *Capacity Contribution* and the curve that represents it is also lifted both by increasing the frequency at which participating students engage in any of the nine areas as well as by their depth of engagement, institutions can put strategies in place to do both. They

may seek to encourage or to support structures that facilitate students who currently participate sporadically or only at one-shot events to become involved more frequently via service trips or regular processes. Second, they may similarly identify those students who are involved more regularly and pave the way for their service to deepen through institutional support or the development of meaningful community partnerships. This is a strategy that many campuses with multiyear community engagement initiatives, such as a Bonner Program or a civic engagement minor, choose to augment. Reorganizing service efforts to promote deeper and long-term engagement, for example, through the adoption of site-based teams or clusters, is a viable strategy.

3. Specifically, institutions can use the individual area capacity contribution graphs to first see the relative contribution in each area and then to target specific areas that they want to target for enhancement. For example, in this case, the institution could say it is satisfied with its contribution to *Youth Services*, but seeing the relative weakness of service to assist *Elderly* or with *Homelessness* and *Hunger*, they could stipulate moving their *POP* scores in those three areas. This can be done by increasing the participation, frequency, and depth of participating students in each of these areas. Often times, these strategies are adopted in tandem with an analysis of the local community context. When a campus finds that its service is failing to address a key need (i.e., drop-out prevention) or demographic (i.e., growing elderly population or immigrant group), the campus programs can make important shifts.

Conclusion

The strategic permutations an institution can take are endless, but analysis of the NASCE helps institutions focus their efforts by providing them with concrete numbers. With the help of the NASCE, schools can have informed discussions and generate meaningful goals aimed at enhancing community engagement and its institution's capacity contribution. Decisions such as whether or not service should be required of all students or whether or not structures that support service should be funded can be pursued, informed by quantitative evidence as opposed to theoretical ideals.

In conclusion, the *POP* values suggest potential strategies for how to mobilize broader and deeper community engagement. Similar to other measures that institutions use to assess their progress and success, the NASCE can be used to strategically inform the direction, programs, and initiatives for moving community engagement forward. Finally, the NASCE can also be completed periodically as a benchmark to gauge an institution's contribution over time.

Notes

1. The NASCE uses community service expressed across nine need areas and performed at any of the three levels of intensity as a proxy for community engagement. The authors recognize that others have conceptualized community engagement somewhat differently and may include other indicators. In this analysis, civic engagement is considered one component of community engagement, and community engagement is derived from service performed with that service aimed at addressing legitimate unmet human needs.
2. Across the entire sample of 19,078 students, 46 percent say that they participate in community service. Across the sample of 36 institutions, however, the average rate of participation is 51.7 percent. This distinction is explained by the fact that larger institutions, which have a disproportionately higher number of student responses, tend to have lower service participation rates, which drives the student sample number lower than the mean college number.
3. "Units of service" is a computation of the raw score, which serves as the basis for the POP score. In some cases, looking at units of service on its own can be very helpful for an institution seeking to understand the total service that their students express and contribute. If the mean service across an institution's survey sample is assumed to be representative of the entire student body, the school can multiply the sample mean units of service by the total number of students to calculate their student body's overall service output in terms of units of service. This number can then be used as a baseline for improvement.

References

Siena College Research Institute. *National Assessment of Service and Community Engagement* (NASCE), 2009–2012.

The National Task Force on Civic Learning and Democratic Engagement, *A Crucible Moment: College Learning and Democracy's Future*. Washington, DC: Association of American Colleges and Universities, 2012.

Colby, Anne et al., *Educating Citizens: Preparing America's Undergraduates for Lives of Moral and Civic Responsibility*. San Francisco: Jossey-Bass, 2003.

Stanton, T.K., and J.W. Wagner, *Educating for Democratic Citizenship: Renewing the Civic Mission of Graduate and Professional Education at Research Universities*. California Campus Compact: Stanford, CA, 2006.

Eyler, Janet S., et al., *At A Glance: What We Know about The Effects of Service-Learning on College Students, Faculty, Institutions and Communities, 1993–2000: Third Edition*. Corporation for National Service: Vanderbilt University, 2001

Institutions and Communities, 1993–2000: Third Edition. Corporation for National Service, Vanderbilt University.

PART II

Developmental, Engaged, and Educational Partnerships

CHAPTER 5

Building Deep Partnerships and Community-Centered Centers

David Roncolato

Introduction

After completing a remarkable summer internship at the Corporation for National and Community Service in the fall of 1999, an energetic student service leader returned to the campus of Allegheny College. Back on campus, one of her first tasks was to meet for coffee in the student union with the college's director of community service. With great fervor, she began the conversation with a vivid description of what she believed should be the next undertaking of the college's service movement. With great conviction she argued, "what we need to do is to build a building between the college and the community with two front doors—one front door opening toward the community and one front door opening toward the college." Her excitement over this idea left her unaware of her surroundings, the volume of her voice, and gestures of conviction accompanying her words. Suddenly, this came into her awareness. She stopped for a significant pause. With an altogether different intonation, she asked; "Does all this sound crazy to you?" No, I assured her, it did not. This was not about a floor plan but about a vision for sustained partnerships. As the administrator for a growing center, I shared this vision.

Over the next decade, Allegheny College purchased a house on the plot of land located on the central town square where the town's original log cabin courthouse once stood. The legal proceedings for the establishment of the college took place in this courthouse. Yes, the current structure on this plot has two front doors. One door leads to the offices of the local Chamber of Commerce. The second leads to an apartment that houses fifth-year Service Leaders and AmeriCorps VISTAs (Volunteers in Service to America) who stay on to continue their work in Meadville. This building has a different physical structure than that originally envisioned by the student. Yet, the house on the town square clearly symbolizes the vision expressed with such passion 13 years ago. The college's willingness to purchase property in the center of Meadville sent a very clear message to the community beyond the campus. Allegheny College resides not just on the hill above the town but in the midst of the community. This building, named the Founders House, symbolizes the college's openness to honest communication with partners in the community, or a community-wide "open door policy." As the current home of Meadville Area Chamber of Commerce, much traffic travels through the doors every day having to do with the life and vitality of the community. The pictures and history on the walls of the hallway and conference room illustrate the shared history of the college and the community.

In her 2003 article "Educating for Citizenship" in *Peer Review*, Caryn McTighe Musil offers six faces or phases of citizenship. The six express different understandings of community, values, and knowledge. The first phase, exclusionary citizenship, "is produced by gated academic environments, which lock students in and all other entities out. It can also be produced by a curriculum that ferociously guards traditional borders" (Musil, 2003, 5). The second face or phase, "oblivious," is marked by civic detachment. The phases then move through naive, charitable, reciprocal, and finally generative.

This chapter explores the symbolic and structural characteristics of deep partnerships between institutions of higher education and the institutions of the surrounding communities. The exclusionary phase and the oblivious phase were predominant faces of Allegheny College's citizenship in the 1990s. Through the accounting of Allegheny College's journey toward authentic deep partnerships contributing to generative citizenship, essential characteristics of such partnerships will be brought into focus. Allegheny's walk into the community can inform this common journey in different locations, with a variety of institutions and in diverse community.

The Allegheny College Narrative

In 2000, the Council of Independent Colleges (CIC) offered four Teaching and Learning conferences on *Active Learning in the World* as part of a larger initiative called *Engaging Communities and Campuses.* The preparatory working paper for this event outlined four key "capacities" necessary for "strong experiential learning in community settings as a major pedagogical practice." These capacities included:

- Faculty Knowledge and Skills;
- Institutional Infrastructure;
- Academic Culture;
- Partner Relationships with Community Organizations.

The fourth capacity was not only the last treated in the working paper but also the smallest section. At the time, less could be said about partner relationships and community organization because for many years it had been a low priority within higher education. Then, the service-learning movement focused on giving institutional legitimation within the academy for this innovative experiential learning pedagogy. The communities beyond the campus were a secondary priority. Allegheny College sent a team to the May, 2000, CIC conference in Raleigh, North Carolina. Having conducted self-assessments on the four capacities prior to participating in the conference, Allegheny's team assessed the fourth capacity as the most underdeveloped. While there was evidence of reciprocity in individual relationships between the community and particular Allegheny projects, there was no structure of reciprocity on an institutional level. The team recognized the power imbalance, whether real or perceived, between the community and the college. Allegheny's assessment of the fourth capacity mirrored the assessment of most if not all of the other 18 schools in attendance. The presenters and the participants at this conference wrestled with the difficulty of establishing sustained and reciprocal relationships. They acknowledged that colleges and communities live in segregated worlds. Indicative of this, while it was the expectation of the conference organizers that the college teams would include community partners, only three of the schools were successful at having a community partner attend.

At the core of deep partnerships is the issue of parity. The CIC's "Building Partnerships with College Campuses: Community Perspectives" published the insights of 21 community leaders from around the country at a 2002 convention. The document speaks to the challenge of parity; "For community partners, issues of parity—actual and perceived—are always part of the partnerships, even if they are not addressed overtly. Community partners particularly value campus partners who recognize and address these issues" (Leiderman et al., 2003, 12). The participants generated four indicators of parity.

Of particular significance was the opposite list, the five indicators of practices that demonstrate a lack of parity. The five indicators can be briefly summarized:

- Higher education receiving funding through grants since they are located in economically distressed communities and those dollars not directly benefiting the people behind the data;
- Using the community as a laboratory of study or students being assigned to "tour" a neighborhood without proper context or preparation;
- Academic community engagement projects that are created without first assessing community interest or needs;
- Lack of communication between community and campus partners on the requirements of shared accountability in order to avoid overburdening either partner;
- When the higher education institution takes a position counter to that of key stakeholders in the community without informing or engaging these stakeholders about the institution's position (Council of Independent Colleges, 2000).

The message was clear: "campus partners have not taken the time to understand how community organizations or processes work, and are distanced from community residents, when push comes to shove, student and campus needs appear to take precedence over community needs" (Council of Independent Colleges, 2000, 14).

During the previous decade, colleges and universities created campus structures to support service-learning and civic engagement. With the support of Campus Compact, Jennifer M. Pigza and Marie L. Troppe developed a theoretical framework for campus infrastructures with three models of development: the concentrated model, the fragmented model, and the integrated model. Although the first two have valuable aspects, the third—the integrated model—clearly has the most to offer (Jacoby, 2003). Here it is helpful to compare just two aspects of the three models—communication and access. In the concentrated model, communication is one directional and controlled by the academy. In the fragmented model, communication is significant with community partners but not among the various individuals in the campus community; every faculty, administrative unit, or program charts its own course. In the integrated model, communication is integrated within established connections between the college and the community. Access also differs across the three models. In the concentrated model, there are barriers to access for community partners. In the second model, access is made possible through the establishment of individual partnerships. In the third model, the university boundaries are made permeable consistent with the paradigm shift as the university or college is viewed as a part of the wider community.

Moving from Fragmented to Integrated

The Allegheny College story can be told in relation to these three models. In fact, analyzing one's institutional context and history through this lens has the potential to generate key insights, as well as strategies for moving forward. During the past decade, several strong "centers" of civic engagement developed on the campus. These centers developed significant partnerships based on their particular focus. The Center for Economic and Environmental Development (established in 1995) developed partnerships around environmental initiatives. The Center for Experiential Learning (formed in 1998) created partnerships for cocurricular student engagement through social service agencies. The Center for Political Participation (opened in 2002) developed partnerships related to political and electoral agendas. While clearly having a "fragmented infrastructure," the long-term partnerships between certain community constituencies and certain college constituencies contributed to the cultivation of goodwill and mutual trust. As with the development of any relationship, the essential dimension of trust cannot be "ramped up" for a particular event or project. Trust must be cultivated over a significant period of congruent interactions infused with integrity and authentic communication.

Allegheny College began a Bonner Leader Program with the opening of the Center for Experiential Learning in 1998. According to Caryn Musil's schema, Allegheny College was progressing into new phases of citizenship—from "oblivious," through "naïve" into "charitable." With great intention, college administrators listened to community partners in developing this program. The directors of Meadville's low-income housing developments clearly voiced that if this program was going to assist in meeting the needs of youth, the college student volunteers needed to work with them throughout the summer and not just during the academic year. The request for extra support and assistance with summer lunch programs meant that Allegheny College had to create a strong summer component to the Bonner Leader Program. Doing so built trust with these partners, recognizing their importance.

Community partners taught the Allegheny College engagement effort a second lesson. After 2000, a small but significant group of Allegheny College faculty became committed to integrating service components in academic courses. From the perspective of the college, this was a very positive development. The more that service was embedded in the academic program, the more established it would become across the institution. Community partners began to voice some resistance to accepting student "help" for semester-long service hours connected with academic courses. The return on the investment of orienting, training, and supporting these short-term student volunteers was just not worth it. One example will suffice. At our local soup kitchen, regular monthly volunteers from the community were displaced or overwhelmed in order to accommodate a one-time group of student volunteers from a class studying poverty. While there was some valuable learning for these students in making a single visit to the soup kitchen, the exercise was burdensome and caused harm to the ongoing volunteer base of the organization.

Community partners articulated their appreciation of student volunteers and service leaders who committed for a set number of hours every week for at least a full year. The sustained commitment of the Bonner Service Leaders, the Davies Service Leaders, and the Allegheny Volunteer Service Leaders community partners developed confidence in the work of Allegheny College students. Student volunteers from academic courses are able to integrate into regular, ongoing service programs without adding additional burden to the staff of the nonprofit partners.

Community Partners at the Heart of a Paradigm Shift

While the trajectory toward an integrated model of civic engagement was moving slowly at Allegheny College, a different vector emerged. The Allegheny College experience of the formation of Partners in Education (PiE) and Meadville Medical Center and Allegheny College Collaborative (MAC) demonstrate a paradigm shift in the integrated model for structuring engagement. During the 2006–2007 academic year, as Allegheny's Director of Community Service, I was asked to participate as a community member in the Crawford Central School District's strategic planning process. In the midst of this process, Charlie Heller, the assistant superintendent suggested forming an ongoing partnership with the college. The response to this invitation gave birth to PiE. Now this sustained, 30-plus member collaborative with monthly meetings is moving into its fifth year. The partnership has a mission to "foster the intellectual and ethical development for all learners, with a focus on those most at promise." Heller, now the superintendent, writes:

> PiE has been successful because it began small, strong relationships were built, and common goals established. Together we have experienced

success. Patience is a virtue as we together solve problems and overcome barriers. As PiE continues to evolve, I am confident that the future impact will enhance the quality of life in the Meadville community as business and industry become more active in the organization. I believe the structure serves our shared mission by meeting the needs of the members. The infrastructure now has expanded support and breadth. It will better serve the community, students and families.

This sustainable structure of engagement and partnership not only meets critical needs but also gradually transforms both institutions.

In 2009, again as director of community service, I was asked to volunteer on the hospital's Institutional Review Board (IRB) committee. Assuming a minimal commitment, I agreed as a gesture of cooperation. I was the only nonmedical staff on the IRB committee. According to the IRB regulations, if this "layperson" did not show up, the meeting could not proceed. A relationship of trust developed. In the spring of 2010, the new hospital chief executive officer in communication with the new Allegheny College president suggested creating an ongoing partnership between the two institutions. The required trust was already in place. The MAC was formed. Again the invitation to create this structure for engagement came from the community not the college. Constituencies from the college and the hospital meet monthly in the boardroom of the hospital to promote a mission of building and sustaining a healthy community.

According to Denise Johnson, MD, chief medical officer:

Meadville Medical Center is invested in this partnership because its mission is to meet the needs of the community we serve. To us, that means not only the medical needs, but others as well. We see Allegheny College as an ideal partner as this organization also seeks to improve the Meadville Community. We believe that by cooperating in our efforts, we have the ability to achieve much more towards this goal. Both of our missions involve community engagement and interaction. By getting together as a shared partnership, we are demonstrating participatory collaboration. All members of the group are equally cooperating and sharing in the efforts. This new structure works because there is a very strong commitment by our CEO, Mr. Pandolph as well as by Allegheny's president, Dr. Mullen. The whole group is also very enthusiastic and passionate about the partnership. There are regular meetings, goals are set with accountability, and annual meetings with the medical center's CEO and the college president. Even though the college and medical center are the primary collaborators, it will take many more stakeholders to be fully engaged to tackle some of the issues already identified.

The Allegheny College experience of the formation of PiE and MAC demonstrates that when the "centers" move off campus, new characteristics of deep partnerships emerge. The development of these two consortia demonstrated an intentional effort to move into authentic sustained, reciprocal partnerships. We began to see the emergence of Caryn Musil's sixth phase, "generative citizenship."

The Characteristics of Community-Centered Centers

The characteristics of community-centered centers are indicators of the shift from reciprocal to generative citizenship. This cumulative phase, "draws deeply from reciprocal citizenship but has a more all-encompassing scope with an eye to the future public good. The community is understood not as something separate and apart but as one and the same, an interdependent resource filled with possibilities." The goal is civic prosperity, seeking the "well being of the whole, and integrated social network in which all flourish" (Musil, 2003, 7). Arguably, the establishment of ongoing community-centered centers is necessary to establish the generative phase of citizenship.

We can glean from the Allegheny College experience five significant characteristics of community-centered, civic engagement centers that make generative citizenship possible.

At the Community's Invitation

Trust cannot be "ramped up" when necessary for partnership engagement for a particular research project or academic course. Trust develops with demonstrated evidence of effect communication and follow-through over an extended period of time. Engagement that ends with the semester or academic year works against the development of trust. Community partners may agree to work with higher education institutions for quite diverse reasons. Shannon M. Bell and Rebecca Carlson discuss four motivations for why community partners say "yes" in their chapter "Motivations of Community Organizations for Service Learning" in *The Unheard Voices: Community Organizations and Service Learning* (edited by Stoecker and Tyron, 2009). These include the Altruistic motive, the Long-Term Motive, the Capacity-Building Motive, and the Higher Education Relationship motive (Bell and Carlson, 2009, 20). Sometimes, community partners may think that they cannot afford to say "No." Partnerships that develop out of the invitation of the community and not the agenda of the college or university build on established relationships of trust. These relationships can be fostered from curricular engagement, cocurricular initiatives, and senior leadership. In all cases, the credibility is established over time. Community-centered centers, formed by invitation from the community, not the college, make parity possible from the beginning.

Formed around Relationships

When the centers move off campus, they are constructed around relationships and not projects. Sustainability is based on relationship and commitment, not on project or program. There is a significant difference between *being in* relationship with the community beyond the campus and simply *having a* relationship with the community beyond the campus. Being "in relationship" makes overcoming barriers and resolving conflicts much easier. The "problem" is understood not as "their problem" but as "our collective problem." Evidence of a shift toward a deeper, more reciprocal relationship is when interaction is regular, occurring in diverse settings and not isolated to organized meetings. This dimension however can differ depending on the size of the community beyond the campus and the proximity of the campus to that community.

The Allegheny College experience also offers another insight. Not every initiative of these centers is of equal benefit to the community and to the college. Some are more demanding for the college to meet with a greater benefit to the community while others have greater demand on the community partners with a greater benefit for the college. Authentic relationships are elastic and responsive. They remain in tack even when demands and burdens are not equally felt in every program.

Regular Meetings

Ongoing regular meetings make it possible for different institutions with different values, guidelines, and operating procedures to understand each other. In the case of Allegheny College, the formation of the partnership with both the school district and the medical center required becoming literate of the language, procedural timelines, and external structures within which each institution operates. The school district must be attentive to the teacher unions and the state's accreditation procedures. The medical center is required to conduct periodic community health need assessments and shape their initiatives based on these findings. Representatives from these two institutions needed to be educated about the tenure and promotion processes within higher education. The recognition and appreciation of the different institutional cultures, though never the focus, have been a significant benefit of ongoing, regular meetings.

Shared Mission Statement

The process of writing a shared mission statement clarifies the investment of the stakeholders, focuses the work, and builds community. The mission statement must be reviewed and rewritten on a regular basis. Such a process maintains the elasticity that such community-centered centers require. There may be new members from participating organizations joining the work of the center or completely new organizations joining in the collaborative. It is important to understand the writing of the mission statement as not the prelude to getting to the shared tasks of the center but as the foundational task of the center.

Grappling with Ill-Structured Problems

According to Eyler and Giles, ill-structured problems are "complex and open ended: their solution creates new conditions and new problems. Such problems require, first and foremost, the ability to recognize that the problems are complicated and are embedded in a complex social context, the ability to evaluate conflicting information and expert views, and the understanding that there is no simple or definitive solution" (Eyler and Giles, 1999, 16). Complex ill-structured problems in our postindustrial society require centers of engagement that include multiple and varied constituents. By locating the center for the work of addressing problems in the community, it is possible to draw together the diverse expertise and resources necessary to move toward solutions. At this metaphorical table, the higher education institutions can offer the expertise of faculty research, the significant resources of their student bodies, off-campus work study positions, community-based research projects, and political advocacy efforts as the community seeks to address ill-structured problems. The PiE effort is currently working to create a virtual neighborhood center to meet critical needs of students and families living in the downtown area. The partnership with the Medical Center is currently developing a strategy for adding fluoride to the city water supply. While these are just pieces of the collaborative efforts with these organizations, they offer examples of how the work of generative partnerships address ill-structured problems and serve the common good.

Conclusion

The final chapter of Association of American Colleges and Universities' *A Crucible Moment* offers three pedagogies that promote civic learning. They include intergroup and deliberative dialogue, service-learning, and collective civic problem solving. Community-centered centers of engagement offer the structure for the third pedagogy to take place. The chapter acknowledges that most higher education continues to operate in the charitable and reciprocal phase of citizenship. Yet, there is evidence and hope as the new phase of generative partnerships are developing. This vision is best illustrated in the following:

> Whatever the language adopted, where generative partnerships exist, the impact on communities can be transformative, on public scholarship far reaching, and on student learning empowering. Interdependency, innovation, multiple perspectives and a commitment to a long-range investment in the public good define the partnership's core values; higher education no longer sees itself as going out into the community, but as part of the community, whether that community is local, national or global.
>
> These partnerships create new public space for democratic engagement. The academy and the community are required to eschew their traditional boundaries in order to forge a new alliance with each other. The new space becomes, in effect, a public square for democratic co-creation. (National Task Force on Civic Learning, 2012, 64).

For Allegheny College and Meadville, this new space is more than the house with two front doors, or the house on the town square. Although still in their infancy, the community-centered centers with the school district and the hospital actualize the vision and values of the generative partnerships envisioned by students and administrators in 1999. Indeed, this is the vision for a new public space addressing critical problems within the shared community of a college and a small town in northwest Pennsylvania.

References

Bell, Shannon M., and Rebecca Carlson, "Motivations of Community Organizations for Service Learning." In *The Unheard Voices: Community Organizations and Service Learning*, ed. Stoecker and Tyron. Philadelphia, PA: Temple University Press, 2009.

Council of Independent Colleges, Engaging Communities and Campuses, working paper for 14th Annual Teaching and Learning Workshops: Active Learning in the World, 2000.

Eyler, Janet, and Dwight E. Giles, Jr. *Where's the Learning in Service-Learning?* San Francisco, CA: Jossey-Bass, 1999.

Jacoby, Barbara, ed. *Building Partnerships for Service-Learning.* San Francisco, CA: Jossey-Bass, 2003.

Leiderman, Sally, Andrew Furco, Jennifer Zapf, and Megan Goss. "Building partnerships with college campuses: community perspectives." *A Publication of the Consortium for the Advancement of Private Higher Education's Engaging Communities and Campuses Grant Program.* Washington, DC: The Council of Independent Colleges, 2003.

Musil, Caryn McTighe. "Educating for Citizenship." *Peer Review* 5 (2003): 5.

The National Task Force on Civic Learning and Democratic Engagement. *A Crucible Moment: College Learning and Democracy's Future.* Washington, DC: Association of American Colleges and Universities, 2012.

Pigza, Jennifer M., and Marie L. Troppe. "Developing an Infrastructure for Service-Learning and Community Engagement." In *Building Partnerships for Service-Learning*, ed. Barbara Jacoby. San Francisco, CA: Jossey-Bass, 2003.

CHAPTER 6

"Walking a Different Way": Coeducators, Co-learners, and Democratic Engagement Renaming the World

Talmage A. Stanley

The Thorns of a Thicket

From the earliest days of the American republic, higher education has been charged with the public duty to prepare persons for effective citizenship and to use its resources for the good of the people in the places in which colleges and universities are located. Twenty years ago, many educators regarded service learning as a means to help colleges and universities better prepare those citizens and better serve the places in which they were located. Yet, in the first decades of the twenty-first century, American higher education is a thicket of thorny contradictions, struggles, and failures to fulfill its civic obligations and overcome the divisions, silences, and elitisms that have long defined it. Many have come to regard service learning equally as part of the problem and as part of the solution.

In *The Unheard Voices: Community Organizations and Service Learning* (2009), Randy Stoecker and Elizabeth Tryon trace the uneven relationship between colleges and universities and the places in which they are located. While American higher education has embraced the practices of service learning, *Unheard Voices* uses the voices of community activists and organizations to ask how this has improved the places that those institutions say they serve. Stoecker, Tryon, and their collaborators describe relationships in which little actual benefit accrues to the place and its people, and the organizations in which students serve often shoulder significant burdens for the benefit of students and the public relations efforts of the institutions.

Further charting this thicket of contradictions, from the perspective of a rural, working-class, woman of color, bell hooks describes the insularity and abstractions of education in America. In *Teaching to Transgress: Education as the Practice of Freedom* (1994), hooks argues that the traditional model of teaching in which knowledge is passed from those who have it to those who do not, so that they can regurgitate it for those who contend they have this knowledge, destroys any excitement for learning and any sense of civic responsibility for the knowledge. American education disconnects the lives of those allowed into the classroom as well as those excluded from that classroom from the social and cultural realities in which they exercise their citizenship.

Echoing these same questions, in their 2009 white paper, *Democratic Engagement*, John Saltmarsh, Matt Hartley, and Patti Clayton argue that "this nation faces significant societal challenges, and higher education must play a role in responding to them" (Saltmarsh et al., 2009, 3–4). The "civic engagement movement has not realized its full potential" to transform higher education and enliven and enrich American democracy and to respond to the "societal challenges" facing us (Saltmarsh et al., 2009, 3). *Democratic Engagement* posits that most American colleges and universities fail to join service learning and civic engagement with "our democracy," neglecting to address "the democratic purpose of higher education." Moreover, too often teaching in the academy focuses on expertise, specialization, and narrow disciplinary divisions and methods, all of which combine to limit the kinds of knowledge and scholarship valued and accepted in the classroom (Saltmarsh at al., 2009, 4–5).

In *College: What It Was, Is, and Should Be* (2012), Andrew Delbanco contends that it is the moral, ethical, and civic obligation of American higher education to ensure that it remains a "transit point" at which people come to understand better and to practice more effectively what it means to be a citizen of the democratic republic. American higher education, the art and craft of teaching, and the places in which our institutions are located are caught on the thorns of this thicket.

Education for a Place

Founded in 1836 to educate a citizenry for the American frontier, Emory & Henry College has long been regarded for the quality of its education and the civic leaders it produces. Over the generations, many people in this place have also understood Emory & Henry as out of touch, elitist, and unwilling to be engaged in the systemic issues, questions, and conflicts defining this place. The college's Appalachian Center for Community Service and the degree program in Public Policy and Community Service, both established in 1996 on the cutting edge of the service-learning movement, were in part a response to this legacy of service and the isolation that had come to define Emory & Henry in particular and American higher education in general.

At that stage of the development of service learning, there was considerable attention given to community. Service to the community was the golden door for colleges and universities, as the naming of the center and department would suggest. However, these first developmental stages largely ignored the complexities of those same communities. Emory & Henry set itself apart by ensuring that the defining, foundational principle for this work was not community but the conflicted realities of place. As the result of the three-part interaction of the natural environment, the built environment, and human culture and history, this place, any place, is a social process. Because it is a social process and the defining nature of all human relationships is conflict, place becomes the product of prolonged social conflict lived out and experienced across, shaped by and shaping, a particular geography. In addition to a location on a map, the Emory & Henry model puts forward place as a lens through which to see and a paradigm by which to interpret the world. *Place* as both a *finite, social, and geographic reality* and as a *theoretical framework* defines this educational process, the goal of which is to equip persons for an effective citizenship of place with the civic and intellectual skills to enter meaningfully into the thickets of forces and conflicts, contradictions, questions, and issues that are always at work in every place.

The Emory & Henry model of a place-based education relies heavily on Paulo Freire's concept of problem-solving education (Freire, 1970). Freire calls for the dismantling of the walls between the academy and the place and for the inclusion of the world, the lived place, as a participant in the classroom. At Emory & Henry, this has meant, among other things, that the people of this place are our teachers. We have regarded our partners as members of our faculty, teaching us and learning with us what it means to be citizens of this place or any place. In a place-based model of teaching and learning, just as the walls between classroom and place are pulled down, the learning process becomes the ground on which traditional categories of student, faculty, staff, and community member collapse. All are engaged in the work of teaching and learning as coeducators and co-learners. In words that would later echo those of *Democratic Engagement*, Freire argues that an education that aspires to be relevant and beneficial to a democratic citizenship requires everyone in the classroom to learn from and to be teachers of each other. Co-learners and coeducators bring lived experiences, family stories, experiences of service placements, and personal understandings into the classroom so that these become part of the course material, pointing to the problems to be solved, the issues and questions to be addressed.

Because part of the work of the Appalachian Center is to integrate this place-based model of teaching and learning across the college's curriculum, the practice of coeducators and co-teachers is supported in 25–30 percent of the college's course offerings each year. Because 93–98 percent of the college's student body participates in some form of service during the academic year and little, if any, distinction is made between curricular service and cocurricular service, the model of education suggested here is available to many persons who otherwise would not have the opportunity.

While the college's place partnerships are with several distinct places, in a more general sense, the place the college works to serve is Southwest Virginia. Long regarded as the unwanted stepchild to the more populous and wealthier sections of eastern Virginia, Southwest Virginia is part of the Appalachian region. Looking to intensify its work and to make more deliberate commitments and partnerships focused on the larger conflicts and issues defining this place, in March and April of 2008, the Appalachian Center hosted a series of focus group conversations across the 12 counties of Southwest Virginia, to which were invited community leaders, nonprofit representatives, elected officials, and other citizens. These twelve 90-minute long conversations, focused on four questions, designed to ensure that the work of the college was grounded in and responsive to this place. What are the needs and issues facing this place? What are the assets and resources of this place? Working together, how can we build on those assets and resources to meet those needs and issues? What are the educational needs of leaders in this place to equip them for twenty-first-century leadership? The persons of the region were clear in their assessment of the larger, systemic issues: poverty, lack of child care, drug abuse, lack of meaningful work, lack of investment in health care and education, declining economic base, a collapsing agricultural infrastructure, shrinking population, and environmental crises wrought from industrial practices. They were equally clear in their eagerness to have the help and assistance of Emory & Henry as they worked to secure a better, more sustainable, more socially just, and more democratic future for all the people of this place.

Building Blocks for Coeducators and Co-learners

More than giving input at public forums and more than identifying needs that students can address, the practice of coeducators and co-learners has required particular structures and deliberate actions. Too often, the demands on the time of faculty members and the cultural assumptions of the academy have prevented ongoing communication and relationship building between the college and its coeducators from beyond the walls of the academy. Members of the Appalachian Center's staff carry this responsibility for the faculty member, maintaining and building relationships with persons from outside the academy. When representatives from the local place are in class, a member of the Appalachian Center's staff meets them prior to class, accompanies them to the class, and is usually present throughout the class. The staff member makes logistical arrangements for the visiting coeducator, serving as a liaison between the college and its faculty and the community member. Following class, the staff member usually writes a follow-up thank you. Unfortunately, faculty cannot always be relied upon to undertake this work or to do so in such a way that will challenge the long-held perceptions of the college as an unwelcoming and closed institution.

Commensurate with this relationship building is the Appalachian Center's commitment of funds in its operating budget to underwrite honoraria for visiting coeducators. To ask a place-based coeducator into the classroom without the commitment to offer a professional honorarium is to underwrite and extend the same class silences for which hooks clearly indicts higher education.

The coeducator's time in the classroom must also be part of the trust- and relationship-building process, requiring adequate preparation of students and professional teachers. All must be prepared to interact with each other on a meaningful level that acknowledges the coeducator's expertise, though the academy and the market economy may not. The Appalachian Center's staff representative acquaints the coeducator with the class dynamics, expectations, and goals before the visit; that same staff member works to acquaint the class with the coeducator, the person's work, involvement in the community, how other students and other classes have worked with this person, and what they have learned.

As coeducators and co-learners, both professional teachers and students must understand how this model differs from every other practice of education, whether in the public schools or in higher education. Raising this awareness is the work of all involved, but it must be undertaken, before the coeducator from the place comes to class. Professional teachers and students alike must understand and acknowledge that they are part of the place, part of its processes. The way they interact with the coeducator can help with the building of trust or they can extend the silences and marginalizations at work in this place. The most effective inclusions of a coeducator from this place involve not one-time visits to a class but several visits over the semester, the involvement of the coeducator in class discussions over time, and the development of a trustful, reciprocal familiarity between all coeducators and co-learners. This, of course, underscores the importance of all the elements that go into building this relationship. Whether for long-term work in a class or for the single visit, to take on this work challenges the ways of power and silence in a higher education institution and the accepted norms of American higher education. As Freire suggests, and as implied in *Democratic Engagement*, these relationships become deliberate political acts.

For What Good?

Years later, Stoecker and Tryon, and hooks and Delbanco, the writers of *Democratic Engagement*, the people of this place, ask us, "What good have we done?" "How have this place and its people grown stronger, more just, and more democratic because of the work of the Appalachian Center and the Department of Public Policy and Community Service?" The Appalachian region is embroiled in what amounts to a civil war over the future of coal mining, and whether coal and mountaintop removal offer a viable future for the people and places of this region. While Emory & Henry has adopted the goal of becoming carbon-free, with many people involved in this effort through many projects, the institution is on the sidelines of the ongoing debate about coal.

The health and well-being of families and individuals in the region continues to decline, though a federal health-care law has been signed into law and upheld by the Supreme Court. Emory & Henry's Appalachian Center for Community Service was instrumental in the development of a federally subsidized, sliding scale community health clinic, located less than two miles from the campus. The college is developing a school of Health Sciences with programs to serve Southwest Virginia. However, the institution has not been able to help shape the regional or national debate on the accessibility of rural health care.

With students in civic engagement placements and using its other resources, the college has been an active partner in the efforts to build a creative economy in Southwest Virginia. Focused on the traditional arts and culture of this place, this asset-based economy is taking root. In dozens of other civic engagement projects and partnerships, Emory & Henry students work in the places of the region, seeking to address systemic issues and problems for the long-term public good. Yet, hundreds of communities, among them the same places in which students are engaged and with which the college has partnership agreements, face a loss of vitality and increasingly limited options for sustainable development, their civic life diminished and lessened.

To paraphrase the authors of *Democratic Engagement*, the building of a culture of service at Emory & Henry College "has sidestepped the political dimensions of civic engagement" (Saltmarsh et al., 2009, 5). Although many of our students are daily engaged in all manner of civic engagement initiatives, the college is failing its "democratic purpose" in the hard, complex questions that roil our common life in Southwest Virginia. As with American higher education more generally, Emory & Henry has attained first-order change, or civic engagement framed by activity and place (Saltmarsh et al., 2009, 7-9, 11–13).

Second-order change, what these writers describe as *democratic engagement*, is more difficult to achieve, involving both the *process* of engagement and its *purposes*. Democratic engagement builds from a *process* by which all the members of a campus learning community—staff, students, faculty, administrators—relate to those beyond the campus community, outside the academy, those without the credentials or the resources for access to that community. The *purposes* of democratic engagement "refer specifically to enhancing a public culture of democracy on and off campus and alleviating public problems through democratic means." We learn and teach democracy by practicing democracy throughout the educational process.

Taken together, all of this suggests that Emory & Henry may have reached the limits of what can be accomplished through civic engagement. Despite all its work for a place-based model, despite an ongoing commitment to an educational process that understands participants from inside and outside the academy, professional teachers, students, and civic representatives as educators and learners, Emory & Henry remains within first-order change. The people and places of this region and our democratic civic life continue to be buffeted by increasingly grave "societal challenges." We may be on our way to an effective implementation of a model of coeducators and co-learners, but it does not change the structures of this education institution and its self-conceptions remain largely unchanged.

The change called for in the second order of democratic engagement is slow, uneven, and may come too late, while the urgency for this change, both inside and outside the academy, intensifies. Moreover, this slowness relegates entire generations of students to an educational process that does not equip them fully for effective engagement with the issues of our time and place. Southwest Virginia needs leaders, citizens, and critical thinkers to chart a way through the societal challenges we face. Time is running out; we cannot wait for entrenched practices and ideas to be challenged before new ideas and processes can be adopted and integrated. What then is there to do in the thickets of Southwest Virginia, Emory & Henry, and American higher education? Perhaps, Paulo Freire offers us yet another way, a radically different way of walking this journey.

Walking a Different Way

Freire argues that part of the work of the problem-solving model, what *Democratic Engagement*'s authors describe as *process*, is to dismantle the walls between the academy and the place. At Emory & Henry, we are beginning to discern that to undertake the education called for by Saltmarsh and his colleagues, by Stoecker and Tryon, and by hooks and Delbanco, with the urgency that our places demand, may mean a radical implementation of Freire's call to dismantle the walls between the academy and this place. Perhaps, we must focus less on the academy and its professoriate and more on the place itself, depending on our coeducators and co-learners from this place.

Through its Appalachian Center for Community Service, Emory & Henry has begun a process of working with our coeducators to provide them with the training so that they feel comfortable in their role as educators and learners. This entails confronting the power dynamics between teachers and students, and between those inside the academy and those outside. Here, we have come to understand the lasting social damages and enduring silences that the American higher education system has produced and that serve the power of the isolated professoriate. The only way to confront the residual silences and marginalization that have resulted from these dynamics is relational training and capacity building. This is the work of the Appalachian Center's staff. Only partially achieved through training events and workshops, it is more nearly a process of intensive individual one-on-one work, building confidence, offering ideas.

If teaching is a relational process, then the coeducator–co-learner exchange is preeminently one of mutual relationship, reciprocity. However, with a succession of students in placements, and having coeducators from the place in the classroom only once or twice each semester, there was little opportunity for these necessary relationships to develop and even less learning could take place. We have realized that an incentivization is necessary in order to foster and encourage extended student involvement in a site. While this might more easily be done with service-based scholarship programs, such as the Bonner Scholar Program, and in the relatively brief span of a semester's engagement, for long-term democratic engagement across the curriculum that enacts a reciprocal model of coeducator–co-learner, the task is somewhat more complex. In all of its civic engagement and service-learning programs and initiatives, Emory & Henry is implementing a developmental model by which students are encouraged to take on long-term engagements in a placement, assuming leadership responsibilities and roles as their knowledge and understanding deepen. Part of the leadership training they receive from this place's coeducators and co-learners focuses on what is necessary for honest confrontation with the challenges threatening to limit and diminish this place. Simultaneous with this, a relationship of reciprocal trust develops between coeducator and co-learner, making learning and teaching possible.

Our coeducators have often had difficulty understanding the educational potential of their work or that of the mission of their organization. To address that, we are in the process of developing curriculum resources for our coeducators. One aim of these resources is to help persons make the connection between the daily work and questions faced in that site to larger, global issues and questions, and to what *Democratic Engagement* describes as the *purpose* of higher education. These resources are developed in such a way that the coeducator can use them as a means of fostering conversation, pointing out the larger issues and how together we might build collaborations to address those issues. This educational model becomes empowering for the coeducators and co-learners at the placement, helping to make clear the larger importance of the work—both the immediate work and that of democratic engagement.

Contemporaneous with these developments and initiatives, we are redesigning the reflection process so that the coeducator from the place is often an active participant. There are issue-based reflections that involve this place's coeducators, and there are student-designed and led reflections in which they draw on insights and ideas from their work with the coeducators.

Incumbent on the partnership is the expectation to provide substantial in-kind contributions through the meaningful and substantive democratic engagement of Emory & Henry students, faculty, and staff. This holds true for any of the engagements undertaken through the Appalachian Center. The coeducator from the place is recognized for the contribution made to the students learning, ensuring that the relationship is more nearly a mutual collaboration. Moreover, from the outset of any project or initiative, there is the defining expectation and requirement that the place is tangibly, demonstrably better because of the presence and service of persons from Emory & Henry.

Since the inception of the Appalachian Center for Community Service and the Department of Public Policy and Community Service, one of the defining tenets of this work has been that our partners are our teachers, members of our faculty, teaching us and learning with us what it means to be a citizen of this place. Too often, the thickets of higher education, shaped and made thorny with issues of class, privilege, and power, have deadened that educational process and stalled its democratic purposes. However, refusing the academy's walls and limits has moved us further into this place. We are learning that perhaps this work in the thickets of this place has the power to rename and reshape service learning for democratic engagement.

Several years ago, Dan Leidig, a neighbor, friend, and poet, wrote a poem in honor of a fellow coeducator and co-learner. Leidig's poem describes bluebirds singing in a "January thicket." In the poem, Dan compares the work of bluebirds to the work of education and democratic engagement, saying that those bluebirds and the song they sing in that thicket "rename the world." At Emory & Henry, in the thickets of this place and of American higher education, perhaps there are the first notes, gentle and light as a bluebird's song, of an education that could still rename the world.

References

Delbanco, Andrew. *College: What It Was, Is, and Should Be.* Princeton, NJ: Princeton University Press, 2012.

Freire, Paulo. *Pedagogy of the Oppressed,* translated by Myra Bergman Ramos. New York: Herder and Herder, 1970.

Hooks, Bell. *Teaching to Transgress: Education as the Practice of Freedom.* New York: Routledge Press, 1994.

Saltmarsh, John, and Matthew Hartley, eds. *"To Serve a Larger Purpose": Engagement for Democracy and the Transformation of Higher Education.* Philadelphia: Temple University Press, 2011.

Saltmarsh, John; Hartley, Matthew; and Clayton, Patti, "Democratic Engagement White Paper." Boston, MA: *New England Resource Center for Higher Education Publications.* Paper 45, 2009.

Stoecker, Randy, and Elizabeth A. Tryon, eds. *The Unheard Voices: Community Organizations and Service Learning.* Philadelphia: Temple University Press, 2009.

CHAPTER 7

A Growing Edge for Community Engagement: Partnership and Policy Networks

Robert Hackett and Patrick Donohue

Introduction

In the mid-1980s, young people were often labeled the "me generation," a view reinforced by popular culture and media. Unfortunately, this view had some merit. According to the annual Higher Education Research Institute (HERI) data, as cited by Liu, between 1972 and 1984, when incoming freshmen were asked about their personal values, the value showing the greatest increase in importance was "being very well-off financially," while the values showing the greatest decline were "developing a meaningful philosophy of life," "participating in community affairs," "cleaning up the environment," and "promoting racial understanding" (Liu, 1995). This trend disturbed leaders in higher education. Two responses were the foundings of two national organizations that proved crucial to encouraging and supporting the service mission of higher education. The Campus Outreach Opportunity League (COOL) was founded by students and recent college graduates in 1984, and the Campus Compact (www.compact.org) brought together college presidents in 1985. These organizations joined efforts of groups like the National Society for Experiential Education (NSEE; www. nsee.org), which had already been at the task since 1971.

Initial goals were simply to get students engaged in direct, hands-on service in local communities, through both curricular and cocurricular approaches. The infrastructure to support these efforts began modestly enough, with new staff positions for coordination at campus offices, often filled by recent graduates. At the same time, the national organizations organized conferences and produced resource guides to help inform campus efforts.

It is fair to say that these early efforts have been remarkably successful at mobilizing students to serve and in creating an infrastructure and expertise both in campus and in national organizations (which have proliferated) to support their efforts. Centers for community engagement are now commonplace in campuses. A 2008 survey of 1,190 member campuses by the national Campus Compact found that 94 percent of these institutions had at least one office designated for coordination of service and community engagement (Campus Compact, 2008). These centers go by many names, generally using a combination of words and phrases that reflect an evolution of the field from "community service" to "service learning," "community-based learning," "community-based research," and now "civic engagement" or "community engagement."

Reflected in this evolution of approaches is a clear recognition by many that it is not enough to simply engage students in voluntary service activities. Rather, colleges and universities must play more substantive roles in addressing and helping solve challenges facing our communities, locally, nationally, and globally. The recent publication of the report *A Crucible Moment: Civic Learning and Democracy's Future*, resulting from a series of national round tables with student, faculty, nonprofit organization, policy and educational leaders, and widespread acknowledgment of its messages provide a distinct marker in this transition. The report calls for "investing on a massive scale in higher education's capacity to renew this nation's social, intellectual, and civic capital" (The National Task Force on Civic Learning and Democratic Engagement, 2012, 2). The call to action is for every college and university to promote a civic ethos that governs campus life, make civic literacy a goal for every graduate, integrate civic inquiry within general education and majors, and advance civic action as a lifelong practice.

The College of New Jersey Experience

This evolution has been reflected in efforts at The College of New Jersey (TCNJ) and partnerships with community-based and governmental organizations in the City of Trenton. What began as a campus-wide requirement for all freshmen to document ten hours of community service has blossomed into a multifaceted effort led by the Bonner Center for Civic Engagement and Learning that touches on every academic department as part of the school's transformational curriculum change, engages hundreds of students in weekly service commitments, and has transformed the relationship of this public college with its neighboring communities.

TCNJ faculty were among the initial group of institutions whose faculty began integrating community-based research into their academic courses with support from several Learn & Serve America–funded consortium grants led by the Corella and Bertram F. Bonner Foundation. With the formation of the Bonner Center, the College has formed sustained and deep partnership teams with 16 community-based groups coordinated by student leaders based on annual plans developed at the beginning of each school year at a retreat with community partner staff. Issue-based teams are managed in five to six issue-oriented clusters, each of which is supported by a Bonner Center staff member along with a faculty adviser. In addition, the student and campus staff also manage the service requirement of all 1,500+ freshmen through *Community Engaged Learning (CEL) Days* and upper-class students through department-based *CEL II courses*, many of which are structured around a community-based research assignment requested by community partners.

This structure has proven highly effective in mobilizing students and faculty to serve community-defined needs while also developing in our students the skills, experience, and ethic of service. However, we recognize now that our efforts have been one dimensional, largely focusing on meeting the needs of individual service-providing organizations in providing their programs to clients and, in many instances, also helping build their organizational capacity. In response, we have expanded our partnerships for the first time to include support for collaborative efforts that bring together organizations and individuals to address a common issue or opportunity.

Collective Impact: A Growing Edge for Community Engagement

Collaborations are often the driving force behind systemic change in communities. A particular model of social change, known as collective impact, has developed in response to the lack of progress being made toward solving complex community-wide problems (Kania and Kramer, 2011). These efforts can be found in many forms: *alliance, coalition, committee, commission, council, initiative, network*, and *workgroup*. The virtues of collective impact are being highlighted in a range of publications and organizations targeted for nonprofit, foundation, and public-sector audiences, including the Stanford Innovation Review, the Monitor Institute, the Foundation

Strategy Group, and many others. In response, community groups are coming together seeking to form small- or large-scale networks that can more effectively address challenges that the member groups can succeed in overcoming on their own.

Efforts organized for collective impact involve the commitment of a group of important representatives from different sectors who share a common agenda for solving a specific social problem. In the best-case scenario, these initiatives typically involve a centralized infrastructure, a committed staff, and structured processes that lead to common agendas, continuous communication, and mutually reinforcing activities among involved parties. These "backbone organizations" focus on planning, managing, and supporting the initiative through ongoing facilitation, technology and communications support, data collection and reporting, and handling the logistical and administrative details needed for the process to run smoothly.

However, in reality, most local collaborations have little to no funds nor staffing, relying instead on the volunteer labor of their most active members who have full-time positions elsewhere. As a result, these collaborative efforts often become unproductive spaces, with the participants too busy to research information to inform their discussions or manage the many small yet essential steps that move them from deliberation to action. The lack of supporting infrastructure is a frequent reason for failure.

Building Capacity for Collective Impact

As we began meeting with local collaboratives here in New Jersey, we saw immediately that colleges and universities have unique assets that, if mobilized, could help address community capacity needs. What are these assets? After several decades of outreach to local community partners, higher education institutions now have faculty, staff, and students who:

- already partner in productive ways with a wide range of local, service-providing groups;
- are considered, for the most part, neutral players who are not competing for the same funds;
- have expertise and credibility in community-based research;
- are experienced organizing and facilitating meetings; and
- are (or can be) skilled in using the Internet to communicate and coordinate.

With this foundation in place, TCNJ has begun to form campus teams to provide logistical, communication, research, and fundraising assistance for two existing and emerging collaborative efforts, one of which we will describe in depth as follows. The specific support activities include:

- Research:
  - community-based research such as neighborhood or organizational surveys, data analysis, Geographic Information Systems (GIS) mapping, oral histories, program assessments;
  - policy and funding research to inform collaborative decision making and grant writing for new initiatives of the collaborative;

- Logistics:
  - consortium meetings on logistics, including hosting policy forums;
  - ongoing communication among collaborative partners;
  - website and social media development to promote the collaboration efforts;
  - volunteer recruitment and coordination for new collaborative programs; and
  - networking with other collaboratives locally, statewide, and nationally.

In addition to mobilizing campus staff, faculty, and students into projects with nonprofit and governmental partners, TCNJ and the Bonner Network of campuses in New Jersey have developed several other valuable resources integral to the success of our partnerships with local collaboratives:

- secured full-time AmeriCorps VISTA (Volunteers in Service to America) members who provide ongoing staff capacity for coordinating the work of the collaborative and the campus connections;
- utilized a website, the PolicyOptions wiki (http://policyoptions. pbworks.com/), for organizing and sharing issue briefs on topics under consideration by the collaboratives;
- established a community information hub website and moderated e-mail list (www.policyoptions.org/) to provide digests of local policy news and community calendar; research on model programs and data sources; and a directory of organizations, programs, and key individuals.

In the following section, we profile one of the most innovative local partnerships, which addresses long-term prevention and policy, and then conclude with some lessons learned in this emerging area.

Win Win: Student Learning in Collaborative Partnerships

For obvious reasons, this type of work needs to enhance student learning. In a recent survey of TCNJ students, 73 percent agreed that the CEL component made the overall class experience more interesting than a regular class. It is not surprising then that 51.8 percent stated that the CEL experience also made it easier for them to participate in classroom discussions. In addition, compared to other courses, 59 percent agreed that they often talked more with other students outside the classroom about ideas that were raised in the class. Finally, 53 percent agreed that the CEL project class helped them to better understand some of the learning objectives, lectures, or course readings.

Their professors have observed the difference between CEL course and traditional ones as well, according to a preliminary analysis of a survey of professors at TCNJ. Ninety-two percent of faculty members have agreed or strongly agreed that CEL "advanced the overall teaching experience"; that it "advanced or enriched the overall learning experience for students (85%)"; that it helped them (the professors) reach or exceed one or more of the course's learning objectives (88%); and that it had a positive impact on the quality or depth of the work of the students (61–72%). Finally, 85 percent reported that they would teach another CEL course in the future.

Case Study: The Trenton Prevention Policy Board

Envision a room with six large round tables with individuals engaged in productive dialogue across organizations and roles to identify better solutions for a city's policy, in this case Trenton, New Jersey. At one table called "Education," individuals included the principal of an alternative high school and training program for out-of-school youth; an alumni of that program; the cofounder of the comprehensive nonprofit community development corporation that houses that program; the principal of the city's main high school; the school board president, who is also a reverend who counsels former gang members; a graduate of the high school who now attends the local four-year public college; an alumni of that college and its four-year service-based scholarship program who has a teacher's certificate and now helps run that program; an urban education professor from that college; and the director of the County's Health and Human Service's Division. This convening of individuals to focus on more effective policy—in concert with others focusing on employment, domestic violence, juvenile crime, health, and mentoring—forms the heart of the Trenton Prevention Policy Board (TPPB)—a unique, grassroots policy-making project.

The Attorney General's Office of Community Justice sparked the creation of the TPPB and planning boards in five different cities in New Jersey (Newark, Trenton, Camden, Asbury Park, and Vineland). Each local board's role is to tackle two related tasks: (1) to make policy, practice, and programmatic recommendations to city, county, and state officials that can reduce juvenile crime as well as promote positive youth development and (2) to look for opportunities to collaborate to implement some of those recommendations based on the resources available to them at their "day jobs."

The Trenton Board meets once a month at one of two locations: Trenton Central High School or the Trenton Police Department. The TPPB "full board meetings" engage outside experts or members to deliver presentations. In addition to meeting as a larger group, the TPPB breaks down into its six issue-based working committees 30–40 percent of the time. The participants attend because it is part of their "job" to learn more about the needs of young city residents—in particular those at risk of interacting with law enforcement at some point—as well as the systems and programs that aim to serve them. In addition, based on that knowledge, the Bonner Center for Civic and Community Engagement strives to "cultivate the common ground that exists between the teaching and civic missions of the College and the needs as well as interests of the local community." This ties back to the larger institutional mission of TCNJ, which emphasizes graduating leaders for the public and private sectors, strong citizens, and persons who will help "sustain and advance the communities in which they live." As a result, the college has a strong CEL program that includes eight hours of engagement for all first-year students and an effort to create one upper-level community-engaged learning course in every major or department.

The Role of Campus Centers

So the TCNJ's Bonner Center Director began serving as co-facilitator of the Prevention Board, with the distinct advantage of being considered a neutral professional. In addition, Bonner Center staff serve as professional facilitators for each working committee. The Center's organization mirrors the TPPB structure to some degree, which is helpful, with five CEL coordinators who lead issue-based divisions: Education, Health and Human Services, Individual and Family Self-Sufficiency, Juvenile Justice and Reentry, and Environment and Community Development. Each program coordinator supervises at least three teams of scholarship students (Bonner Community Scholars) whose work is based at an equal number of key nonprofit organizations in the city.

TCNJ's mission and the focus of the Bonner Center made it easier to fill the challenge many grassroots policy efforts struggle with: How do you ensure that the ideas that move forward are those that are based on solid research—as opposed to those that are simply popular or known by some participants? In response, the Center has recruited a team of professors and created the *Bonner Academic Fellows*; each one picked a committee and a leader agreed to guide the TPPB Steering Committee. These faculty members' main roles are to complete literature reviews on ideas bubbling up from the working group—allowing the participants to move them forward or end them based on the best available evidence.

The Bonner Center staff were also well positioned to recruit additional partners to join the cause—and they did. Within a short time, some key missing constituents were at the table—including, for example for the education group, the principal of the alternative high school, the principal of the main campus, the school board president—to name a few. In addition, a few TCNJ Bonner students themselves, as well as the young people they work with in the city, started to attend meetings intermittently—providing encouragement to the seasoned professional veterans. Some key nonprofit staff partners volunteered to bring program participants to join committees—including high school dropouts and formerly incarcerated persons. As a result, the monthly meetings have begun to attract as many as 75 individuals with active, productive participation in smaller working-group sessions.

The resurgence of the Board (and the fact that some respected original members remained) made it easier to recruit additional members with far-reaching public responsibilities—most notably the new director of the Trenton Police Department and the president of the school board. There was a bit of a buzz in town that reached their ears—which added another level of credibility and influence in both the halls of power and on the streets.

The Bonner Center's first major action step upon taking a leading role in the TPPB was to develop a six-month *Action Plan*. More importantly, perhaps, was the inclusion of one meaningful, concrete, and achievable annual goal. Since the beginning, the main audience was the mayor; Center staff consulted with colleagues who had worked in City Hall to better understand how to proceed when mayors ask cabinet members to think about the next year's budget and priorities for spending funds. The Center later proposed that the TPPB produce an annual report that captured all of its recommendations, setting a target of three to four solid ideas per working group. The ability to point toward a tangible, relevant, and visible product—and deadline—added urgency and focus to our efforts.

The end result of this work—which is still ongoing—was much more than the production of a report. As the group labored to make recommendations, it started to turn some into reality before the ink was dry. For example, the school board president (who is a TPPB participant) worked with the school district administration to enter into a contract with a researcher from Rutgers University. Her team is now leading an effort to ensure that staff have accurate data on kids who are most likely to drop out of school, so as to develop effective intervention strategies. In addition, juvenile probation officials have agreed to ask parents of offenders entering their system if they have younger children they are concerned about—and work with TCNJ and TPPB to link them to an interdisciplinary team of professionals who may respond to their needs to prevent them from following the same path. These are examples of how these new partnerships are resulting in more far-reaching, policy-oriented types of engagement.

As the TPPB continues with a dual purpose of making some recommendations and implementing others, there are more opportunities for class-based CEL projects. Three professors and their classes got involved in September 2012 including:

- An Interactive Multimedia course, which is developing a phone application that would allow high school administrators and their TCNJ Bonner colleagues to send students information about services that are available to them in the building—as well as inspire them with success stories and possibly quotes.
- An Applied Sociology class, which is working to help develop the protocols and tools that would allow the TPPB to identify the kids who are the most at risk of dropping out of one of the district's middle schools and how the large Bonner program might be able to provide each one with a mentor.
- Finally, two Cost Accounting sections working with a TPPB and Bonner partner organization—Isles Inc.—conduct research on a few possible business ventures it could create (e.g., a Community Supported Agriculture site) and thereby employ graduates of its YouthBuild program. YouthBuild helps out-of-school youth get their degree or General Educational Development (GED) test and receive job readiness training—among other forms of assistance.

Other "policy" classes will get involved in the Spring of 2013 or shortly thereafter. Bonner Center staff have begun conversations with political science faculty. The TPPB will be a source of research questions that could be clearly linked to course learning objectives.

Lessons for Replication

Other colleges and universities interested in replicating a structure like the TPPB may want to consider these lessons.

Provide student training: In order for undergraduates to play an effective role in supporting our local collaborative partners, most of them will need to further develop some hard skills, including the ability to deliver high-quality presentations or facilitate working-group conversations with individuals with diverse characteristics (age, profession, race, etc.).

A long-term perspective and staffing plan: This work is built on relationships and trust, yet our AmeriCorps VISTA members and many of our students might be involved for only a year or semester. Campuses must craft strategies to identify key staff who remain at the center of the collaboration and can have ongoing dialogue with community participants. Part of that dialogue acknowledges that some members of the campus team will come and go but they can be useful resources in the fight to get things done.

Transforming the traditional higher education calendar: As with all community–campus partnerships, we have to find ways to address the gaps caused by the academic calendar. Students are not usually available during semester breaks and the summer. Full-time AmeriCorps, VISTA members, and staff can help. Or, community cochairs of working groups may step up during those times as well, in order to provide continuity year round.

A little funding goes a long way: Collaboratives often lack funding to support their work. However, there are obvious benefits to having access to even small amounts of funding. This can cover expenses for food, printing brochures and reports, hiring a consultant to lead a retreat, or even to help refine a funding proposal.

Being grounded to the community: The college or university—via faculty or staff members—needs to be connected to the community in real and concrete ways. Among other things, it needs to have the right amount of credibility to start and sustain such a project via relationships that have been built on trust, mutual respect, and/or past victories.

Leverage the role in providing research: Key community partners and funders asked the college to fill facilitator roles because of the perception that they are more neutral, especially if they are not depending on funding from local government. In addition, city officials like the fact that its independent experts can chime in with research that informs decisions.

The symbolism of logistics for community: The board decided to hold monthly meetings at two locations: the high school and the police department.

The former sent a message that the board cared about the involvement of school leaders and students. The latter responded to the new police director's desire to let the community know that his force cares about prevention and positive youth development—helping people—not just law enforcement.

Make concrete, small victories: Systemic change takes time. So do asking for and seeing changes in programs and practices. The board's decision to produce and present an annual report helped keep constituents connected and invested. In addition, when the group realized that it had the people and abilities to implement recommendations, it fueled the process.

Understand enlightened self-interests: Recognizing that most of the members who attend the TPPB meetings get paid by their employers for attending the 3:15 p.m. meetings, its leaders offered stipends to out-of-school youth and young reentry program participants.

Think hard about who really represents the community: Do nonprofit leaders in a city truly represent the will of the residents? This is a valid question. In response, the TPPB will soon start organizing mid- and end-of-year "stakeholder meetings" to get input from residents because many non-profit leaders, while respected, and often living in the city, are not always residents or taking a holistic view of the community.

Tap community organizers: This work calls for higher education representatives to lead these efforts or to empower community partners who have the skills and resources to stay involved for the long haul. The bottom line is that *participatory democracy work is messy*. Among other things, it requires individuals who can communicate effectively, anticipate reactions or spot political and personal landmines in advance, navigate around them, and have a thick skin. They must know that there will be misunderstandings as well as informed and uninformed criticisms that are not always delivered gently.

Provide continuous education: As the process is open and transparent, allowing participants to join discussion when they wish to do so, there is an unexpected result: Some people show up thinking that the TPPB is something that it is not. At times, it is like someone showing up at a basketball game asking why the pitcher is not throwing fastballs. Hence, leaders must provide ongoing orientation and training, as well as clarification.

Conclusion

The reimagining and opening of campus–community partnerships to include policy research for community partners, city government, and local collaborations focused on reducing or eliminating the need for ongoing social services is a promising growing edge in our work. Through the work of the Bonner Center and the TPPB, TCNJ, and NJ Bonner Network are developing new models and internal capabilities. While certainly these structures involve new skill sets, organizing models, and investments, they also represent, we believe, a vital way in which colleges and universities may serve a larger purpose for our communities and democracy.

References

Campus Compact (2008). Service Statistics 2008: Highlights and Trends from Campus Compact's Annual Membership Survey. Retrieved from www.compact.org/wp-content/uploads/2009/10/2008-statistics1.pdf.

Kania, John, and Mark Kramer. "Collective impact." *Stanford Social Innovation Review* Winter (2011): 36–41.

Liu, Goodwin. "Origins, Evolution, and Progress: Reflections on a Movement." Providence College, 1995.

The National Task Force on Civic Learning and Democratic Engagement. *A Crucible Moment: Civic Learning and Democracy's Future.* Washington, DC: Association of American Colleges & Universities, 2012.

Useful Sources for Additional Information

Articles and Papers

- Building the Field of Dreams: Social Networks as a Source of Sector-Level Capacity in the After-School World—www.barrfoundation.org/news/building-the-field-of-dreams/
- Building Smart Communities through Network Weaving—www.orgnet.com/BuildingNetworks.pdf
- Community Collaboratives Whitepaper: A Promising Approach to Addressing America's Biggest Challenges—www.serve.gov/new-images/council/pdf/CommunityCollaborativesWhitepaper.pdf
- Connected Citizens: The Power, Peril, and Potential of Networks—www.knightfoundation.org/media/uploads/publication_pdfs/Connected_Citizens_-_final_draft_online_edition.pdf
- NET GAINS: A Handbook for Network Builders Seeking Social Change—www.barrfoundation.org/news/net-gains-a-handbook-for-network-builders-seeking-social-change/
- Transformer: How to Build a Network to Change a System—A Case Study of the ReAMP Energy Network—http://monitorinstitute.com/downloads/ReAmp_Case_Study_by_Monitor_Institute.pdf

Website and Blogs

- Foundation Strategy Group: Collective Impact articles & resources—www.fsg.org/tabid/191/ArticleId/211/Default.aspx?srpush=true
- Working Wikily: Network Tools and Approaches Are Creating New Opportunities for Powerful Social Impact. Social Innovators are Pioneering the Art of *Working Wikily*, Embracing Openness, Transparency, and Decentralization—http://workingwikily.net
- Beth Kanter's Blog—www.bethkanter.org
- Network Weaver—www.networkweaver.com

CHAPTER 8

"One Partnership, One Place": Building and Scaling Sustained Student-Led, Community-Driven International Partnerships

Kelly Elizabeth Behrend and Stephen Darr

Introduction

In the past few decades, research about the effects of engagement in learning has suggested that community engagement and service-learning, including in international contexts, can have a powerful effect on students' learning outcomes. For example, in 1995, George Kuh in a seminal article "The Other Curriculum" looked at a variety of educational experiences that occur outside the traditional classroom context during college, pointing to their effects. Citing the emerging research by Alexander Astin on the impacts of student involvement in the landmark book *Four Critical Years: Effects of College on Beliefs, Attitudes, and Knowledge* (1977) and Pace (1984) on understanding student effort as part of quality assessment, Kuh then proposed the Involvement Principle, which is "simple but powerful: the more time and energy students expend in educationally purposeful activities, the more they benefit." Kuh goes on to describe the various out-of-classroom activities that impact students, citing international travel as one of those activities and demonstrating how it had affected students' sense of Humanitarianism, Interpersonal Competence, Knowledge and Academic Skills, as well as Cognitive Complexity (Kuh, 1995). More recently, the Association of American Colleges and Universities

(AAC&U) has captured Diversity and Global Learning as one of the core High-Impact Practices (HIPs), which maximize student learning outcomes, arguing that students who engage in international experiences have a broadened worldview, develop intercultural competencies, sustain difficult conversations in the face of highly emotional differences, and "explore the relational nature of their identities" (Hovland, 2010).

We believe that these unique benefits can be best realized with the provision of a series of key values that mitigate international challenges while also maximizing impact for participants and communities. To do so, we assert that partnership practices, which are *strategic, reciprocal,* and *sustainable,* together with cross-cultural understanding, are indispensable values in the development of long-term effective international engagement programs.

First and foremost, international community development must happen in a localized and collaborative environment, which promotes a *strategic* approach that upholds inclusivity and result-driven projects. As Boland and McIlraith argue, universities must undertake such localized approaches, even if it means adapting their typical learning style or pedagogies while on site. As such, the authors advocate for a strategy "whereby the philosophy, principles, and practices of a particular curriculum innovation are adapted (or even subverted) to reflect and serve local culture, context, and conceptions" (Boland and McIlraith, 2007). This is a fundamental practice for international engagement that can lead to collaborative strategic design, implementation, and results.

The second key recommendation is that civic engagement should be a truly *reciprocal* experience, with deep meaning and relevance to all stakeholders involved—a strategy that promotes mutual growth and development for all parties. Practitioners who do not embrace this essential value may find their efforts to be "lost in translation," unsustainable in the long term, and potentially one sided. As Merrill suggests, practitioners must embrace a culturally aware approach of "doing *with,*" also defined as:

> Having the intellectual knowledge, the empathetic understanding, and the personal modesty and desire to move *from* one's own certainty about why people act in the ways they do *to* explanations for behavior that are rooted in the cultural context of another society. (Merrill, 2005)

Finally, the international partnership must involve a deep kind of learning for participants, such as those outlined in the HIP by AAC&U and its Liberal Education and America's Promise (LEAP) Report. This commitment to transformative learning for students is typically coupled with a commitment to long-term partnership with a given community. Projects that maintain a commitment to mutual learning can form the basis of *sustainable* partnerships, a relationship that Sheffield calls "a two-way service ethic" (Sheffield, 2005). With the commitment to ongoing impactful student learning and to strategic community engagement, we assert that these practices lay the foundation for effective *sustainable* partnerships among all parties involved. Enos and Morton describe the effect of this trifold commitment to strategic, reciprocal, and ultimately sustainable partnerships, writing:

> Higher education's failure and best self can be found by engaging community partners in mutually transformative work that allows us to reimagine, in ways both creative and practical, sustainable communities. Our choice of partners and our visions of what may be accomplished together create opportunities for us to become members of communities and of a world of which we would like to be part. (Enos and Morton, 2003)

Strategic, Reciprocal, and Sustainable International Partnerships

As these scholars and the experience of the Bonner Network suggests, the practice of *strategic, reciprocal*, and *sustainable* international partnerships grounded in cross-cultural understanding produce unparalleled leadership, learning, and impact opportunities for students and communities alike. Institutions in the Bonner Network gathered these lessons from the practice of community partnerships on the local level and found innovative ways to meaningfully reproduce, contextualize, and adapt them to the international scale. Examples include the College of Saint Benedict's annual semester of service exchange program with St. Xavier's College in Calcutta, India; Lynchburg College's long-standing multidisciplinary International Service Learning May Term program with a network of nonprofits in St. Lucia; Siena College's annual International Community Development summer internship program with a series of community partnerships established in Bangalore, India; Ursinus College's ongoing alternative spring break community development program in Beeston Springs, Jamaica; and Washburn University's year-round partnership with a multidimensional grassroots community development organization in the city of Managua, Nicaragua.

Inspired by the existing work of participating campuses, the Bonner Foundation and Peacework formed a partnership in 2011 to apply a combined 50 years of research and practice in the field of service learning and build a model for international engagement. The approach was grounded in the organizations' complementary commitments to uphold student leadership (the Bonner model's core focus) as well as local community leadership (the core practice of the Peacework development strategy). Combined, this partnership has brought enormous potential to expand and deepen the student-led, community-driven international engagement efforts of nearly 75 American colleges and universities that are part of the Bonner Network through connecting them with a series of international communities in long-term development partnerships.

Although there are clear benefits for campuses and communities to collaborate within this guided framework, the *outcomes for student learning* are what have been most prominent to date and will therefore be the focus of this work. This investigation into the effects of international engagement was comprised of exploratory pilot interviews designed to study the impact on student participants in order to discern what additional benefits civic engagement in an *international context* can provide. The sample for this pilot study was seven students from five campuses who participated in a student-led, community-driven service immersion and strategic planning retreat in the community of Orange Walk, Belize.

What we found is that this collaboration not only provided the space for students to lead international partnerships in structured and transformative ways for their campuses and communities, but also empowered students to have unparalleled learning experiences and skill-based development opportunities by being true stakeholders in the partnership's design and development. As we will describe, the approach produced a series of critical learning outcomes for participating students that *differed from those of their domestic experiences*, particularly in terms of ownership and accountability, dialogue across diversity, strategic planning and assessment, and an applied understanding of how to build and manage community partnerships. The experiences of the students, in their own words, will illustrate the depth of these new learnings and underscore the added value of global engagement in the context of sustained, student-led, and community-driven international partnerships.

Student Leadership in Global Immersions: An Engagement Approach that Promotes Deeper Learning

The service immersion was prompted by the local development goals of the Ministry of Education of Belize, who in conversation with Peacework had identified youth engagement programming (specifically in character education and entrepreneurship) as a development priority for youth education in Belize. Given that the majority of Bonner students serve in youth programs domestically, this need prompted Peacework to approach the Bonner Network with the opportunity to exercise their service expertise of working with youth in a global context. As a result, Bonner students (also called "participants") engaged in multicampus immersion experience in Orange Walk, Belize, to serve the local community, participate in a training series focused on international development and global engagement, and strategize about the future of a network-wide international engagement model. The aim of the conference portion was to engage participants in thoughtful and collaborative discussions with a variety of stakeholders on international development theory, the potential for partnership in the Orange Walk community, and the strategic design and implementation of the model in other communities around the world.

As a result of this community-driven development project, student participants spent the months leading up to the immersion designing a character-building curriculum that was built on the trip participants' shared value set, also known as the Bonner Program's Common Commitments (Civic Engagement, Community Building, Diversity, International Perspective, Social Justice, and Spiritual Exploration). The curriculum was designed to engage global youth in an exploration of personal values and the identification of their place in their communities as citizens, as contributors to the economy, and as activators of positive social change. The goal of the immersion was to activate the shared commitments that have inspired and empowered Bonner students to serve their communities and reapply them through empowering global youth to do the same. Participating Bonner students wrote the curriculum, implemented it in two primary schools in Orange Walk, made revisions, and strategized about its potential reapplication to other communities and contexts.

In the years of her developmental community engagement prior to this trip, participants like Amelia Lumpkin (Davidson College) had already engaged in profound international experiences through her participation in the Bonner Program. Amelia's primary placement while on campus was with a local community center as an after-school academic support assistant for area youth. Her passions for education, art, and youth were later extended to global contexts through her summer service experiences working with disabled youth in Syria and serving with a youth arts program in Nicaragua. Despite this variety of deep international experiences, Amelia reflects:

> I had done service abroad, I had gone to conferences, and I had engaged in teaching experiences before. This experience included all of those elements, yet it was really intensive. We did a lot of planning beforehand,

and we were participating in a conference while we were engaging in service with the community in a very collaborative way. (Lumpkin, 2012)

Her peers brought similar knowledge and experiences to the table, ready to conceptualize the founding of a new international program for fellow students in the Bonner Network. Not only did participants meet the project's goals of strategic program design and engage in a meaningful service immersion with primary school youth, but they also walked away with profound learning experiences of their own, four of which we have focused on for this study.

Ownership and Accountability

A common takeaway for participating students was their sense of ownership and accountability in the project, which they agreed was markedly different from their community engagement back on campus. When asked what they generally considered to be the most significant difference between this experience and their previous service experiences, three students replied with similar answers:

This was different because we had a more direct ability to determine what we did and how we approached it. Normally with our service sites back home, those elements are already decided. This enabled us to really direct our impact, find out what worked and what didn't, and try new things. (Murlo, 2012)

We were required to listen to the community and incorporate their needs in a collaborative way, which seemed different than the pre-developed plans and strategies with my domestic community service position on campus. That was new and it taught me a lot. (Helmbrecht, 2012)

The "large unknown" of the project was a huge challenge for me—we didn't know if the curriculum or schedule would work, we hadn't met each other beforehand, we didn't know if the students would respond to the program. It was a good challenge, because each of us stood up and took leadership at different times. Unlike other service experiences, we knew we had the challenge, and also the responsibility, to create the results. (Lumpkin, 2012)

Experience with Dialogue across Diversity

Additional learning outcomes that emerged from this experience were increased competencies in dialogue across diversity and encounters with "otherness," outcomes that have been found to be among the greatest contributors to the program's effectiveness. Cheryl Keen's research of the Bonner Program's impact on student learning concluded that:

> The core experience of service is not the service itself but the sustained dialogue across boundaries of perceived difference that happens during service and in reflection along the way, including with people students serve, with the people they serve alongside of, with their supervisors at the service site, with the college staff, and, centrally, with their peers…with these dialogue partners, students can construct new understandings of what is compassionate and just and what is required of them now and in their future. (Keen and Hall, 2009)

This experience produced similar outcomes as Keen describes and resulted from the series of structured and unstructured reflection opportunities with multiple stakeholders including peers, community partners, local experts, and youth. The Belize Minister of Education, Dr Patrick Faber, led a community town-hall meeting on the direction of the education system in Belize, and students sat in on this round-table discussion to gather locally determined development goals. The students took these recommendations from the federal level and then interviewed local practitioners of education and development, including school principals and teachers. During the evenings, participants reflected together on their experiences, made edits to the curriculum, strategized about the global engagement strategy with Peacework field staff, as well as led their own structured reflections on self-directed topics such as ethnocentrism, sustainability, poverty, and economic opportunity. This intentional diversity of perspectives and interactions gave students a platform to think critically and collaboratively about the potential for meaningful strategic partnership in the community.

One student took note of the combination of structured and unstructured reflection, specifically the advantages of experiencing a service immersion and a conference at the same time, saying:

> I was expected to collaborate with people that I hadn't had the opportunity to get to know beforehand, but we had a common goal. This common goal ultimately meant providing a service to a community, but also meant committing to a set of learning outcomes for ourselves. It was a conference within a conference. Our performance and presentation was important, but our reflection and conversations after the direct service was just as important to the experience. I think the merger of those two

priorities and commitments—to both the community and to ourselves—was really important, and also new. (Grego, 2012)

Skills in Strategic Planning and Assessment

Another strong outcome for student participants was their experience with strategic planning and assessment. Participants had undergone a virtual training series before the conference that emphasized Belizian culture, curriculum review, and the management of students' individual leadership roles and contributions (the lead team consisted of positions such as curriculum designer, sustainability analyst, and social media coordinator). Once on site, the conference portion of the experience consisted of two all-day training series on the first and last days, as well as evening discussions throughout the five-day service immersion in the primary schools. Finally, students engaged in an ongoing curriculum and program evaluation process, putting together an assessment report and strategic plan for review by the Bonner Foundation and Network. Students cited these experiences in strategic planning and assessment as an important lesson in leadership:

> During one of our last reflection sessions together, we really had to refine a vision of what we wanted to do with this project and curriculum, especially how we wanted to present it at our individual schools and the network. I guess it was that we knew we each had a stake in the project and we were passionate about doing it right. (Moehring, 2012).
>
> My leadership abilities definitely were both developed and challenged during this experience...My specific position as the Sustainability Analyst pushed me even further, as I knew I was going to have to document what we did, and that my documentation of the project would be setting the tone for the continuation of this program on the network level—both in Belize and in the extension of the [global engagement strategy] more broadly. (Lumpkin, 2012)

Strategies for Building and Managing International Partnerships

After the project, we interviewed participants and asked them what they considered to be the most significant values and practices to uphold when engaging with an international community. Their responses echo those of the theorists and practitioners in the field of civic engagement, who have often had the applied experience of engaging with local leadership and program design in the same ways these students had experienced in the international setting. In other words, participants had gained an applied and accurate understanding of how to build and manage international partnerships because they now had the experience of designing and developing an international partnership as project leaders. As a result of their applied leadership on a global scale, students noted the following values and practices as significant to effective community partnerships:

> The first priority is respect—knowing your own boundaries and having a sense of self-respect—as well as having each stakeholder respect each other in the project through mutuality and reciprocity in each activity. It should be seen that way by each stakeholder, with each party interested in the benefits for all involved. Awareness and study is also important; we should be committed to studying ourselves, our perspectives, and those of others. It's important to really do your homework. (Lumpkin, 2012)It's important to build bridges before you go and know how to walk across them in intentional and respectful ways, alongside the community, even when you're not present with the community. That's the challenge. But if you are committed to really getting to know these partners, it can be done. (Grego, 2012)

The student-generated assessment report and strategic plan produced after the conference included extensive notes on the partnership possibilities in Orange Walk and through the global engagement strategy more broadly. Although the effects on the community and the potential for future multi-campus collaboration is promising, the effects of the intensity of the learning experience for participating students was immediately evident. Beyond their acquired skills in project ownership and accountability; dialogue across diversity, strategic planning, and assessment; and an applied understanding of how to build and manage community partnerships, student participants had become advocates for the program and committed a portion of their service hours for the following academic year toward the program's continued management and development.

Perhaps, the greatest lesson learned through this experience for student participants was not just serving to learn, but *learning to serve humbly in a new and different context*. Students, as project stakeholders in an international context, had learned how to better engage with community partnerships like the one established in Orange Walk and are undoubtedly committed to its continuation.

Conclusion

International development partnerships are certainly not a new idea within the civic engagement field and have been widely challenged for their financial, logistical, and relational complexities. What we discuss here is a model that has not only lessened these challenges, but also maximized results for stakeholders. The program financial costs were met with creative cost-sharing between the Bonner Foundation and Bonner programs. Logistical concerns were mitigated by an experienced partner organization, Peacework, equipped with an applied local knowledge of the community and its resources. The program minimized relational challenges (such as gaps in cultural competency) with an intentional student training series, knowledgeable Peacework staff on the ground, and the early and ongoing participation of community members. In exchange for this unique collaboration, the project gained increased potential for student voice, engaging opportunities for community collaboration, cross-campus experiential learning outcomes, effective community engagement on the global level, and ultimately the stage for program expansion.

One may ask how a handful of students could make a tangible difference worth the time, effort, and resources put into such a project. The students' strategic plan answers this question with a simple, yet significant consideration: "our plan starts small: with *one* partnership in *one* place." The advantages of a small student group meant including each participant in an intentional planning process, thereby enabling them to explore the complicated dynamics of establishing a partnership. Students were involved in critical conversations about otherness, contributed to a curriculum grounded in their shared values, suggested culturally relevant modifications to the curriculum through their applied research, engaged in discussions around project sustainability, and adapted these learnings through critical engagement and analysis during the project's evening reflections and strategic planning sessions. As a result, this small group was able to engage in learning experiences perhaps unseen by other formalized international programs, while also having just enough voices at the table to provide a clear and diverse student-led direction for the future of a global engagement program.

The students' descriptions of the project reminds us that international engagement need not be a massive undertaking across multiple countries and projects—it can and should start as simply and significantly as one partnership and in one place—just like civic engagement through community practices in the domestic context. With this in mind, Orange Walk then becomes the model for engagement through collaborative student-led and community-driven partnership in the global context—transferable to communities around the world and transformative for students for years to come.

References

Astin, A. W. *Four Critical Years: Effects of College on Beliefs, Attitudes, and Knowledge.* San Francisco, CA: Jossey-Bass Publishers, Inc., 1977.

Boland, J. A., and L. McIlrath. "The Process of Localizing Pedagogies for Civic Engagement in Ireland: The Significance of Conceptions, Culture and Context." In *Higher Education and Civic Engagement: International Perspectives*, ed. L. McIlrath and I. MacLabhrainn. Galway, Ireland, 2007, pp. 83–99.

Enos, S., and K. Morton. "Developing a Theory and Practice of Campus-Community Partnerships." In *Building Partnerships for Service-Learning*, ed. B. Jacoby. San Francisco, CA: Jossey-Bass, 2003, pp. 20–41.

Grego, Clay. Interview by Kelly Elizabeth Behrend [Phone Interview]. New York City, NY, August 22, 2012.

Helmbrecht, Meghan. Interview by Kelly Elizabeth Behrend [Phone Interview]. New York City, NY, August 22, 2012.

Hovland, Kevin. "Global learning: aligning student learning outcomes with study abroad." *Report for The Center for Capacity Building in Study Abroad.* May 2010.

Keen, C., and K. Hall. "Engaging with difference matters: longitudinal student outcomes of co-curricular service-learning programs." *The Journal of Higher Education* 80, no. 1 (January/February 2009): 59–79.

Kuh, George. "The other curriculum." *The Journal of Higher Education* 66, no. 2 (March–April 1995): 125–141.

Lumpkin, Amelia. Interview by Kelly Elizabeth Behrend [Phone Interview]. New York City, NY, August 23, 2012.

Merrill, M. C. "The Cultural and Intercultural Contexts of Service-Learning." In *Knowing and Doing: The Theory and Practice of Service-Learning*, ed. L. A. Chisholm. 2005, pp. 177–201.

Moehring, Jenna. Interview by Kelly Elizabeth Behrend [Phone Interview]. New York City, NY, August 23, 2012.

Murlo, Nicole. Interview by Kelly Elizabeth Behrend [Phone Interview]. New York City, NY, August 24, 2012.

Pace, C. R. "Student effort: a new key to assessing quality." University of California, Higher Education Research Institute Report No. 1 (1984).

Sheffield, E. C. "Service in service-learning education: the need for philosophical understanding." *The High School Journal* (2005): 46–53.

PART III

Faculty: Exploring New
Epistemologies for Academic
Community Engagement

CHAPTER 9

Developing Faculty for Community Engagement across the Curriculum

Paul Schadewald and Karin Aguilar-San Juan

Introduction

The civic engagement movement in higher education has given special attention to campus models that develop the civic leadership capacity of students. These models build student skills and develop cohorts of students committed to integrating civic engagement in the academy and contributing to the public good. One recent report, *A Crucible Moment*, advocates that civic engagement be integrated holistically into higher education institutions (National Task Force on Civic Learning and Democratic Engagement, 2012). The report focuses especially on approaches to student curricular and cocurricular civic learning.[1] Scholars and practitioners have paid less attention to interdisciplinary campus models that might develop the capacity of faculty members for civic engagement work, or to models that form a cohort of faculty on a campus for mutual support, curricular development, and institutional change.

We contend that for the civic and community engagement movement to mature and grow, colleges and universities cannot assume that faculty members will gain needed skills, knowledge, and voice through their own individual efforts, individual collaborations with civic engagement staff, or individual participation in larger consortia. An individual approach risks only attracting the most interested and motivated faculty members. Without a base of support on their own campuses, faculty may not be able to develop their own interests or create a place for themselves within their institution or in the broader profession. Moreover, because of the transient nature of higher education, faculty members may lack the knowledge of the local context in which they work unless an intentional learning community is created that invites and instructs faculty how to understand the social and cultural fabric around them and engage local communities, organizations, and residents respectfully and productively.

This essay describes an interdisciplinary faculty development seminar, Macalester College's Urban Faculty Colloquium (UFC), which introduces and prepares faculty for civic engagement and which connects them to their urban context as scholars, teachers, mentors, and local citizens. Over eight years, beginning in 2005, Macalester College has supported 11 iterations of the UFC with various themes. The trainings have varied in length from three to eight days, depending on the time of year and the focus. An annual summer UFC has engaged faculty in Macalester's local context, and three "national" colloquia over winter break or immediately after spring graduation have built on Macalester faculty, staff, students, and institutional connections in New Orleans, Chicago, and Detroit. In all, over 83 Macalester faculty, staff, or partners of the college have participated in at least one local or national UFC. The UFC has provided ongoing curricular support that has enabled professors to design assignments, activities, and courses about issues that related to some aspect of urban or civic engagement.

We observe that this intensive approach to faculty development facilitates the creation of a cohort. By learning together and traveling together to off-campus sites (in the Twin Cities or other cities) when school is not in session, faculty form relationships across departmental or divisional lines, and faculty also interact meaningfully with staff. Especially for the faculty, the UFC creates a necessary learning community in which they are able to reflect on their roles on campus and on their place in the larger profession. The metaphor of a pathway resonates for faculty as they develop themselves into "civic professionals," and as they mentor students on their paths through the liberal arts and beyond.

Building a Faculty-Oriented Learning Community

We are not proposing a "cookie-cutter" approach to campus-based faculty trainings. Rather, in describing our experiences working with Macalester's UFC, we identify several overarching themes in our work. Three key factors allow the UFC to evolve into a generative space for a faculty-oriented learning community. First, the UFC engages with and builds upon the college's values and history. Second, the UFC draws support from campus leadership and strategically included both "rank-and-file" faculty and staff as well as higher-level administrators in its programming. Third, the UFC intentionally draws participants from across campus and is intentionally coled by faculty and staff to serve as a model for the respectful and interdependent relationships that are often necessary for engagement work.

A campus-level approach to building a cohort must be adapted to the specific mission, values, history, and institutional structure of an institution. Macalester College is a small, private liberal arts college located in St. Paul, Minnesota. It serves a mostly traditional-age, full-time undergraduate student population. Macalester no longer offers typical preprofessional programs such as journalism or teacher licensing. Indeed, as part of a rise to national prominence, specific vocational outcomes have been generally downplayed. As a result, contemporary civic initiatives must instead engage the liberal arts around a notion of citizenship, emphasizing the skills, knowledge, and dispositions that students should acquire as part of their discipline-based education.

As an academic community based on an urban campus, we live in the midst of abundant resources for teaching and learning about "real world" issues, such as local urban development, environmentalism, migration, internationalism, and multiculturalism. In the past two decades, we have engaged our urban context out of a sense of possibility for student civic learning and institutional responsibility. Our college mission explicitly states our commitments to internationalism, multiculturalism, service, and academic excellence. Yet, the precise mechanisms for engaging others and for expressing implementing our commitments to the people, organizations, and communities beyond our campus have been in a constant state of evolution and conversation.

Since 1988, the Civic Engagement Center, through the work of Director Karin Trail-Johnson, student leaders, and a network of supportive faculty and staff members has created a strong foundation of community partners and a history of civic engagement work. Faculty members in individual departments, such as American Studies, have also evinced important examples of civic and urban engagement curricular work. Macalester's collaboration with Project Pericles, a national consortium of colleges committed to civic engagement, provided an important early example of faculty and staff coming together for the shared project of deepening and institutionalizing community engagement.

The UFC continues this history by putting both academic staff and faculty in key positions of leadership and decision making. This integrated approach set the tone for the interdependent relationships that are necessary to sustain community partnerships, to support faculty forays into the community, and to demonstrate that we take the skills of engagement, such as empathy and critical thinking seriously. Even a small campus can be fractured between reporting lines and academic divisions. Yet, from its inception, the college treated the UFC as a partnership between an academic department (American Studies) and academic staff office (the Civic Engagement Center), and allowed the UFC to be codirected by faculty and staff. Although many faculty and staff provided leadership, American Studies Professor Karin Aguilar-San Juan and Civic Engagement Center Associate Director Paul Schadewald provide consistent leadership throughout the iterations.

The duties of faculty and staff leaders in the UFC are comingled so that essential tasks are shared, such as facilitating discussions, driving vans, leading neighborhood tours, or presenting to the group. Training focuses on faculty issues and development. But because the UFC allows full participation by staff, we are able to send a message that civic engagement should and can involve people from many corners of the institution.

The evolution of the UFC also depended upon the strategic support of higher-level administrators. In 2005, President Brian Rosenberg asked each department chair to describe his or her current engagement with the urban environment. He also asked how additional resources would enhance that engagement. Rosenberg recognized Macalester's urban location as a distinctive opportunity for engaged student learning at a liberal arts college. Many of the first urban and civic engagement classes that grew from the UFC relied upon seed funding from his office, and subsequently the UFC was integrated into proposals for large external grants.[2] Consequently, "soft money" has been the UFC's lifeline, allowing for faculty participation stipends for the local summer trainings, and support for civic engagement activities in specific courses. Since external funding is never guaranteed, however, the precise future of our efforts is uncertain, and the degree to which various constituencies on campus will continue to work collaboratively is also unclear. We feel that we have made the strongest case possible for a faculty-oriented development program on civic engagement and have included the Deans of the college as well as the Provost within programming to widen the circle of support.

Creating and Implementing a Relevant Program

Participants

Participation in the UFC has ranged from a small, intimate group of 8 to a much more diverse and wide-ranging group of 23 during the training in

Detroit. The Twin Cities training followed a developmental arc: The UFC started with a seminar format in which one faculty and one staff member led the training. Once faculty had gained a familiarity with the Twin Cities and could design projects to share with the group, we changed the UFC to a colloquia format. In this format, new participants would gain a basic introduction to the Twin Cities and civic engagement work and established participants would have the opportunity to lead sections of the training, share their knowledge, and mentor newer faculty.

We avoid centering the program in any one area or division of college but instead seek to make it interdisciplinary and trans/cross-disciplinary, providing a model to faculty of bringing their own skills and frameworks to larger civic issues. We do not worry about how to entice our detractors. Rather, we welcome both curious novices and the more experienced individuals who were already committed to urban and civic engagement. At the beginning, we briefly debated about which new faculty to include, since untenured faculty are the most vulnerable, and it is often assumed that visiting faculty have less institutional commitment. Yet, across campus, departments began to encourage new faculty regardless of rank or status to participate in the UFC either as a way to be oriented to the Twin Cities or as a way to learn the culture and structures of campus, or both. In the end, we rationalized the inclusion of visiting and adjunct faculty members as equal co-participants with tenure and tenure-track faculty on the basis that many visiting and adjunct faculty were strongly connected to the Twin Cities and that, precisely because they were not on a tenure schedule, they often had more freedom to create civic and urban engagement activities for their students. Furthermore, we realized that their students would benefit from their developing stronger ties to their colleagues and to the institution as a whole. Still a tension persists between the apparent enthusiasm for UFC as an initiative that has tremendous value, and the tenure and promotion cycle in which many junior faculty members feel unsure about the consequences of their investment in civic engagement activities.

We do not want to create a civic engagement movement at Macalester that was dependent upon a few very prominent "stars." The risk to a star strategy of faculty development is that if or when such stars leave or retire, the college would not have anyone under them to continue this work. Worse, the idea of campus–community partnership focused on a handful of well-known individuals would defeat the purpose of demonstrating to our students a broad notion of "global citizenship" and shared contributions to the "common good." The collaborative approach to civic engagement is part of what makes it desirable for faculty to join the effort; the UFC offers a community and a new framework for understanding what our work is and how we do it.

Over time, the UFC developed basic components and rhythms to the training. Each training included discussions of readings on civic engagement and the urban context; presentations on curricular issues; travels off campus to engage the social, cultural, and physical context; meetings with community partners; and time to work on syllabi or curricular concerns. We intend for each day to have an experiential off-campus component and to conclude with a constructive, critical reflection session that would allow faculty to engage broader themes. The goals are to engage many learning styles and also to provide faculty with experiences analogous to what students might encounter in a curricular setting.

In the past three years, Macalester supplemented the local UFC by developing yearly national-level UFCs in three additional cities, New Orleans, Chicago, and Detroit. We choose cities where we can build on existing curricular or cocurricular connections. We want to help faculty consider their own local context with a fresh perspective after intentionally engaging a different urban context. In addition, we hope that comparative courses, partnerships, or projects in other cities might develop. We structure these national-level colloquia in the same manner as the Twin Cities colloquia with readings, discussions, and meetings with community organizations. When possible, trainings engage faculty and staff with knowledge of each city to lead the sessions.

Whether in the local context or in a comparative context, the UFC focuses on three learning goals: engaging the distinctions of "place"; creating engaged learning opportunities; and supporting inquiries into faculty members' roles as "civic professionals."

The Distinctiveness of Place

Civic engagement work is not only building partnerships, but it is also reorienting and valuing work that takes into account the context. While Macalester's urban location is a source of distinction for faculty who come from more remote locations, getting faculty out of the classroom and into an engagement with the urban context proved challenging. The challenge in the first years of the program was a sheer lack of knowledge. On one early faculty training through Project Pericles, a Macalester faculty member admitted that he had never stopped to explore one of the central commercial corridors of the Twin Cities. In fact, the faculty member never had a reason to explore neighborhoods around the corridor, which ran east–west across the Twin Cities. This faculty lived in a southern suburb of St. Paul and his mental map ran north to south. As this example suggests, faculty members construct their mental maps around the places where they go for family obligations, work, and cultural events, not necessarily around neighborhoods where our community partners are located. As a result, large areas of the Twin Cities remain blank on their mental maps.

On a level that appears mundane but was in fact, essential and profound, we make the observation of the physical, social, and cultural environment a core component of the UFC. By heightening faculty awareness of the "placefulness" of any particular neighborhood, we accomplish the basic task of helping to fill in otherwise blank spaces on their mental maps. We want faculty members to think about *place* from a variety of perspectives— including from the perspectives of students who might be entering into that space as part of their classes, from the perspective of the diverse communities who might live and work there, and from the perspective of those who might work in schools, nonprofits, or community organizations. To this end, even the transportation we utilize to get faculty members off campus become learning experiences. We transport faculty members in college vans, in part, because this is the method that their students might use for their own engagement work. Vans facilitate group conversations and processing but also can disconnect students from the actual experience of the street and changing neighborhoods. We ask faculty to pay attention to the journey itself, because the act of travel replicates the student experience and also provides reflection on the relationship between campus and community. We seek to draw on the faculty members' various disciplinary approaches to understand the place, including approaches that value the arts, humanities, and geography. We then invite them to share their disciplinary approaches to think of new ways that they might utilize the arts or simple observations in their reflection exercises with students.

For example, one year we focused on a particular commercial corridor and asked faculty members to walk up and down the street to pay attention to aspects of street culture that they (and their students) might otherwise miss. We also provided public bus passes so that they could gain the experience of observing the street from the bus window. That year, we trained them in the act of documenting their observations with an urban street photographer. We invited each of them to represent the fine-grained texture of life on the street and the neighborhoods, and we concluded the training with an urban photography slide show. The result was their getting to know a place better.

We try to model for faculty members a way of engaging *place* that relies on multiple perspectives. We include broader historic and geographic overviews, address demographic trends, and often utilize demographic maps and artistic and historical resources for understanding neighborhoods, such as the visual arts, poetry, or local histories. The goal is to model for faculty what we tell our students: They are entering a story that began before them, that they will add their own voices to it, and that the story will continue after them. Whenever possible, we provide time for residents and those working in the community to talk directly with faculty. Even as faculty members send students to work in sites or they themselves mentor students in internships or community-based research projects, rarely do residents or organizational leaders interact with faculty directly or introduce their neighborhoods.

As one example of this process, North Minneapolis is most often referenced in the media as the area of Minneapolis with the highest concentration of poverty and home foreclosures. When we introduced faculty to North Minneapolis—an area that many of them had never visited before the training—we engaged the neighborhoods' challenges through demographic maps and reports. Yet, we also utilized other ways for understanding the place. We connected the faculty to the neighborhood through public art tours, alums who worked there, and nonprofits that had hosted our students.

Creating Engaged Learning Opportunities

For faculty, the barriers to creating engaged learning opportunities are pedagogical and logistical. On the logistical side, faculty members are often mystified with the technicalities of reserving or driving vans, or arranging for the payment of honoraria or room rentals. Alongside helping faculty engage the world off campus, we find that we needed to devote significant time to helping faculty members map the campus itself. Thus, we help faculty understand such mundane but essential topics as reporting lines or how staff members could support their efforts.

Pedagogically, the primary barriers in recruiting faculty are concerns that civic engagement is not rigorous enough or consummate with Macalester's liberal arts curriculum, or that it might entail enlisting students into a narrow version of political activism. We find that faculty do not want to be given rules or how-to booklets that might violate the culture of professional autonomy or academic freedom that are core components of the academic profession.

Consequently, we strike a balance between offering structure and community, while respecting individual choice. Instead of abstract best-practice discussions, we try to engage broader themes around the purposes and values of engaged education. We utilized William Cronon's "Only Connect," a piece that invites readers to consider how a liberal arts education helps students relate to the world (Cronon, 1998). We set aside time for faculty to share specific experiences and examples of engaged work and for faculty to work on their own syllabi and to receive feedback from their colleagues. Since no one was cast as an "expert," the risk of embarrassment is minimized.

One of the benefits of going off campus is that we ask faculty members to step out of their professional roles and to leave behind their disciplinary identifications and see themselves in another role as citizens. We do this by encouraging active participation rather than observation, so that theorizing the larger meaning starts from their own experience. This process also allows faculty members to understand what students experience on stepping into the unknown and struggling to adapt into roles within the organization or community. We intentionally utilize sites where students are currently involved. As one example, one of our most successful sites for the UFC is the Jane Addams School for Democracy, which supports learning circles between people from higher education institutions and new American communities. One of our faculty members became an active participant in the Hmong circles and was asked by a participant, "What do you do?" The faculty member visibly struggled to explain in nonacademic jargon what a "social psychologist" did. In the ensuing conversation, we fulfilled the goal of changing a faculty from an "expert" to a co-learner.

Faculty come to the training with different understanding of such terms as "service," "civic engagement," and "urban engagement." We find it useful not to offer strict definitions of these terms but to offer general distinctions between curricular activities that provide some degree of reciprocity and benefit to the community (civic engagement) and those activities that utilize the city as a resource for student learning through field trips, observation, guest speakers, or attendance at events (urban engagement). We do not wish to create a hierarchy between urban engagement and civic engagement. Each has its appropriate place in the curriculum according to the learning goals of classes and the time available. Yet, we also want faculty to understand that if their own activities and the larger college's "portfolio" of interaction begins to draw too heavily on experiential activities alone, then residents and communities might feel less like partners and more like participants in an urban laboratory for the benefit of students. We want faculty members to grapple with the notion of what reciprocity might mean in relation to neighborhoods, individuals, and community organizations.

Pathways toward a New Professionalism

Whether they are based in the Twin Cities or in other US cities, the Urban Faculty Colloquia expands the prevailing notions of "professionalism" for faculty and for their work with students. An important objective has been to enhance the capacity of faculty to provide substantive advice and support for students in the new interdisciplinary concentrations—Human Rights and Humanitarianism, Community and Global Health, and Urban Studies. Although not technically "pre-professional" programs, these concentrations do encourage students to link their liberal arts background with vocational pathways and to aim toward making a living while also serving the public good. Some faculty members feel ill equipped to help guide students in careers or professions outside of academia. The Urban Faculty Colloquia helps faculty gain knowledge of community resources within the Twin Cities, and in other cities, Macalester alumni provide insights into their vocational paths. We see an emphasis on preparing students for vocational pathways that contribute to the common good as one future direction of the UFC.[3]

Somewhat surprisingly, UFC faculty participants evince a hunger to discuss the mesh between and among their academic career paths, personal lives, and commitments to the common good. An engagement of these topics requires the mutual trust that participants develop through shared activities, conversations, travel, and experiential learning. At one reflection session ostensibly summarizing the activities of the day, a professor openly expressed the difficulty of balancing family obligations with college work and broader commitments. The conversation she started came up organically as part of the common tasks involved in the colloquium. It seemed refreshing and normal to everyone to talk about family life in this context. However, in other campus settings, mentioning family as a high priority hovers perilously close to admitting professional incompetency or disloyalty, especially among women. We found that there are few places on campus to have these honest conversations. In many other ways, participants want to bring their personal experiences to bear in thinking about what it meant to be a professional and a member of the academic community.

The concept of "pathway" not only has strong resonance for our students but also for our faculty participants. Most entered the profession with a passion for their disciplines and strong commitments to the common good. Yet, their pathway through academia often centered on questions of tenure, how their commitments to civic engagement would or would not be recognized by professional colleagues, and how they could synthesize the diverse areas of their lives. In some ways, the UFC took them on an experiential pathway from academic expert, to community learner, and back to the college to engage their own professional work.

In the most recent iteration of the UFC, we devoted time to exploring issues of public scholarship and tenure and the career experiences of civically engaged faculty—tenure track, visiting, and adjunct. The time necessary for these conversations could not be contained in the short time frame of the UFC and needed to be continued in meetings throughout the academic year. This will be one focus moving forward. The issue of how faculty members connect to the wider community and recreate the curriculum around civic engagement is deeply connected to how they recreate their own identities as "civic professionals." Relevant material include the "Tenure Team Report" of Imagining America, studies of faculty motivation for civic engagement by academics such as KerryAnn O'Meara, and critical studies of the concept of professionalism by scholars such as William Sullivan. We hope that creating campus-based and interdisciplinary civic engagement cohorts through intentional colloquia will continue to be an important step in this journey.[4]

Notes

1. For additional information, see the National Task Force on Civic Learning and Democratic Engagement, *A Crucible Moment: College Learning and Democracy's Future*, Washington, DC: Association of American Colleges and Universities, 2012. For examples of campus models that focus on developing a student cohort, see the Bonner Scholars/Leaders program and Project Pericles' Debating for Democracy program.
2. The UFC was supported specifically by the Bush Foundation, a regional foundation established by a retired 3M executive, the Andrew W. Mellon Foundation, and the Teagle Foundation.
3. "Civic Professionalism" is the future direction of Imagining America's "Undergraduate Civic Engagement" collaboratory, funded by the Teagle Foundation. For works on civic professionalism and education, see Harry C. Boyte and Eric Fretz, "Civic professionalism," *Journal of Higher Education, Outreach, and Engagement* 14, no. 2 (2010): 67–90; William M. Sullivan, "Markets vs. professions: value added?," *Daedalus* 134, no. 3 (2005): 19–26; William M. Sullivan, "Can professionalism still be a viable ethic?," *Good Society* 13, no. 1 (2004): 15–20; and William M. Sullivan, "Knowledge and judgment in practice as the twin aims of learning," in *Transforming Undergraduate Education: Theory that Compels and Practices that Succeed*, ed. Donald W. Harward (Lanham: Rowman & Littlefield Publishers, 2012).
4. Julie Ellison and Timothy K. Eatman, *Scholarship in Public: Knowledge Creation and Tenure Policy in the Engaged University* (2008). On the civic dimension to faculty's professions, see KerryAnn O'Meara, L. R. Sandmann, John Saltmarsh, and Dwight Giles, "Studying the professional lives and work of faculty involved in community engagement," *Innovative Higher Education* 36, no. 2 (2011): 83–96; and KerryAnn O'Meara, "Reframing incentives and rewards for community service-learning and academic outreach," *Journal of Higher Education Outreach and Engagement* 8, no. 2 (2003): 201–220.

References

Boyte, Harry C., and Eric Fretz. "Civic professionalism." *Journal of Higher Education, Outreach, and Engagement* 14, no. 2 (2010): 67–90.

Cronon, William. "Only connect: the goals of a liberal education." *American Scholar* 67 (1998): 73–80.

Ellison, Julie, and Timothy K. Eatman. *Scholarship in Public: Knowledge Creation and Tenure Policy in the Engaged University.* Syracuse, NY: Imagining America, 2008.

The National Task Force on Civic Learning and Democratic Engagement, *A Crucible Moment: College Learning and Democracy's Future.* Washington, DC: Association of American Colleges and Universities, 2012.

O'Meara, K. "Reframing incentives and rewards for community service-learning and academic outreach." *Journal of Higher Education Outreach and Engagement* 8, no. 2 (2003): 201–220.

O'Meara, K., L. R. Sandmann, J. Saltmarsh, and D. Giles. "Studying the professional lives and work of faculty involved in community engagement." *Innovative Higher Education* 36, no. 2 (2011): 83–96.

Sullivan, William M. "Can professionalism still be a viable ethic?" *Good Society* 13, no. 1 (2004): 15–20.

Sullivan, William M. "Markets vs. professions: value added?" *Daedalus* 134, no. 3 (2005): 19–26.

Sullivan, William M. "Knowledge and judgment in practice as the twin aims of learning." In *Transforming Undergraduate Education: Theory that Compels and Practices that Succeed*, ed. Donald W. Harward. Lanham: Rowman & Littlefield Publishers, 2012.

CHAPTER 10

Permeable Boundaries: Connecting Coursework and Community Work in Disciplinary Curricula

Emily Kane, Georgia Nigro, Ellen Alcorn, and Holly Lasagna

Introduction

Many colleges and universities today integrate high-impact educational practices with best practices for community engagement to create curricula that are developmentally powerful for students and community partners. Participating in such educational practices, as George Kuh (2008) has argued, leads to positive results for college students of many different backgrounds. Building upon this work, Brownell and Swaner (2010) studied the outcomes for students participating in five of the practices (first-year seminars, learning communities, service learning, undergraduate research, and capstone courses and project) alone or as part of an integrated effort. A special focus of their work was examining the differential outcomes for students from traditionally underserved populations. Common outcomes for students included academic gains, increased civic engagement, higher persistence rates, greater interaction with faculty and peers, and increased tolerance for and engagement with diversity; for students from underserved populations, higher grades and rates of persistence joined with a greater sense of belonging on campus and higher rates of school enrollment as important outcomes.

In recent years, the Bonner Network has introduced an initiative that has articulated a set of best practices for community partnerships. These practices include strategic multiyear relationships with community partners, developmental, multiyear student placements, community-based learning and research that involves multiyear faculty commitments, public policy research with community partners, and capacity building with partners involving evidence-based program assessment and strategic planning. In this chapter, we draw upon examples from two disciplines at Bates College where coursework and community work have been bridged by drawing on best practices, with developmentally powerful results for students, faculty, and community partners.

The Department of Psychology at Bates College began to implement these practices by developing an alternative to its required research methods course, an intensive course that involved the design and execution of three research projects over the course of the semester. In the alternative, students designed and executed their final research project in collaboration with a community partner (thereby integrating service learning and undergraduate research in a manner that actively engages partners in the design of the research and creates a permeable boundary between classroom and community work). This first change in the psychology curriculum came in a course typically taken by sophomores and juniors. From this beginning, the curriculum continued to change at both earlier and later levels. First-year seminars began to include community-based learning with partners who might later work with students in the research methods course, and the department introduced a community-based research alternative to the laboratory-based senior thesis (thereby integrating service learning, undergraduate research, and capstone projects). Enabling these curricular changes was a strong center for community partnerships, with staff members attentive to the long temporal horizon while faculty members attended to the quotidian demands of teaching. Now, for example, a psychology student might begin college with a 20-hour placement in a Head Start classroom as part of a first-year seminar, providing direct service to children and teachers and returning to the college classroom to reflect on connections to coursework. The same student might return to the Head Start classroom as a senior to design an intervention for its Somali refugee population, with the thesis course and community work completely integrated in a single project. Thus, the boundary between coursework and community work becomes more permeable across the developmental span of these courses.

In sociology, curricular change began with the gradual introduction of community-based learning opportunities in various elective courses at the 100 and 200 levels, and eventually resulted in the introduction of a community-based research component in the required sociology research methods course taken by sophomores and juniors. A smaller department than psychology, sociology cannot staff both a traditional and alternative methods course; so the community component is less extensive than that developed in the alternative psychology methods course. Although a community-engaged project is carried out in the methods course, it is completed with little contact between students and community partners and thus a less permeable boundary between coursework and community work. However, this is linked to more fully reciprocal community-based research projects in a 300-level seminar entitled "Public Sociology," an optional course for which the required methods course is a prerequisite. In this seminar, the boundary is more permeable, with community partners participating fully in the crafting of research questions and the co-creation of knowledge, in projects that often lead to senior thesis work with the same partners. Later, a first-year seminar was instituted, exploring social inequality through community engagement developmentally appropriate to first-year students. In conjunction with staff members from our community partnerships center who are fully immersed in the community, projects have been developed that address felt needs in the community and can cut across these various courses and levels. For example, work related to a community food assessment has been incorporated into the research methods course and the public sociology seminar over multiple offerings of each course, and became the foundation for independent senior thesis work in sociology as well.

As the two examples illustrate, the integration of high-impact educational practices with best practices for community engagement offers great promise for students and communities alike. On our campus, fulfilling that promise depends critically on the working relationships forged between faculty and community members with staff of the campus center for community partnerships. Because high-impact educational practices demand so much of faculty members, the assistance and expertise of the staff make their integration with best practices for community engagement feasible. Center staff take a developmental approach with faculty members and community partners, helping to forge relationships that grow over time into multiyear partnerships that may not need further staff assistance. As faculty members introduce changes into their courses, and community partners' needs change over time with shifting funding opportunities and demographics, so the relationship between center staff and the other parties continues to be important.

Navigating Disciplinary and Community Boundaries: Opportunities and Challenges

As the National Task Force on Civic Learning and Democratic Engagement (2012) notes, while community-based learning has expanded tremendously in recent decades, "the vast majority of courses are still random electives that students encounter in no particular order or time sequencing" (59). In our experience at Bates College, situating community-based work squarely within the sequential curriculum of specific disciplines has generated both opportunities and challenges. A primary opportunity is the manner in which it fosters student learning that is both developmental and holistic.

Foundational Courses

This developmental opportunity begins in the first year, as our approach recognizes that unlike most service work in high school, college-level community work requires students to engage critically with disciplinary concepts as well as the ideas, values, and assumptions that animate the work of their community partners (Ross and Boyle, 2007). Through sequenced disciplinary curricula, and supported by intentional reflection and the coordination of our center, we help students make that transition gradually. For example, in a developmental psychology course, a first-year student might have the opportunity to work in a Montessori classroom, helping the teacher document children's learning. Back in the college classroom, that student is asked to reflect on how the Montessori approach to preschool education relates to major theories of child development and how the community work relates to his or her own developing life purpose (Long, 2012). Or, in a first-year seminar offered by the sociology department, students read texts that introduce a sociological perspective on social inequality and investigate the role of higher education in advancing the public good. In the community, they provide direct service in partner organizations that address inequalities. And in the classroom, these strands come together through discussion, written work, and a poster assignment in which small groups synthesize course concepts with their partner organization's approach to challenging inequality.

By sophomore and junior year, both psychology and sociology offer foundational research methods courses and advanced seminars that involve a more permeable boundary between classroom and community work, and engage community partners more explicitly as coeducators and co-creators of knowledge. In the required research methods course for sociology, the instructor works with our community partnerships center and a community partner to develop a research project loosely informed by the partner's needs, but not to the full extent typical of community-based research (Strand et al., 2003). Some elements of the project are specifically designed to answer a question generated by the partner, while others introduce students to the community more generally and ensure exposure to a range of methods common in the discipline. Recently, the focus has been on food security, local

food, and alternative food institutions. Students read the sociological literature on food security and learn about local initiatives. Then, they design and
implement data collection using a standardized survey, a content analysis
of media coverage, field observation, and qualitative interviews. Although
students visit local sites, their research work is coordinated by the instructor
in the classroom and is of limited use to our community partner, creating
only a semipermeable boundary.

Our psychology department is large enough to offer a more traditional
methods course and one focused on community-based research. After the
instructor of the community-based methods course cultivates a few themati-
cally related partnerships, students work in small groups directly with their
partner organization to develop research designs. Methods are selected specifically for answering the partner's questions, rather than using a predetermined
set of methods typical of the discipline. For example, a group of sophomore
psychology students formed a team to evaluate a training program for child-
care providers offered by the Maine Infant Mental Health Association.
Weaving their previous knowledge of psychology and their emerging research
skills with the expertise and needs of the association's staff, the student team
moved between classroom and community as they executed the evaluation.

Advanced Courses

After the foundational methods course, seminars are available to juniors and
seniors. At this stage, students are prepared to conduct more independent
research and question how disciplinary constraints impact publicly engaged
scholarship. One example from our psychology department is an advanced
seminar in developmental psychology, in which a junior psychology major
might work with the head of a preschool to investigate and document how
different states fund and implement universal preschool, while also exploring how psychologists engage in research, policy, and practice related to
education. The student navigates the boundaries between classroom and
community, bringing insights from the partner's expertise back to peers in
the course and conducting the research project based on the partner's goals.
Within the sociology department, a seminar entitled "Public Sociology"
offers similar opportunities. With a basic research goal appropriate to the
students' abilities outlined in advance, students work semi-independently
with various community partners to specify the research question and methods, and then produce a final product designed to meet their partner's needs.
While some reading and classroom discussion are focused on engaging disciplinary debates of greater relevance to academic partners (see Burawoy,
2005), most work takes place at the permeable boundary between classroom

and community through community-based research (Strand et al., 2003). Students work on campus and at their partner organizations, and final products are evaluated for how well they meet partner needs. Formal evaluation is completed by the course instructor based on a definition of partner needs worked out by all parties in writing, but students also receive immediate feedback from partners by presenting drafts before finalizing their products. In recent years, projects in this seminar have been crafted from the partnerships engaged in the first-year and sophomore courses. For example, one group conducted a comprehensive survey of local emergency food providers for the same local food initiative with which the methods course had partnered more loosely. Another group conducted participant interviews and evaluated a resource fair for an economic self-sufficiency program at a local public housing community, a program for which some first-year students had previously engaged in direct service providing child care.

In these seminars, community partners play a key role in the classroom as coeducators and act as full partners in the research process. Moving along this set of sequenced courses, the boundary between classroom and community becomes more permeable and students become better prepared for reciprocal community engagement. Step by step, students, partners, faculty, and staff build trust and the kind of relationships necessary for meaningful co-creation of knowledge. By the time psychology and sociology students arrive at Bates's required senior thesis, seasoned community partners know that they can trust students with sensitive material and at the same time they recognize that seniors are in a transitional and vulnerable state. In the senior thesis, the overlap between coursework and community work is complete, and the boundary highly permeable: Students work individually with their partners, with limited supervision from their thesis adviser. Over the years, sociology students who first learned of the community food initiative in the sophomore methods course have conducted more advanced research in a seminar and then delved deeper in a senior thesis in partnership with that initiative. The same progression has occurred with the economic self-sufficiency program, with which students have partnered at all levels of the sociology curriculum. Psychology students have completed senior thesis projects that build on their previous partnerships and community-based evaluation research too, including a senior who developed, implemented, and evaluated a preliteracy intervention for Somali refugee and immigrant children in a Head Start classroom.

Opportunities and Challenges

The combination of these practices, adjusted to each developmental stage, is exciting to many of our students. As their excitement and capacity for the work grow, they attract more faculty to the enterprise. Students make well-informed requests for community-based opportunities in other relevant departmental courses, engage their favorite professors in independent study projects, and bring new thesis supervisors into community work by arriving at the thesis stage prepared to advocate for the approach. By this point, most students recognize the value of what is increasingly emphasized in the civic engagement literature: their community partners' expertise and the benefits of generating knowledge with rather than only for those partners (see Hoyt, 2011; Saltmarsh and Hartley, 2011; Scobey, 2012). Across the sequence of courses, the curriculum challenges more traditional service-based models of community-engaged learning and challenges disciplinary expertise as the primary form of knowledge generation. A recent graduate captures it well in a reflection on his participation in our Bonner Leaders Program, referring to a specific partnership with a local elementary school, "My learning at Bates College and my learning at Park Avenue School have formed a unique educational experience that neither could provide alone." Addressing all of the Bonner Leader cohort's work at Bates more broadly, he argues that the "value" of their degrees "is based on a reciprocal value between what we've learned in the classroom and what we've learned and done with the community, with our neighbors" (Conwell, 2012, 1).

Along with the many successes we have experienced with this approach, student learning may be limited when community experiences are understood through the lens of coursework within a particular discipline. Addressing this challenge requires cross-disciplinary initiatives that can involve individual faculty, staff, and students, but are even more robust when a strong center for community partnerships facilitates and supports the work. Several programs at our center help faculty and students stretch beyond disciplinary constraints. One is our center's noncredit seminar for students engaged in community-based research, offering a cross-disciplinary opportunity for peer and staff support. In addition, cocurricular leadership programs and training sessions on topics such as effective tutor-mentor strategies, grant-writing and fundraising, and the ethics of community engagement, build a network of community-engaged students across disciplines who learn, over time, to connect their coursework and community work even more fully. These programs encourage intentionality and reflection that allow community-based work to realize its potential for academic learning, cognitive development, and civic engagement (Conway et al., 2009; Zlotkowski and Duffy, 2010).

Another challenge is the risk that community impact and cogeneration of knowledge may be dampened by the application of theories and methods with a strong disciplinary slant. Here again, our center facilitates by taking a wide-angle view, pairing community partners with students and faculty from a variety of disciplines and forging relationships that highlight partners as coeducators. For example, the community food initiative involves many community stakeholders. A staff coauthor of this chapter has served on that initiative's coordinating committee from its earliest stages, allowing a broad perspective on opportunities and fostering the relationships necessary for reciprocity. Therefore, a larger range of classroom/community connections can be crafted, and boundaries can become more meaningfully permeable. Our other staff coauthor specializes in education-related partnerships, with public schools and programs like Head Start. The depth and breadth of her relationships also facilitate cross-disciplinary and multidisciplinary opportunities for community impact and student growth. Working together across various partnerships, these staff members devote time and resources to developing partners' capacity as coeducators and creatively addressing logistical and intellectual problems from liability to transportation, ethics to articulation of partner, and student and faculty responsibilities. These multidisciplinary connections, crafted through authentic reciprocity, encourage recognition of our community partners as important sources of knowledge. Expanding beyond limited emphasis on disciplinary expertise, boundaries between disciplines and between classroom and community become permeable to the benefit of all involved.

Discussion and Conclusions

We close with two questions. First, is our model an adaptation to the status quo of departmental curricula, or is it more transformative? If we take seriously Boyer's (1994) call for "a larger purpose" (48) for higher education, then each and every department of an institution must respond. To be sure, a departmental or disciplinary approach is not new within the civic engagement movement; Edward Zlotkowski linked service-learning with disciplinary aims in his writing and editorial work at the end of 1990s. The American Association of Higher Education's 19-volume series on service-learning in the disciplines is over a decade old, and our college bears fruits from that effort. We believe that the sustained engagement that comes from developmental curricula in departmental homes is transformative. It allows students and faculty members to work together solving problems and generating knowledge, and in so doing, to set aside old, inaccurate worries about rigor versus relevance. As we have seen in our own departments, when faculty members and students approach engaged work with the support and guidance of disciplinary colleagues, the resulting practices grow sturdy roots and sprout strong wings. That is, disciplinary scaffolding affords a firm basis that adds credibility and depth to the scholarship, which in turn, frees student and faculty scholars to tackle harder and more intractable community issues.

Second, is our model sustainable? Institutions of higher education face many challenges to sustaining the kind of best practices in classrooms and communities we describe here. Indeed, new initiatives, such as MOOCs (massive open online courses) and Mozilla's Open Badges Initiative, aim to disrupt the current model of higher education that depends on time- and place-based approaches to learning. Many of these new initiatives take a competency-based approach, whereby students advance when they have demonstrated mastery of a skill, ability, or body of knowledge. Any pedagogical method that moves a student toward mastery is acceptable in this approach, enabling the student to find the best instruction at the lowest cost. Technology is now available to provide competency-based education in some domains. However, we argue that these developments will not help students acquire all the competencies they need to generate new knowledge about critically important issues and solve pressing social problems. There are no shortcuts when it comes to investing in human relationships and building capacity within students, colleges, and community organizations for the hard work of social problem solving. New technologies will change the ways we express those investments, but investments in human relationships will always be central to the enterprise of social change. Colleges and universities that continue to offer time- and place-based approaches to learning may find their social change goals well served by a curriculum model such as ours, especially if combined with a strong center for community partnerships. Given reported declines in civic orientation among young people (National Task Force on Civic Learning and Democratic Engagement, 2012; Twenge et al., 2012), higher education's role in fostering civic outcomes is essential. Although some institutions may choose to add a major, minor, or certificate in civic engagement, we believe that infusing the work broadly across disciplinary structures of the curriculum, as our model begins to do, helps ensure sustainability and has the potential to prepare even more students for democratic participation.

References

Boyer, Ernest. "Creating the new American college." *The Chronicle of Higher Education* A48 (March 9, 1994).

Brownell, Jane E., and Lynne E. Swaner. *Five High-Impact Practices: Research on Learning Outcomes, Completion, and Quality.* Washington, DC: Association of American Colleges and Universities.

Burawoy, Michael. "For public sociology." *American Sociological Review* 70 (2005): 4–28.

Conway, James M., Elise L. Amel, and Daniel P. Gerwien. "Teaching and learning in the social context: A meta-analysis of service-learning's effects on academic, personal, social, and citizenship outcomes." *Teaching of Psychology* 36 (2009): 233–245.

Conwell, Jordan. *Senior address*. Paper presented at the 2012 Bonner Leader Senior Celebration of Learning, Bates College, Lewiston, ME, May 2012.

Hoyt, Lorlene. "Sustained City-Campus Engagement." In *"To Serve a Larger Purpose": Engagement for Democracy and the Transformation of Higher Education*, ed. John Saltmarsh and Matthew Hartley. Philadelphia, PA: Temple University Press, 2011, pp. 265–288.

Kuh, George D. *High-Impact Practices: What They Are, Who Has Access to Them, and Why They Matter*. Washington, DC: Association of American Colleges and Universities, 2008.

Long, Theodore E. 2012. "Evoking Wholeness: To Renew the Ideal of the Educated Person." In *Transforming Undergraduate Education: Theory That Compels and Practices That Succeed*, ed. Donald W. Harward. Lanham, MD: Rowman and Littlefield, pp. 129–140.

National Task Force on Civic Learning and Democratic Engagement. *A Crucible Moment: College Learning and Democracy's Future*. Washington, DC: Association of American Colleges and Universities, 2012.

Ross, Laurie, and Mary-Ellen Boyle. "Transitioning from high school service to college service-learning in a first-year seminar." *Michigan Journal of Community Service Learning* 14 (2007): 53–64.

Saltmarsh, John, and Matthew Hartley. "To Serve a Larger Purpose." In *To Serve a Larger Purpose": Engagement for Democracy and the Transformation of Higher Education*, ed. John Saltmarsh and Matthew Hartley. Philadelphia, PA: Temple University Press, 2011, pp. 1–13.

Scobey, David M. "A Copernican Moment: On the Revolutions in Higher Education." In *Transforming Undergraduate Education: Theory That Compels and Practices That Succeed*, ed. Donald W. Harward. Lanham, MD: Rowman and Littlefield, 2012, pp. 37–49.

Strand, Kerry, Sam Marullo, Nicholas Cutforth, Randy Stoecker, and Patrick Donohue. *Community-Based Research and Higher Education*. San Francisco, CA: Jossey-Bass, 2003.

Twenge, Jean M., W. Keith Campbell, and Elise C. Freeman. "Generational differences in young adults' life goals, concern for others, and civic orientation, 1966–2009." *Journal of Personality and Social Psychology* 102 (2012): 1045–1062.

Zlotkowski, Edward, and Donna Duffy. "Two decades of community-based learning." *New Directions for Teaching and Learning* 123 (2010): 33–43.

CHAPTER 11

Wisdom from the Garden: Exploring Faculty Transformation

Beth Blissman

The pitcher cries for water to carry
and a person for work that is real.

Introduction

In her poem "To be of Use," Marge Piercy (1982) reminds us of the power of intrinsic motivation. Different people have unique pathways to community engagement: Some prefer individual efforts, others like to get engaged as part of group, and still others thrive upon connecting those who typically would not collaborate. Piercy reminds us that:

The work of the world is common as mud
Botched, it smears the hands, crumbles to dust.
But the thing worth doing well done has a shape that satisfies, clean
    and evident.

These difficult-to-measure internal motivators causing humans to put the needs of others in front of their own, as well as various external motivators, are worth exploring as related to faculty involvement in civic engagement activity.

As a practitioner who has been engaged in "making the way by walking" for over 20 years, I offer these reflections on faculty motivation in the hope that they resonate with readers and as a gift back to a network that has nourished and sustained my intellectual journey. I will start with a confession: although I am trained as an ecological ethicist grounded in the Christian tradition, I must admit that I have found just as much wisdom in my home garden as in the academe. Plant-based metaphors help me make sense of the world, and keep my thoughts growing through the seasons and annual cycles. In this chapter, I will briefly review some existing literature pertaining to faculty motivation for civic engagement and then explore several parallels between a healthy garden and a healthy, growing center supporting the integration of service and learning.[1]

What the Research Says

We are seeing a growing number of organized studies that document faculty motivations for involvement in both community-based learning and civic engagement. Although community-based learning[2] (CBL), also called service learning, has been a part of higher education for many decades, especially in Historically Black Colleges and Universities (HBCUs) and faith-based settings, we did not see many studies about why some faculty members chose this particular pedagogy until the 1990s. Several early studies of faculty motivation to incorporate CBL focused, out of necessity, on geographic regions. Hammond (1994) explored the impetus of 130 faculty members at 23 higher education institutions in Michigan who incorporated service-learning into their teaching. She discovered that their key motivating factors related to students' course-based learning, as faculty members perceived that students in their CBL courses found the course materials more relevant, demonstrated self-direction, and experienced improved student satisfaction with their education.

Within a decade, another study of 518 faculty members at 43 colleges and universities in Ohio (Abes et al., 2002) sought to articulate the factors that both motivated and deterred faculty use of CBL. This study expanded on earlier work because it was based on responses from over 500 faculty—approximately half of whom did not use service-learning—and it described factors that not only motivated, but also deterred, faculty use of service-learning. Both confirming and expanding Hammond's work, these authors found the primary motivating factors to be those connected directly to student learning outcomes (such as increasing student understanding of course material, increasing student personal development, and increasing students' understanding of social problems as systemic) and the primary deterring factors to be logistical difficulties and the fact that CBL courses take more time to coordinate well.

Ironically, this study noted that—on the whole—concerns regarding tenure and promotion were not a considerable deterrent to faculty members' decisions to employ CBL. Only one faculty group noted the reward structure as an important consideration: service-learning faculty at research universities. Nearly a third of these faculty members indicated that not being rewarded in performance reviews and tenure and promotion decisions might cause them to discontinue using CBL. Although untenured professors were more concerned about the reward structure than were tenured professors, "service-learning faculty appear to be internally motivated and for the most part unlikely to stop using service-learning if they are not rewarded for doing so" (Abes et al., 2002, 15). This finding—of the reward structure's relative unimportance in decisions to use CBL—is the most striking difference between the 2002 study's results and much of the prior literature from the 1990s (Morton and Troppe, 1996; Stanton, 1994; Ward, 1998).

In essence, what is coming to the fore is that there is no one indicator or characteristic of faculty engagement. The reasons that faculty members choose to get involved—and stay involved—bridging campus and community are influenced by a number of factors and the ways in which these factors intersect. The motivations are myriad and there is no one factor, no one pathway, and no one common experience that characterize the creation of a civically engaged faculty member. Researchers have been able to tease out some patterns, however. The Publicly Engaged Scholars (PES) Study, led by Timothy K. Eatman, research director of Imagining America, explores both the graduate school experiences and career aspirations and decisions of early career faculty and staff as a way to enhance our understanding about the career arc for publicly engaged scholarship and practice. As part of the PES study, Eatman is investigating, and categorizing, different professional pathways to engagement in order to characterize profiles of publicly engaged scholars in humanities, arts, and design. He and his research team have developed seven profiles to convey the different pathways publicly engaged scholars may take throughout the early stages of their career.[3]

Finally, O'Meara (2012) provides a fine summary of scholarly documentation regarding the wide variety of motivations for faculty involvement in community engagement, as well as theoretical and conceptual frameworks for these motivations. She outlines the research that suggests certain demographic factors (gender, race, class, etc.) and/or participatory epistemologies as indicators of involvement—as well as the research that brings these conclusions into question. O'Meara looks beyond motivation for initial involvement in community engagement and posits the possibility that it is the "dynamic interaction among an individual's characteristics, institutional factors, and environmental factors" that affects whether or not faculty members continue involvement and integrate it into their own professional growth (O'Meara, 2012, 221). These emerging patterns are helpful in starting to sort out the mystery of motivations, and while I do agree with O'Meara (2008) that we can learn from exemplars, experience has also taught me that a close reading of one's local social, economic, ecological, and political setting is key to success when attempting to motivate faculty members.

Wisdom from the Garden

At Oberlin College's (OC) Bonner Center for Service & Learning (BCSL), my task is to find, train, encourage, support, and recognize faculty members undertaking CBL. I try my best to keep up with the literature, and speak with as many colleagues as possible on those rare occasions when I can afford the time to attend conferences. One particular challenge we have is juggling an expanding CBL effort slowly and sustainably among a rich group of cocurricular and extracurricular programs. Similar to other civic engagement centers, we are not blessed with large amounts of money and have just enough staff to get by. So how have I been able to grow new connections and shepherd the process of doubling our number of CBL courses in less than a decade? Most of the credit for our growth goes to the dedicated faculty members willing to take risks, along with our energetic community partners and enthusiastic undergraduates, but I have learned several valuable lessons along the way.

Explore the Rhizomes

Rhizomes, or hidden stems of plants, connect and expand below ground, invisible to the casual observer.[4] So where are the hidden connections on campus? At a more progressive institution like Oberlin, where many married or partnered couples would not dream of taking each others' surnames, just figuring out who lives with whom can be a delightful challenge. I have also found faculty members willing to make connections of various sorts with their child's school and/or early childhood center because it is a place where they spend time anyway. (Sometimes a faculty member's first foray into community engagement is serving on a PTO [parent–teacher organization] or board of a nonprofit organization that serves children.) There are also connections to be made based on getting to know research agendas, favorite foods, common interests, and—especially for new faculty members—a desire to get to know the area. I have found that being in the right place at the right time to do a little research and friendly Q and A, when combined with decent record-keeping, can really pay off when connecting campus and community.

Plant the Seeds—Continuously

Mustard seeds are amazing—this summer I have gown mustard leaves nearly 18" long from a seed that is smaller than a grain of rice. Sometimes, a seed that is planted comes up one year—or several years—after it is placed in the ground. Patience and persistence are the friends of any good gardener. Some seeds, however, germinate fairly quickly, and if one wants lettuce, or mustard greens, or peas, throughout the entire growing season, then one must sow seeds every two weeks for a continuing harvest—this is called succession planting. I have noticed that faculty members' schedules of academic leaves, administrative appointments, and unexpected tasks make it challenging to keep up consistent long-term relationships with our community partners. Therefore, I have taken to sowing seeds of ideas for CBL wherever and whenever possible. For example, a few ideas for a course that I spoke with a faculty member about over five years ago are now coming to fruition. Another idea is to remind faculty members that their most engaged students may be able to continue involvement with a community partner through a cocurricular pathway or an independent study sponsored by the BCSL. My thinking is that the more seeds of ideas that our staff plants, the greater the chances that these seeds will some day grow into courses, workshops, community-based research agendas, or concentrations.

Perennials Rock!

One of my most joyous discoveries as a gardener has been perennials. These plants, once established, bear fruit every year without much coaxing at all. (Think asparagus, strawberries, sunchokes, and raspberries.) As a campus service director, I deeply appreciate the faculty members who find something that functions well pedagogically, and then work on perfecting a CBL course each year that they are not on leave. Sometimes, these faculty members are deeply connected to the local community, or they have responded to a request from a community partner, or perhaps they grew up in the South in the 1960s and witnessed first hand the power of engaged learning.[5]

Whatever their background, supporting such faculty members is an important and relatively easy task—we advertise these courses to students, do our best to connect them with relevant community partners when appropriate, and recognize their work with occasional awards or free meals. We are also in the process of lifting up the work of these professors through faculty profiles on our website in order to share the best practices they have developed and to seek funding to support at least one of these professors as a CBL mentor to younger faculty members.

Offer Supports

Just as tomatoes, beans, and other vegetables that grow on vines need a great deal of support, faculty members also need assistance in various ways. In Vogelgesang et al.'s (2010) study, we see the importance of faculty perception of institutional support for civic engagement. They claim that it is the primary predictor of involvement, which affirms the need for institutions of higher education to invest in adequate staffing to support faculty members.

At Oberlin, the BCSL offers several ways to support civically engaged faculty members, although we have little sway as of yet over decisions of promotion or tenure. Earlier this decade, with support from Learn and Serve America, we were able to offer small grants and workshops to faculty members interested in creating or revising CBL courses.[6] We always offer free consultations to any faculty member interested in CBL, and host the occasional workshop or brown bag lunch to discuss engaged pedagogy. One pathway that has worked particularly well has been to offer an independent study course for students selected as CBL teaching assistants by faculty members. Typically, our faculty members choose students who have already taken their CBL course to serve as a TA, and these students are often eager to learn more about CBL pedagogy. I work with students to design a course where they learn more about the theory and best practices of CBL, and the service they provide supports other students' experiences in CBL courses.[7] Perhaps most importantly, I make sure our faculty members know that I am available at any point in the semester to listen, support, and offer suggestions for any glitches that arise in their course(s). The BCSL also offers free transportation for students to and from service sites and is willing to cosponsor reflection and/or celebration events.

Try New Flavors

There are as many different ways to do CBL as there are courses at any given college or university. Staff members need to be flexible and support faculty members who wish to enter into CBL cautiously, such as a language professor teaching a first-year seminar on (dis)ability who wished to have her students seek out projects that worked before developing a portfolio of projects that need to be changed. It is also important to take a broad, even global, view of service and lift up faculty members who bring their work to a whole new scale. For example, when OC history professors Carol Lasser and Gary Kornblith accepted an offer to speak at Tel Aviv University in Israel in 2008, they had no idea that the trip would lead to collaborations with two very different universities—one in Palestine and one in Israel—and a brand new course in American Democracy.

The American Democratic Culture Partnerships (ADCP) is an innovative program that brings together students from OC, Al-Quds University in Palestine, and Tel Aviv University in Israel. The program consists of a spring course in the History department at OC that focuses on American democratic values and concepts and the relationship between the United States and the world. Parallel courses are taught the same semester at the two foreign universities. As the culmination of the coursework, the three cohorts meet for a three-week seminar hosted by OC during the following summer to foster cultural exchange, dialogue, and deeper learning both on campus and in Washington, DC.[8] This is only the ADCP's third year and already over 60 undergraduate students from the three universities have taken part in the experience. Fostering cross-cultural dialogue in the context of a multicultural democracy is not your typical CBL course, but it might be the one that provides the skills needed to ease tensions—or even broker peace—in hotspots around our world.

In sum, the challenge is to help keep faculty members learning and growing—keeping it fresh! Similar to the way that vegetables taste the best when served fresh from the garden, faculty members seem to be happiest when they are learning new things and both articulating and practicing their deepest desires for both effective teaching and social change—or perhaps even ecosocial transformation.

Companion Planting (Teams/Couples/Multidisciplinary Projects)

Just as some plants do better when located next to a companion plant that helps to distract insects or attract pollinators, some faculty members work better in teams and/or as part of a larger vision. The Oberlin Project is a joint effort of the City of Oberlin, OC, and private and institutional partners to improve the resilience, prosperity, and sustainability of our community.[9] It is a large multiyear, complex project attracting faculty members from several disciplines. Thus far, Environmental Studies and Psychology have taken the lead, but faculty members from Art, Hispanic Studies, and Politics are also interested in developing opportunities as well. Thus far, students have been involved in asset-mapping, alternative energy design research, and community-based social marketing.

There is no shortage of work to be done. The Oberlin Project's aim is to revitalize the local economy; eliminate carbon emissions; restore local agriculture, food supply, and forestry; and create a new, sustainable base for economic and community development. Project goals include transitioning to a post-carbon energy system based on efficiency and renewable energy, developing a 20,000-acre greenbelt around the city to revive local agriculture and forestry, and using the entire Project as an innovative educational laboratory for the Oberlin public schools, our county vocational school and community college, and OC. The model and lessons of the Project are intended to have broad replicability, both for communities seeking to move toward a sustainable future and for colleges and universities.[10]

Do Not Forget to Weed and Fertilize

Several months ago, one of my staff members asked me about the wisdom of some actions during a service project at a local community garden. The students were asked to weed various garden plots and then place the weeds on the pathways in between cultivated areas. My staff member was worried, thinking that the weeds would then germinate and grow in the pathways. Since it was only mid-summer, and not yet harvest time, I observed that if the weeds were young, just flowering or not yet to the stage of having ripe seeds, the idea of placing them in a compost pile, or on a pathway, allows the weed to gracefully decompose and offer its life to building better soil. Also, I should note that what we call weeds in this country are simply plants that tend to be invasive, or plants that we do not particularly like, or plants that demonstrate great resilience by crowding out other plants to support their own survival. Is this not like working in the academy? Just like many weeds have thorns or spikey exteriors, just about every campus has its prickly personalities. Sometimes, these personalities have hearts of gold, if one but takes the time to get to know them. Furthermore, I have met my fair share of weed-like obstructionists, and have actually learned a great deal from them, as they have forced me to more clearly articulate my goals, objectives, and plans for assessment.

In this process of moving the work forward, I have found that it is essential to enrich our efforts with some compost, and even fertilizer. Whether this be support of faculty members, community partners, student assistants, or ourselves, it is important to make time for rest, reflection, relaxation, professional development, recreation, and spiritual growth. If we are not nourished well as change agents, our work will not flourish. Organic fertilizers are preferred. This may seem ironic, but it is important to remember that sometimes the best fertilizer comes from unexpected sources and looks—and smells—like dung.

Appreciate Ecosystems

In a section lifting up positive sources of encouragement for employing CBL, Abes et al. (2002) noted that—in their interactions with institutional gate-keepers—many campuses had a tough, gristly time even identifying their faculty members who do CBL. Admittedly, working with faculty members is somewhat akin to herding cats (and that's on a good day), but the very assumption that there should be institutional gatekeepers around CBL is somewhat problematic. As a campus service directory, or CSD, I had to find a balance between working to make sure our community partners are not overstretched by enthusiastic, well-meaning, but thoroughly untrained students appearing on their doorstep because an unwise faculty member gave them a two-week assignment to "do good and get to know the local community," and ferreting out the very finest in CBL pedagogy and reward-ing the faculty members collaborating with community partners to produce amazing projects and deliverables.

As you may have guessed by now, I approach this task as a gardener, not as a gatekeeper. I do make plans, plant seeds and nourish seedlings, water regularly, and add fertilizer when needed, but I also try to slow down and pay enough attention so that I delight in noticing a volunteer squash or tomato plant popping out of the compost pile, unbidden but beautiful and vigorous. Taking the perspective of a gardener is also helpful regarding building slow, sustainable growth. Just as each new growing season provides the opportunity to install new supports, think through companion plant-ing, and consider ever more appropriate fertilizers, each new academic year offers the opportunity to explore the life cycle of curricular, cocurricular, and extracurricular community engagement programming. As we seek the necessary staffing and fiscal infrastructure to grow additional high-impact programs, each year offers our staff the opportunity to further develop and learn from the previous year's observations. Furthermore, even though OC is a relatively small school, there are plenty of new faculty members each year, and more and more of them are coming with CBL experience and interest. Finally, like any good gardener, I seek plenty of advice for doing the good work.[11] The best move we have made thus far is to form a General Faculty Committee on CBL, who popularize the pedagogy and help the BCSL find faculty members to add to our lists of CBL supporters and practitioners.

New Directions for Practice and Research

While O'Meara (2012) lifts up five key directions for new research on fac-ulty motivation for CBL and civic engagement based in social science theory (and while I agree with her that our research to date has not been grounded as deeply as it could be in theory), I feel compelled to offer an additional alternative perspective. We are the first generation of humans to live with the concept of an emergent universe, that is, the realization that all matter in the universe was created out of a singularity commonly referred to as the Big Bang, or—if you prefer—the Cosmic Birth, and this matters for civic engagement (Blissman, 2002). Based on this view of cosmogenesis, we are slowly but surely recognizing our kinship with all living things on earth, as well as the complex ways in which life is interconnected. However, when we take a step back and examine the social, political, and ecological challenges facing us within and outside of higher education, we see that the systems we have designed are not serving us well. The ways we currently mass produce food and material goods harm the earth's oceanic and land-based support systems and exploit other humans. In essence, "education is at odds with sustainability when modern economies function to damage and destroy the ecological systems that support human and non–human communities."[12] We need new moral insights, new ways of thinking and reflecting that will allow us to articulate values that do not yet even exist and invite them into being through creative imagination and productive action (Happel and Walter, 1986).

I am not entirely confident that there are any quick and easy theories—in higher education or elsewhere—that can easily assist us in solving our challenges. However, I have been engaging with my work over the past decade with more of a systems-based approach, recognizing that we live within eco-systems, and trying my best to integrate the learning I have received from the swampy bioregion in which I live. I am encouraged to see that young scholars are not only thinking systemically, and applying systems theory to civic engagement (O'Meara, 2012; O'Meara and Niehaus, 2009) but are now starting to explore intersections between biomimicry and civic engagement (Sipos et al., 2008). We have only begun to learn how to both think and act locally.

Taking our groundedness in particular bioregions seriously can only enrich our effectiveness as connectors of campus and community, especially as we recognize that "community" includes plants, trees, bees, and bats in addition to other humans. For faculty members, and those who support them, a good exercise is to slow down and intentionally notice more detail about both the work that you do and the current state of campus–community relations in your locale. Use all of your senses to check in with both assets and challenges of your area, and stretch yourself to explore potential cross-disciplinary or interdisciplinary responses to challenges. Imagine that tenure has been redefined to reflect community wellness and wholeness instead of purely individual achievement. Reflect on the type of legacy you wish to leave in the particular place in which you live.

It is true that the work of the world is common as mud, and it is also true that we have the ability, skills, and the responsibility to turn that mud into bowls, pitchers, fertile soil, adobe bricks, plaster for straw bale buildings, art that transforms culture, and other organic and innovative tools to see us through this rich and challenging time of discovery and transition.

Notes

1. Although I have taught at both mid-sized universities and a community college, the majority of my experience has emerged from directing the BCSL at Oberlin College since the 2000–2001 academic year.
2. Oberlin College's definition of CBL is a pedagogy in which faculty members integrate community-based research and/or community service in guiding students to meet the academic goals of a course. Best practices include rich and varied opportunities for orientation, reflection and even celebration whenever possible We chose the term community-based learning over the terms service-learning, academic service-learning, or academic community service because CBL is an emerging term used in higher education to denote rigorous course-based pedagogy, whereas service-learning is also used at the K-12 level and is oftentimes linked to both curricular and cocurricular activities. Furthermore, several early adopters at our institution were perceived (rightly or wrongly) by their peers as focusing too much on service and not enough on learning. Finally, we see CBL as more closely linked to a social justice orientation in contrast to a charity orientation, which suits our campus ethos. For the purposes of this chapter, however, the terms community-based learning and service-learning are used interchangeably and both refer to credit-bearing, course-based experiences grounded in the academic curriculum.
3. See both http://imaginingamerica.org/research/engaged-scholars/ and http://imaginingamerica.org/research/engaged-scholars/about-the-study/
4. Common plants that use rhizomes to propagate are asparagus, bamboo, ginger, and even certain types of trees. Quaking Aspen colonies in both Colorado and Utah are rumored to be hundreds of thousands of years old, as fires or insects might damage the above-ground parts of the trees, but the rhizomes continue to thrive and propagate. So if you are new to a campus that has experienced transition or loss, do not despair, simply seek out the hidden places of growth.
5. My absolute favorite quote on this topic occurred during an informal conversation with a professor in the humanities. When I asked why she practiced CBL, she promptly responded "it was obvious. Why do people put one foot in front of the other when they walk? It's good pedagogy, with benefits to both parties."
6. Unfortunately, Learn and Serve America, which was an active part of the Corporation for National and Community Service's funding of service-learning in both K-12 and higher education settings since 1994, has not had funds

appropriated since 2011 (see www.nationalservice.gov/about/programs/learnand
serve.asp).

7. Another extremely well-developed model of this type of faculty support can be
found at St. Mary's College, where their student assistants are called Engaged
Learning Facilitators (ELFs).

8. Amanda Nagy, Mideast meets Midwest. Oberlin Alumni Magazine, Summer–
Fall 2010, Vol. 105, No. 4 (see online at www.oberlin.edu/alummag/summer
-fall2010/features/mideast.html).

9. For more information, see www.oberlinproject.org. On the basis of this Project,
Oberlin, Ohio, in 2010 became one of 17 communities worldwide participating in the Clinton Climate Positive Development Program, which seeks to set
new standards for environmentally responsible urban development. (For more
information, please see www.clintonfoundation.org)

10. See Oberlin, Ohio: Laboratory for a New Way of Life (November 6, 2011),
Chronicle of Higher Education by Scott Carlson.

11. Just as excellent soil contains thousands upon thousands of microorganisms,
so a great civic engagement center is based on the small actions of many, many
supporters from both campus and community. This includes community partners; staff and faculty members; students and alumni; and sometimes even parents, high-level administrators, and/or angel investors. We are just beginning
to celebrate several important anniversaries associated with several of our programs at OC's BCSL, and I see it as the task of our staff to lift up and celebrate
the cast of thousands—literally—who have contributed to the successful work
our students do daily in Lorain County, Ohio, and beyond.

12. Sipos et al., 2008, 69.

References

Abes, E. S., G. Jackson, and S. Jones. "Factors that motivate and deter faculty use
of service-learning." *Michigan Journal of Community Service Learning* 9(1) (2002):
5–17.

Blissman, M. E. (2002). "Expanding the Horizon of Engagement: Pioneering
Work at the University of Denver," in Devine, Richard, Joseph A. Favazza,
and F. Michael McLain. *From Cloister to Commons: Concepts and Models for
Service-Learning in Religious Studies.* AAHE's Series on Service-Learning in the
Disciplines. Merryfield, VA: American Association for Higher Education.

Colbeck, C. L., K. O'Meara, and A. Austin (eds). "Educating integrated professionals: theory and practice on preparation for the professoriate. *New Directions for
Teaching and Learning* 113 (2008): 27–42.

Driscoll, A. "Studying faculty and service-learning: directions for inquiry and development." *Michigan Journal of Community Service Learning*, Special Issue (2000): 35–41.

Eyler, J., and D. Giles. *Where's the Learning in Service-Learning?* San Francisco, CA:
Jossey-Bass, 1999.

Giles, D. E., and J. S. Eyler. "A Service-Learning Research Agenda for the Next Five Years. In *Academic Service-Learning: A Pedagogy of Action and Reflection*, ed. R. Rhoads and J. Howard. San Francisco, CA: Jossey-Bass, 1998, pp. 65–72.

Hammond, C. "Faculty motivation and satisfaction in Michigan higher education." *Michigan Journal of Community Service Learning* 12, no. 1 (1994): 41–51.

Happel, Stephen, and James Walter. *Conversion and Discipleship: A Christian Foundation for Ethic and Doctrine*. Philadelphia, PA: Fortress Press, 1986.

McKay, V. C., and P. D. Rozee. "Characteristics of faculty who adopt community service learning pedagogy." *Michigan Journal of Community Service Learning* 10, no. 2 (2004): 21–33.

Morton, Keith, and Marie Troppe. "From the margin to the mainstream: Campus Compact's project on Integrating Service with Academic Study." *Journal of Business Ethics* 15, no. 1 (1996): 21–32.

National Service-Learning Clearinghouse (2011). *What is Service-Learning?* Retrieved from www.servicelearning.org/

O'Meara, K. "Uncovering the values in faculty evaluation of service as scholarship." *Review of Higher Education* 26, no. 1 (2002): 57–80.

O'Meara, K. "Stepping up: how one faculty learning community influenced faculty members' understanding and use of active learning methods and course design." *Journal on Excellence in College Teaching* 18, no. 2 (2007): 97–118.

O'Meara, K. "Motivation for public scholarship and engagement: listening to exemplars." *Journal of Higher Education Outreach and Engagement* 12, no. 1 (2008): 7–29.

O'Meara, KerryAnn. "Graduate education and community engagement." *New Directions for Teaching and Learning*, no. 113 (2008): 27–42.

O'Meara, K. "Rewarding Multiple Forms of Scholarship: Promotion and Tenure." In *Handbook of Engaged Scholarship, Volume I: Institutional Change*, ed. H. Fitzgerald, C. Burack, and S. Seifer. East Lansing, MI: Michigan State University Press, 2010, pp. 271–294.

O'Meara, K. "Research on Faculty Motivations for Service Learning and Community Engagement." In *Research on Service Learning: Conceptual Frameworks and Assessment*, ed. Clayton, Bringle, and Hatcher. Sterling, VA: Stylus, 2012, pp. 215–244.

O'Meara, K., and A. Jaeger. "Preparing future faculty for community engagement: history, barriers, facilitators, models and recommendations." *Journal of Higher Education Outreach and Engagement* 11, no. 4 (2007): 3–26.

O'Meara, K., and E. Niehaus. "Service-learning is… How faculty explain their practice." *Michigan Journal of Community Service-Learning* 16, no. 1 (2009): 1–16.

O'Meara, K., A. L. Terosky, and A. Neumann. *Faculty Careers and Work Lives: A Professional Growth Perspective. ASHE Higher Education Report, 34 (3).* San Francisco, CA: Jossey-Bass, 2008.

O'Meara, K., L. R. Sandmann, J. Saltmarsh, and D. E. Giles. "Studying the professional lives and work of faculty involved in community engagement." *Innovative Higher Education* 36, no. 2 (2011): 83–96.

Sandmann, L., J. Saltmarsh, and K. O'Meara. "Creating academic homes: an integrated model for advancing the scholarship of engagement." *Journal of Higher Education Outreach and Engagement* 12, no. 1 (2008): 47–63.

Simons, L., and B. Clearly. "The influence of service learning on students' personal and social development." *College Teaching* 54, no. 4 (2006): 307–319.

Sipos, Y., B. Battisti, and K. Grimm. "Achieving transformative sustainability learning: engaging head, hands and heart." *International Journal of Sustainability in Higher Education* 9, no. 1 (2008): 68–86.

Vogelgesang, Lori J., Nida Denson, and Uma M. Jayakumar. "What determines faculty-engaged scholarship?." *The Review of Higher Education* 33, no. 4 (2010): 437–472.

Ward, K. W. *Faculty Service Roles and the Scholarship of Engagement.* San Francisco, CA: Jossey-Bass, 2003.

Stanton, T. K. "The experience of faculty participants in an instructional development seminar on service-learning." *Michigan Journal of Community Service Learning* 1 (1994): 7–20.

CHAPTER 12

Community Engagement across the Curriculum: Boyer, Integration, and the Challenges of Institutionalization

Thomas G. McGowan, Suzanne Bonefas, and Anthony C. Siracusa

Introduction

Community engagement now occupies a central place in American higher education. However, challenges related to assessment, alignment, and ethics continue to limit its institutionalization, even among colleges and universities recognized for their accomplishments in community engagement (Driscoll, 2011). Addressing these challenges will require nothing less than what Butin (2010) calls an "intellectual movement"—a self-reflexive intellectual inquiry into the numerous assumptions undergirding service-learning and related pedagogies. This chapter presents an intellectual investigation of Ernest Boyer's work on the *scholarship of integration* and applies his ideas to reconceptualize the meaning of community engagement for students, faculty, and institutional practice.

A Case Study of Reflexive Institutionalization

At Rhodes College, two initiatives are addressing issues that limit institutionalization: (1) a grant-funded project involving the creation of a college consortium[1] and (2) a working group consisting of students, faculty, staff, and administrators that studies internal institutional practices related to community engagement. The main goal of the first initiative is to establish a sustainable consortium of colleges committed to developing and sharing effective community-based learning (CBL) approaches to practice and assessment. In order to understand baseline institutionalization of community engagement at our colleges, consortium members have used the Furco rubric (Furco, 2002). Although most of our members scored in Stage 2 ("quality building") or even Stage 3 ("sustained institutionalization"), the overall consensus has been that course-based community engagement, though it may be a priority in our mission statements, is not widely practiced by faculty on our campuses.

In order to improve how we assess community engagement, the consortium developed the CBL Scorecard, which began as a list of "success factors" or best practices based on the literature about characteristics of service learning/CBL that correlate with student learning gains.[2] The Scorecard has proven useful to consortium members by providing course-level benchmark assessments of how closely their courses in community engagement align with best practices. However, one identified shortcoming of the Scorecard is its limited ability to measure the value-added impact of CBL on student development.

A central feature of consortium meetings is the ongoing, reflexive discussion of community engagement models and their practical relevance to smaller colleges and universities. These discussions identified institutional alignment as a primary concern, specifically, the need to bridge institutional mission, the academic curriculum and CBL practice. Additionally, these discussions identified the need to improve discourse and collaboration among college offices and stakeholders already working on community engagement within member institutions.

Our primary strategy to advance the institutionalization of community engagement within our institution is to conduct research, foster shared intellectual discourse, and promote the development of conceptual frameworks that help us to understand the added value of community engagement for both students and faculty. This effort is supported by the work of the Community-Integrative Education (CIE) Working Group. This group had its origins as the steering committee for a large-scale grant-funded project that supported relationship development and programming in the neighborhoods surrounding our campus, a project that we ultimately institutionalized. At Rhodes, we have generally avoided a centralized model for CBL initiatives, preferring a decentralized approach that encourages cross-departmental and interdisciplinary dialogue. The CIE working group is our primary vehicle for coordination and communication across departments, offices, and programs.

Working group discussions gained momentum during the 2011–2012 academic year as our research increasingly became the focus of biweekly meetings and monthly presentations to the campus community. As with the larger consortial group, these conversations began as mechanisms for communication about research on the operational aspects of community engagement, but gained traction as the topic broadened to encompass an investigation into the intellectual framework underlying our shared work.

The efforts of the consortium and working group benefited directly from scholarly research conducted by the authors of this chapter. In order to address the challenges of institutionalization, we undertook a close reading of Ernest Boyer's *Scholarship Reconsidered* with the hope of informing our ongoing assessment of the meaning and scope of community engagement. This effort was guided by three specific questions. First, how might the effort to define and assess the value-added impact of community engagement on student development be informed through Boyer's work? Second, might Boyer provide insight regarding the challenge of bringing more faculty into the practice of community-engaged learning? Finally, how might Boyer inform our institutional practices related to the development of community engagement?

The Scholarship of Integration Reconsidered

Ernest Boyer's impact on higher education is largely the result of the expanded view of scholarship he introduces in *Scholarship Reconsidered* (1990). In this seminal work, Boyer describes how the focus of higher education has developed and changed over time. During the American colonial period, higher education focused primarily on the *scholarship of teaching* and its principal purpose was to educate a morally astute leadership class for an emerging nation. As industrialization intensified, the scope of higher education expanded through the creation of land grant universities, which emphasized more applied fields of study (e.g., engineering and agriculture) to meet the needs of industry and nation building. During this period, the *scholarship of application* (practical knowledge applied to meet social needs) was added to the *scholarship of teaching* as an important priority. In the early twentieth century, basic research and publication became increasingly important. As a result, the *scholarship of discovery* emerged as a priority of higher education and a key criterion for evaluating and rewarding faculty performance. In the latter part of the twentieth century, Boyer discerned

172 • Thomas G. McGowan et al.

the emergence of a fourth type of scholarship, *the scholarship of integration*, as scholars increasingly sought to understand the broader significance of the knowledge they produce and became involved in interdisciplinary collaboration and research.

More than 100 publications focus on Boyer's ideas regarding the scholarships of discovery, application, and teaching, but only a handful discuss the scholarship of integration (Braxton et al., 2002). This is intriguing because one year before his death, Boyer expressed the belief that the *scholarship of integration* is the domain most relevant to the future of higher education (Johnston, 1998). Moreover, Boyer located integration at the center of his vision of the New American College in which the curriculum would be organized around research topics and social issues rather than academic divisions and disciplines (Boyer, 1994).

Given the importance Boyer attributes to the scholarship of integration, it is surprising that integration is by far the least studied, and the least understood, of the four scholarship domains. We attribute this to the fact that Boyer's description of integration is conceptually diffuse and unwieldy.

Boyer's description of integration consists of several interrelated but distinct conceptual dimensions. According to Boyer, integration is interpretive scholarly activity that "give(s) meaning to isolated facts, putting them in perspective" (1990, 18). It is "serious, disciplined work that seeks to interpret, draw together, and bring new insight to bear on original research" (1990, 19). While the scholarship of discovery *produces* new knowledge, integration involves interpreting the meaning and significance of knowledge, those engaged in discovery ask, "What is to be known, what is yet to be found?" Those engaged in integration ask, "What do the findings *mean?* Is it possible to interpret what's been discovered in ways that provide a larger, more comprehensive understanding?" Questions such as these call for the power of critical analysis and interpretation (1990, 19–20). The scholarship of integration also involves "making connections across the disciplines, placing the specialties in larger context, illuminating data in a revealing way, often educating nonspecialists, too" (1990, 18).

Boyer's multidimensional conceptualization of the scholarship of integration makes it difficult to operationalize and assess. For example, Braxton et al. (2002) needed to develop a long list of scholarly products to assess the extent to which the scholarship of integration is institutionalized in higher education. Their list includes three types of scholarly products: (1) critical/theoretical reviews of existing research, (2) interdisciplinary research, and (3) public scholarship. These types of scholarly products share a common *interpretive* dimension, and clarifying this interpretive dimension may open new opportunities to conceptualize the meaning of integration and its relation to community engagement.

The interpretation of meaning is a basic human ability, whereas critical-theoretical reviews, interdisciplinary work, and public scholarship are particular scholarly activities in which scholars interpret the meaning of knowledge beyond a given epistemological or paradigmatic standpoint. Critical-theoretical reviews of research bring new meaning to existing work. Interdisciplinary research involves translating the meaning of knowledge across disciplinary or paradigmatic frames of reference. Similarly, public scholarship involves translating the meaning or significance of formal, disciplinary knowledge into a vocabulary understandable to nonacademics. In all cases, these acts of integrative scholarship involve a *generative interpretive* activity that creates new, holistic meanings by bridging the boundaries of two or more interpretive positions. This implies that the core conceptual dimension of integration is interpretation that generates new meaning beyond or across particular interpretive standpoints.

Identifying *generative interpretation* as the conceptual core of integration is important for at least two reasons. First, since interpretation is a reflexive (self-referential) act that involves the internal mediation of what a scholar previously understood, it follows that integrative scholarship may be understood as a form of self-development. Herein lies the value-added quality of integrative scholarship. The integrative scholar is transformed by the experience of integration itself. The field of philosophical hermeneutics describes this process of self-development in ontological terms: Changes in our interpretation of meaning are synonymous with changes in our self-understanding (Palmer, 1969). This point has relevance for assessing the value-added impact of community engagement on student development and will be discussed later in this chapter.

This reading of Boyer also suggests that integration is evident whenever scholarship is conducted in a way that produces interpretations that are more holistic than those which came before. Critical-theoretical reviews, interdisciplinary work, and public scholarship are thus *several* among many potential expressions of integrative scholarship, expressions that may be found within the three traditional scholarly domains. For example, integration is presupposed within the scholarship of application (since application involves translating the meaning of academic research across contexts), and may be present in the scholarships of teaching and discovery. In the case of teaching, integrative teachers go beyond the dissemination of knowledge to help students understand the broader meaning and significance of knowledge. In the case of discovery, integrative researchers explore the implications of their research beyond discipline and academia. In sum, our reading of Boyer suggests that integration is best understood as a scholarly disposition that adds value to traditional scholarly practice.

This interpretation of the scholarship of integration aligns with the work of Paulsen and Feldman (1995), who read Boyer's four-domain typology from the perspective of Talcott Parsons's *social action system* model. According to Paulsen and Feldman, integration is best understood not as a self-standing scholarship domain, but rather, as a value-added quality that connects the more traditional functions of faculty scholarship (discovery, teaching, and application) by integrating them into the social action system of higher education. This functionalist approach places integration within important institutional activities of the professoriate such as committee work related to the norms governing curriculum development and faculty peer evaluation, tenure, and promotion. Their approach problematizes Boyer's notion of integration as a separate and distinct scholarship domain, yet acknowledges its interpretive function at the institutional level (faculty members engage in interpretive, integrative activity and meaningfully construct the norms that define the curriculum and scholarly ethos of their institution). However, by limiting *meaning* to institutional *function*, Paulsen and Feldman consequently displace consideration of the value of integration as a generative and developmental activity with implications for the quality and meaning of individual scholarly practice.

The Value-Added Impact of Community Engagement on Student Development

Students of higher education are being socialized to practice the same scholarly activities as their professors, albeit in a preparatory sense. Students are taught to conduct research (discovery) and to write and speak about what they have learned (teaching). In the case of community-engaged learning, students are taught to apply their knowledge through public, civic practice in the community (application). Through guided reflection, students engaged in the community are taught to interpret the meaning of their community *and* classroom experiences, an interpretive activity that involves integrating intellectual and personal development. Ideally, community-engaged students will become *students of integrity* as they learn to integrate the meaning of their community experience into their self-development through internalization and reflection. It is for this reason that we find the language of integration to be an effective way to articulate the value-added impact of student community engagement on our campus.

In their classic contribution to the literature on service-learning, Eyler and Giles (1999) present research on the value-added impact of community engagement that aligns closely with our understanding of integration and holistic student development. Their description of the impact of service-learning on student development illustrates how the interpretive integration of community experience has a circular and transformative structure. Philosophers describe this interpretive process as a "hermeneutic circle," a productive, circular process whereby individuals are transformed by interpretive experience and in turn experience change in their understanding of self and world (Palmer, 1969). In the case of community engagement, the process of making sense of their community experience changes students and this change is evident in the way students understand in general.

The transformative experience of community-engaged students begins with encounters with different types of people in the community. According to Eyler and Giles, "Coming into contact with people whose life experiences and assumptions about the world are different calls one's own world into question" (1999, 34). Encountering difference through community interaction is therefore important because it serves as a catalyst for reflexive experience and the self-questioning of assumptions. According to Eyler and Giles, "Transformational learning occurs when individuals confront disorienting dilemmas; perspective transformation becomes possible when this dilemma raises questions about fundamental assumptions" (1999, 141).

The impact of reflexive experience often includes the realization that students share more in common with people in the community than they had previously imagined. Eyler and Giles found that student involvement in community service "has a powerful impact on how they see themselves and others" (1999, 25). They report that "students recognize the value of service-learning in their own personal understanding... knowing themselves better was among the most important outcomes of their experience" (1999, 35). Change in student self-understanding is thus directly related to change in their interpretations of others, which is marked by "the reduction of negative stereotypes and the increase in tolerance for diversity" (1999, 29).

The reflexive self-development of students is inherently related to and inseparable from their intellectual development. Eyler and Giles report that through community engagement "Some people leave service-learning with a new set of lenses for seeing the world" (1999, 129). This is because their experience of community engagement "reframed their understanding of social issues and social change" (1999, 131). According to Eyler and Giles, "it is this questioning of the assumptions about how society is organized and how these assumptions underlie social problems that is at the heart of transformational learning" (1999, 132). This underscores the importance of reflexive discourse and interpretation for actualizing the transformative potential of community engagement.

This view of community engagement as a catalyst for the personal and intellectual development of students is relevant to the contemporary call for a shift from *civic engagement* to *democratic engagement*. Building on Walt Whitman's view of democracy as a way of life (rather than a political act or classification), the United States Department of Education's report *A Crucible Moment: College Learning and Democracy's Future* affirms Whitman's conception of democracy as "the highest form of interaction between (humans)" (Whitman, 1993). Whitman's expansive understanding of democracy emphasizes the importance of interaction in different contexts and underscores the value-added potential of community engagement for student development. Colleges committed to community engagement are thus positioned to effectively respond to the National Call to Action issued by the *Crucible Moment* report, which pushes colleges and universities to "reclaim and reinvest in the fundamental civic and democratic mission" of higher education (The National Task Force on Civic Learning and Democratic Engagement, 2012, 46). Following the direction of Saltmarsh et al. (2009), institutions of higher education must move from a model of civic engagement to democratic engagement, a pedagogy that supports the whole development of students and improved civic health of American society.

Preparing students for a democratic way of life requires a commitment to helping students develop their ability to integrate the meaning of their encounters with both texts and people into an expanded understanding of self and world. Integrative students come to understand themselves differently through interaction with off-campus partners and in the process expand their intellectual understanding of social issues. These meaningful interactions democratize students by socializing them into an interpretively competent ethos of interaction in which the opinions and interests of others are respected, grappled with, internalized, and responded to through practice.

In his foundational text, *Democracy in America*, Alexis de Tocqueville speaks to the transformational quality and ethos of democratic human interaction and the importance of fostering institutions and voluntary associations:

> Feelings and opinions are recruited, the heart is enlarged, and the human mind is developed by no other means than by the reciprocal influence of (humans) upon each other. I have shown that these influences are almost null in democratic countries; they must therefore be artificially created, and this can only be accomplished by associations. (de Tocqueville 2000, 491)

Here, de Tocqueville warns of the potential peril within the individualist spirit and particularist ethos of a budding democratic America, a country that does not force association among institutions in the way previous feudal societies might have done. De Tocqueville's antidote to the pitfalls of an individualistic society is voluntary association and democratic interaction. Community engagement facilitates association through meaningful encounters with difference, and, as a result, "democratic knowledge and capabilities...are honed through hands on, face to face, active engagement in the midst of differing perspectives about how to address common problems that affect the well-being of the nation and the world" (de Tocqueville, 2002). In other words, community engagement may be understood as a socializing process through which students become democratized. Naming the importance of integration in this way suggests that community engagement can advance the mission of higher education by cultivating students of integrity, that is, students who have internalized a democratic ethos as their way of being in the world.

Relevance to Institutional Practice

Our research also allowed us to define and promote integration as a principle to guide institutional discourse and interaction related to community engagement. Our study of Boyer has led us to rename our institutional effort regarding community engagement under a single, unifying rubric: *community-integrative education*. This title is as much a directive as it is a name. As a name, community-integrative education has helped us to collapse unnecessary and counterproductive distinctions between various off-campus programs by focusing on the shared goal of graduating students of integrity. For example, following a campus presentation of our research on Boyer and integration, representatives of different programs and campus offices began an ongoing discussion of the potential benefits of integrative dialogue and intra-institutional collaboration. The directors of internships, student fellowships, external programs, and service scholarships now share information and strategy on a weekly basis with an eye toward the shared goal of integrating all of these programs more closely into the academic curriculum. As a directive, community-integrative education guides students, faculty, and community stakeholders to practice democratic interaction toward the common goal of personal, institutional, and community integration. This research is being broadened to include questions related to the quality and ethical concerns of our community partnerships.

   In practical terms, integration is pursued through an institutional discursive process that is dialogical and inclusive across hierarchical domains and programs related to community engagement. Biweekly meetings held during the academic year solicit input through the democratic participation of students, faculty, staff, and administrators. This approach has allowed the CIE working group to develop initiatives that are increasingly transparent and inclusive, and which model reflexive interpretation as an institutional ethos. For example, the principle of integration is guiding the reorganization of the Rhodes Urban Studies program and the development of a new concentration in urban and community health. The concept of integration is also guiding an emergent initiative to infuse the college's first-year core curriculum with community-integrative student experiences.

Conclusion

The theoretical appropriation of Boyer presented in this chapter is helping us to address several challenges to the institutionalization of community engagement. First, our understanding of the value-added impact of community-integrative education on student development has been broadened through the concepts of integration and democratic interaction. Rather than limiting the goal of community engagement to helping students to become more civically engaged, we now understand our goal to be more fundamental and comprehensive: to graduate students of integrity, students who have experienced personal and intellectual development by integrating the meaning of their classroom and community experience into their self-development. Such students are more inclined to practice democracy as a way of life and to demonstrate the ability to interact openly and dialogically with people both inside and outside the academy. In order to better prepare students for community-integrative education, we have created a curriculum on interpretive competence that is being taught to students actively engaged in the community.

Our reading of Boyer also provides insight regarding the challenge of bringing more faculty into the practice of community engagement. By identifying integration as a value-added quality that enhances the traditional scholarships of discovery, teaching, and application, our work suggests a new *ideal type* of American scholar well suited to meet the professorial needs of the New American College (Boyer, 1994). Integrative scholarship is a *way* of practicing the scholarships of discovery, application, and teaching in a holistic manner that is transformative for both faculty and students. Integrative scholars integrate the meaning of their work into who they are and act on the broader implications of this meaning through practice. Integrative scholars seek to engage in research that has broad meaning and significance. They teach to change lives and apply their knowledge and understanding to real-world needs through various strategies that include community-engaged practice, interdisciplinary collaboration, and public scholarship. It is our hope that by naming integration as a quality that distinguishes *integrative scholars* from *traditional scholars*, more faculty members will aspire to become integrative scholars and, in time, the value-added quality of their work will gain institutional appreciation and recognition.

Finally, the concept of integration has allowed us to inform the process of institutional discourse around community engagement and improve communication among offices and programs that were previously siloed. By synthesizing our various off-campus programs and initiatives under the rubric of *community-integrative education*, we have taken an important step toward furthering the institutionalization of community engagement at our college.

Notes

1. This consortium was established with funding from the Teagle Foundation's Outcomes and Assessment program.
2. During the implementation phase, we worked with John Braxton (Vanderbilt) and Willis Jones (University of Kentucky), who reworked the Scorecard as a set of survey items and validated the resulting instrument.

References

Boyer, E. *Scholarship Reconsidered: Priorities of the Professoriate.* Princeton, NJ: Carnegie Foundation for the Advancement of Teaching, 1990.

Boyer, E. "Creating the new American college." *The Chronicle of Higher Education* A48 (March 9, 1994).

Braxton, J. M., W. Luckey, and P. Helland.. *Institutionalizing a Broader View of Scholarship Through Boyer's Four Domains.* ASHE-ERIC Higher Education Report: Volume 29, Number 2, 2002.

Butin, D. W. *Service-Learning in Theory and Practice: The Future of Community Engagement in Higher Education.* New York: Palgrave Macmillan, 2010.

de Tocqueville, A. *Democracy in America*, ed. and trans. Harvey C. Mansfield and Delba Winthrop. Chicago, IL: University of Chicago Press, 2000. Quoted in The National Task Force on Civic Learning and Democratic Engagement, 2012, 3.

Driscoll, A. 2011. As quoted in Carnegie Selects Colleges and Universities for 2010 Community Engagement Classification. Retrieved April 21, 2012 from http://www.carnegiefoundation.org/newsroom/press-releases/carnegie-selects-colleges-and-universities-2010-community- engagement-classification National Service-Learning Clearinghouse.

Eyler, J., and D. E. Giles, Jr. 1999. *Where's the Learning in Service-Learning?* San Francisco, CA: Jossey-Bass.

Furco, A. *Self-Assessment Rubric for the Institutionalization of Service-Learning in Higher Education.* Berkeley, CA: University of California Press, 2002.

Johnston, Rita. "The university of the future: Boyer revisited." *Higher Education* 36, no. 3 (1998): 253–272.

Palmer, Richard E. *Hermeneutics.* Evanston: Northwestern University Press, 1969.

Paulsen, M. B., and K. A. Feldman. "Toward a conceptualization of scholarship: a human action system with functional imperatives." *Journal of Higher Education* 66, no. 6 (1995): 615–640.

Saltmarsh, J., M. Hartley, and P. H. Clayton. *Democratic Engagement White Paper.* Boston, MA: New England Resource Center for Higher Education, 2009.

The National Task Force on Civic Learning and Democratic Engagement. *A Crucible Moment: College Learning and Democracy's Future.* Washington, DC: American Association of Colleges and Universities, 2012.

Whitman, W. "Democratic Vistas." In *Education for Democracy*, ed. Barber, R. Benjamin, and Richard M. Battistoni. Dubuque, IO: Kendall Hunt Publishing Company, 1993, p. 63. Quoted in The National Task Force on Civic Learning and Democratic Engagement, 2012, 5.

PART IV

Centers

CHAPTER 13

Best Practices and Infrastructures for Campus Centers of Community Engagement

Marshall Welch and John Saltmarsh

Introduction

On many campuses, community engagement centers emerged out of student affairs, further developed as units of academic affairs, and in both cases were focused on "service" as the organizing purpose, whether community service or service learning. Community "engagement" has recently been framed as reciprocal, two-way relationships (as articulated in the Carnegie Community Engagement classification, in the "Democratic Engagement White Paper" [Saltmarsh et al., 2009] as "publicly engaged scholarship" as articulated in the report Scholarship in Public [Ellison and Eatman, 2008], and in other recent framings). This is in contrast to what has historically been characterized as a one-way, charitable, noblese-oblige, expert-driven, service relationship. The reframing of community engagement has challenged those who are leading and staffing existing structures to think about their work, and their operations, differently.

In 2006, the Carnegie Foundation established the elective classification of community engagement by creating and incorporating a set of benchmarks to assist in designating institutions for this classification. The application for classification requires evidence of campus practice, structures, and policies designed to deepen community engagement and make it more pervasive across the institution. As a result, more and more campuses strive to expand its cocurricular service and curricular service-learning programs in ways that promote broader civic community engagement coordinated by a campus center.

However, these campus centers often lack the infrastructure or resources necessary to maintain quality programs and partnerships. Defining features such as organizational structure, reporting lines, funding, student programming, faculty professional development, community partnership development, policy, and procedures are critical elements for a successful center. Additionally, community agencies face an array of challenges in their own work that may complicate establishing and maintaining meaningful partnerships with institutions of higher education (IHEs) and centers of community engagement. Institutional differences in mission, structures, culture, and communication can have the potential to either enhance or minimize partnerships between the community and academy.

Community Center Profiles

This study is timely as it may very well be that IHEs and the field as a whole implicitly assume that campus centers originally designed for cocurricular volunteering and later service-learning have the necessary structure and resources to also coordinate newer civic engagement efforts. Therefore, this investigation was designed to answer the following questions:

What are the defining features of the organizational structures created by campuses for the purpose of facilitating connections to communities at the local, regional, national, and global levels?

What are the purposes and goals of campus–community partnerships expressed through the structure?

To what extent are the activities undertaken through these institutional structures connected to institutional or community change initiatives?

This chapter is designed to provide an overview of critical components and essential infrastructure to guide campus administrators and center directors as they establish and continue to advance community engagement as part of the college experience.

A Review of Critical Components and Essential Infrastructure

We began by reviewing the literature to identify the critical components and essential infrastructure enumerated in the earlier phases of the field. The review also included analyzing over 100 successful applications for the

Carnegie Foundation for the Advancement of Teaching elective Community Engagement Classification (Carnegie Foundation, 2012). A total of 66 key characteristics and their prevalence at community engagement centers on college campuses were identified and are summarized in Table 13.1. A handful of other examples of best practice were derived anecdotally from personal conversations and included. We categorized these characteristics into six sections to assist in the organizational structure and format of the survey instrument: (1) institutional architecture/policy, (2) center infrastructure, (3) center operations, (4) center programs for faculty, (5) center programs for students, and (6) center programs for community partners. Institutional architecture/policy is characterized as a systemic structure within the institution as a whole, including things such as organizational flowcharts, strategic plans, policy and procedure manuals/handbooks, and governance. Center infrastructure on the other hand includes administration, personnel background/roles, physical space, and operational tools to maintain the center's existence and work. Related is the category of center operations, which includes day-to-day functions that maintain overall center programming. This category was then subcategorized into operations pertaining to specific stakeholders associated with the center, including faculty, students, and community partners. Survey items in these categories focused on specific operational activities.

This list of "best practices" was used to generate the survey instrument. A prototype instrument was field tested by two practitioners in the field who then provided feedback used to make revisions. The sample for this study was the campuses that received the Elective Community Engagement Classification from the Carnegie Foundation for the Advancement of Teaching. The revised survey consisting of 66 items was sent via e-mail to the current center director at the 311 IHEs receiving Carnegie Classification for Community Engagement in 2006, 2008, and 2010. The Survey items were constructed using a modified Likert scale allowing for respondents to indicate if each component was: (1) in place for operation, (2) in the process of being in place for operation, (3) were hoped to be in place, or (4) were not in place. Any responses indicating that the component was in place or in the process were deemed to be essential to a center's operation.

We were also interested to know the opinion of directors as to what they felt were the most essential components of a community center. This presents a unique perspective from practitioners as an alternative to the theoretical perspective found in professional literature. Respondents were also asked to list what they considered to be their "Top Ten" essential components of a campus community service center. These responses were compared to the

Table 13.1 Review of best practices for campus centers

Best practice	Source
Institutional architecture/policy	
Academic affairs reporting line	Battistoni, 1998
Budgeted institutional funds	Carnegie; Hollander et al., 2002; Walshok, 1999
Campus-wide commitment to civic engagement	Carnegie
Central coordinating center/office	Carnegie; Bucco and Busch, 1996
Civic engagement in institutional strategic plans	Carnegie
Course designation process	Carnegie
Institutional leadership promotes civic engagement as a priority	Carnegie
Institutional mission statement includes community engagement	Carnegie
Official/operational definitions of service-learning, CBR, engagement	Carnegie
Transcript notation of engaged courses	Carnegie
Center infrastructure	
Adequate office space	Walshok, 1999
Advisory/governing board	Carnegie; Fisher, 1998
Annual report	
Center vision/mission statement	Fisher, 1998; Furco, 2002; Hollander et al., 2002
Center alumni association	
Center director background (faculty, Student affairs, community)	
Center director credential/degree (terminal degree, graduate degree)	Other
Clear internal/external access entry points to the center	Pigza and Troppe, 2003
Community representative to advisory board	Bringle and Hatcher, 1996
Database tracking system/hardware	Carnegie; Bringle and Hatcher, 1996
Development officer	
Faculty advisory committee/board	Carnegie; Fisher, 1998
Faculty liaison to academic units	Bringle and Hatcher, 1996
Full-time administrator	Bucco and Busch, 1996
Full-time administrative assistant	Bucco and Busch, 1996
Newsletter/web updates	Other
Support programming staff	Walshok, 1999
Center operations	
Assessment mechanisms/procedures	Carnegie; Hatcher and Bringle, 2010
Announce/provide resource materials	Bringle and Hatcher, 1996
Community voice/input	Carnegie; Furco, 2002 ; Bringle and Hatcher, 1996; Hollander et al., 2002
Conduct research on faculty involvement	Bringle and Hatcher, 1996
Conduct surveys on student involvement	Bringle and Hatcher, 1996
Create student course assistants	Bringle and Hatcher, 1996

Table 13.1 Continued

Best practice	Source
Provide course development grants	Furco, 2002; Bringle and Hatcher, 1996
Maintain course syllabi file/database	Bringle and Hatcher, 1996
Database on faculty involvement	Bringle and Hatcher, 1996
Establish faculty award	Carnegie; Bringle and Hatcher, 1996; Hollander et al., 2002
Evaluate community partner satisfaction	Bringle and Hatcher, 1996
Evaluate student satisfaction with Service LearningBringle and Hatcher, 1996	
Facilitate faculty research on service learning/community/civic engagement Bringle and Hatcher, 1996	
Fundraising mechanisms	Carnegie; Holland and Langseth, 2010
Involve students in creating SL courses	Bringle and Hatcher, 1996
Presentations at student orientations	Bringle and Hatcher, 1996
Publicize faculty accomplishments	Bringle and Hatcher, 1996
Risk management policy/procedures	Rue, 1996
Recognition of student accomplishments	Rubin, 1996
Recognition of faculty accomplishments	Bringle and Hatcher, 1996; Rubin, 1996
Student leadership and decision making	Furco, 2002; Bringle and Hatcher, 1996
Transportation coordination/policy	Rue, 1996
Center programming—faculty	
One-on-one consultation/support	Furco, 2002 ; Bringle and Hatcher, 1996
Faculty fellowships	Furco, 2002; Fisher, 1998
Faculty professional development program	Carnegie; Clayton and O'Steen, 2010; Bringle and Hatcher, 1996; Hollander et al., 2002; Rue, 1996
Faculty mentor program	Fisher, 1998; Bringle and Hatcher, 1996
Center programming—students	
Opportunity for student research	Carnegie
Opportunity for student leadership	Carnegie
Opportunity for student internships	Carnegie
Opportunity for student study abroad	Carnegie
Cocurricular programs and opportunities	Pigza and Troppe, 2003
Offer service-learning minor/emphasis	Bringle and Hatcher, 1996
Service-learning/CBR student scholars	Fisher, 1998
Center programming—community partners	
Presentation/publications with partners	Bringle and Hatcher, 1996
Award to community partner	Bringle and Hatcher, 1996
Collaborative grant proposals with partners	Bringle and Hatcher, 1996
Educate partners on engaged pedagogy	Bringle and Hatcher, 1996
Initiate site visit/meetings with partners	Bringle and Hatcher, 1996
Community incentives and rewards	Furco, 2002

list of best practices that generated the 66 survey items as a form of recipro-cal validity (Welch et al., 2005) in which practitioners socially validate best practices enumerated in the professional literature.

Each of the "Top Ten" lists was individually reviewed to identify and cat-egorize responses that most closely reflected the survey items. The essential components from the open-ended lists was tabulated by calculating the total number of times a response was listed.

The data were examined to identify promising and emergent practices as well as essential components initially enumerated in the literature that do not appear to be viewed as essential by practitioners.

Results

Descriptive Statistics—A Profile of Centers

Survey data indicate that there are predominant characteristics that emerge providing a profile of a "typical" civic engagement center. The findings are summarized in the following list:

Institutional Architecture/Policy Context
- Exists in an environment of a campus-wide commitment to civic engagement
- Is structured as a central coordinating office reporting to academic affairs with a budget from operational funds
- The director of the Center has a graduate degree and is professionally aligned with academic affairs
- Civic engagement is included in the campus's strategic plan and is part of the criteria used in accreditation processes
- Campus has an institutional operational definition of service-learning and/or engagement

Center Infrastructure
- Has a physical space on campus but is in need of more space
- Has an articulated mission/vision to guide its work
- Has staff paid for out of institutional funds that consist of a full-time administrator without faculty status, a full-time administrative assis-tant, and a part-time administrative staff
- Involves faculty through a faculty liaison and an advisory board with faculty representation
- Gathers data in a systematic way and reports on its activities through an annual report and newsletter

- It aspires to greater community partner and student representation on its advisory committee, is moving to greater faculty involvement in center operations, and it is seeking to increase its fundraising capacity and ability to involve alumni in supporting the center

Center Operations
- Has responsibility of overseeing campus civic engagement requirements
- Is taking on increased risk management functions
- Provides resources for capacity building, particularly among faculty
- Gathers assessment data for accountability and improvement
- All of these operations point to increasingly complex functions and the need for more staff and more resources to carry them out

Center Programming
- Has academic, cocurricular, and partnership programming functions.
- Provides significant programming aimed at faculty and students
- Provides programming that nurtures student's leadership development
- Works with both faculty and students around community partnerships, and works with community partners as coeducators

Top Ten List of Essential Components

A total of 17 themes or factors consistently emerged from their "Top Ten" lists. Of these, five items fell within the Center Operations (Cop) category, four items were within the Institutional Architecture/Policy (IAP) and Center Infrastructure (CI) category, and one item was categorized as Center Programming for Faculty (CPF). Three additional items emerged from the reciprocal validity process not included in the survey items or categories. The ranking and frequency of responses are presented in Table 13.2. We present a description of these results by category as follows. The results are ranked in terms of frequency of responses rather than importance.

Analysis and Implications

Institutional Architecture/Policy Context

There is some indication in the data that the existence of a center may be a factor in propelling the campus to greater institution-wide commitment to civic engagement. While just three-fourth of the campuses reported that

Table 13.2 Top Ten responses for essential components for community engagement centers

Rank	Category	Essential component	No. responses
1	IAP	Budgeted institutional funds	49
2	IAP	Administrative support	47
3	CI	Programming staff	33
4	CPF	Faculty development	32
5	*	Faculty leadership/buy-in	24
6	COP	Student leadership/decision making	23
7	COP	Assessment mechanism/procedures	21
	CI	Full-time administrator	21
	IAP	Academic affairs reporting line	21
8	CI	Database/tracking system	15
	CI	Adequate office space	15
9	IAP	Define/designate courses	12
	COP	Fundraising mechanisms	12
	*	Communication/outreach	12
10	COP	Transportation coordination/policy	11
	*	Cross-campus collaboration	11
	COP	Course development grants	11

*Responses not included in survey items.

IAP = Institutional Architecture/Policy; CI = Center Infrastructure; COP = Center Operations; CPF = Center.

there currently exists a campus-wide commitment, factoring in those that are in process toward a campus-wide commitment and those that hope to establish that commitment, the total rises to 99.3 percent of the respondents. The question of whether creating an infrastructure to support civic engagement is not only an indication of institutional commitment but perhaps a catalyst for institutional commitment warrants further study and has implications for understanding how structures influence institutional commitment.

It may be worth further study to understand the importance of establishing a campus-wide operational definition of civic engagement activities. The survey data indicate that only 70.2 percent of the respondents currently have an operational definition. What is the role of creating an operational definition of civic engagement activities in advancing civic engagement as an institutional priority? Do established centers resist official definitions as a way of providing a broad umbrella of civic engagement activities by many units on campus? Is a single official definition an obstacle to the development of disciplinary definitions of civic engagement and thus a detriment to encouraging departments to commit to civic engagement? Is there a process that opens up space for many definitions on campus that then evolves into a move to conceptual clarity for the campus as a whole: while just over 70 percent of the campuses have an official definition, another 24.1 percent are in the process of creating one and another 4.3 percent would like to (for a total of 98.4%).

The data on the budgeting of civic engagement centers indicate that these centers are institutional priorities and that they are part of the longer-term identity of the campus. The use of operational funds, or "hard dollars," instead of grant monies, or "soft dollars," indicates that the effort is not something that will disappear when the grant dollars are no longer available. It is worth considering the question of whether, in times of economic crisis, civic engagement funds are vulnerable to the budget axe. One might hypothesize that if the civic engagement efforts are part of the core academic work of the campus (83.3% of the campuses either currently report to academic affairs or are in the process of establishing an academic affairs reporting line), they are less subject to reduction or elimination. The campuses selected for this study, independently recognized for their commitment to community engagement, likely overrepresent this core academic commitment. A comparative study of Carnegie-classified campuses with those that are not classified to examine sustainability of community engagement could possibly address this question: Are campuses where civic engagement is not tied closely to faculty work and the curriculum more likely to scale back on a civic engagement commitment in tight economic circumstances than campuses where civic engagement is established as central to the academic enterprise (teaching, learning, and research)?

The data on the background of the director deserve further study. What the survey does not reveal is potentially significant information about career pathway into a center director position. For example, faculty who have moved into administration to lead/administer civic engagement activity on campus may have claimed a background in both academic affairs and in the faculty. Similarly, a community leader may have received an advanced degree, taken a faculty position, and moved into directing civic engagement, and may have checked multiple boxes. It would be useful to know more about the career pathway of civic engagement center directors.

Finally, while the results from the reciprocal validity Top Ten list reflect and support these findings, they also reveal the important role of informal faculty leadership to promote this work. This is related yet separate from the topic of faculty development but the cultural and political implications suggest the importance of a critical mass of influential faculty. As such, center directors must be cognizant of and use this as an approach to garner support for programming. Similarly, the Top Ten responses revealed the important role of institutional administrators in publicly advocating centers and their mission to establish legitimacy across campus.

Center Infrastructure

Survey results suggest that the creation of an infrastructure to support civic engagement is an evolving process. As the operations of the center develop, the work of the center becomes more complex and expansive. The data seems to indicate that the evolutionary direction of centers is (1) toward a need for more staff, more space, larger budgets, and more intentional fundraising; (2) toward deeper affiliation with academic affairs and faculty roles and responsibilities; (3) toward better data gathering and reporting/communicating the work of the center and its outcomes; and (4) greater community partner voice and student voice in center planning and operations. The data suggest that centers are in flux; this may be an indication of the growth of the field and the level of importance of civic engagement in higher education at a time of significant challenges and change, it may be typical of organization development, and it may indicate a pattern of development of centers that could be useful in center planning.

The findings also suggest that it would be useful to know more about how centers develop and evolve. What is the ordering of activities that lead to effective operations and maximize the outcomes of center activities? What is the time frame for center development, and what are the strongest indicators of predicting the time frame for center development? The data also suggest that current centers may benefit from assessing the current state of their development in relationship to the survey data as a way of evaluating future directions for their work.

Center Programming

Perhaps not surprisingly, because the sample in this study is highly engaged campuses, there is strong emphasis on civic engagement as a core academic enterprise and therefore a part of the work of faculty. Center programming is heavily focused on faculty: building capacity, creating wider curricular options, and providing recognition. There is a strong faculty development dimension to programming, which is critical in assuring high-quality pedagogical practices. Results did not, however, elaborate on the content and scope of faculty development other than mentioning formats such as workshops, retreats, and one-on-one technical assistance. This merits further investigation on how faculty development occurs. Therefore, the greater the capacity of the faculty to deliver high-quality civic engagement courses, the more opportunity for providing greater curricular options for students. Thus, community engagement minors and certificates are emerging as curricular options. There is also widespread effort to provide recognition for faculty who participate in civic engagement through fellowships, grants, awards, and through making their work visible. This may raise issues beyond the scope of this study to address. If faculty are not being recognized and rewarded for civic engagement though the official reward structures for promotion, is there an effort to provide other forms of recognition being offered by the centers? If civic engagement were rewarded as part of the scholarly work of faculty, would centers be focused as much on providing recognition for civic engagement work?

Centers in this study appear to be attentive to greater student involvement in leadership positions in all aspects of community engagement. There appear to be opportunities for student voice, student input, and student participation in the delivery of curricular and cocurricular civic engagement. These kinds of activity, especially those that provide opportunities for students to exercise leadership in courses, working with faculty, reflects enacting the logic of reciprocity and cocreation with students and reflects the literature in the field on "students as colleagues." The data also indicate that programming around community partners and partnerships lags behind programming for faculty and students. At the same time, there appears to be recognition that this is potentially problematic since the aspirational, "hope to," responses are high in all of these survey items.

It also appears that campuses make the distinction between service-learning as a pedagogical practice and service-learning as a distinct body of knowledge; service-learning as a pedagogy integrated into courses across majors is common; service-learning as a major is rare.

Other Findings

Finally, the Top Ten list designed for reciprocal validity revealed at least three themes not found in the professional literature and therefore were not included in the survey instrument. Faculty leadership or "buy-in" was articulated in one way or another several times. Respondents noted that respected faculty who had embraced this form of pedagogy had to serve as an advocate or "cheerleader" to their peers and administrators to garner a sense of legitimacy for the center and its work. This response represents a unique relational and/or political element that is outside the structural and operational dimensions that other survey items and open-ended responses revealed. In other words, the survey items derived from the professional literature focused primarily on systemic and operational dimensions of centers while these anecdotal responses suggest that center directors strategically identify and utilize highly respected faculty members for what might be considered "professional evangelism" or marketing to help promote the center and its programs.

A second finding was related to communication and outreach. Analysis of comments revealed that this involved more than reporting on the center's work as public relations such as annual reports, newsletters, or websites. Again, the comments were relational in nature, suggesting the necessity for center administrators and staff to reach out to faculty and community partners not merely to disseminate information and resources or provide technical assistance, but to establish and maintain a relationship. Examples of communication in this context reflected more of a conversational nature in which directors "checked in" with instructors and representatives of community agencies to see how things were going as well as solicit and/or provide input and feedback.

Finally, respondents also indicated that cross-campus collaboration was an essential component of a successful center and program. While the majority of respondents consistently advocated the critical need for a reporting line within academic affairs, equally important was the ability and nature of working with other units within student affairs. Directors provided examples and instances in which their offices worked with nonacademic units such as campus ministry and residential life. These responses most likely are in the context of cocurricular programming, but may, in fact also include the necessity of curricular collaboration across academic disciplines to design, implement, and maintain service-learning courses.

Conclusion

This study was designed to answer to identify defining features of the organizational structures created by campuses for the purpose of facilitating connections to communities at the local, regional, national, and global levels. Likewise, our investigation was an attempt to ascertain purposes and goals of campus–community partnerships expressed through the organization structure of a campus community center. Finally, the survey attempted to determine to what extent are the activities undertaken through these institutional structures connected to institutional or community change initiatives. Based on the descriptive statistics and open-ended responses, we have reported what appear to be critical and salient components for a successful and effective community center on campus.

It appears that the role and structure of campus centers have, indeed, evolved in the past 20 years. The transformation suggests that these centers have not abandoned cocurricular programming that was the original foundation for many colleges. Instead, centers have built upon and expanded those programs. There has, however, been a significant shift and emphasis in housing these centers within academic affairs, and we were somewhat surprised to see a trend in having these centers take responsibility for institutional coordination of most community-based programming. As such, what were once peripheral offices and services a generation ago have evolved into critical and more visible entities on campus with a specific role and mission and an expanded infrastructure. However, we also noted that effective and substantial infrastructure for community engagement is only one aspect of institutionalization. Other key factors have to be in place as well. Centers are not the single key to success; there have to be multiple innovations simultaneously to align institutional practice and culture for community engagement. The coordinating infrastructure of a center is essential to institutionalization but it is not sufficient. It became evident from the qualitative results that relational dynamics through personal contact as well as the social capital of public administrative advocacy and visibility of highly respected faculty as practitioners are equally important.

Another surprise was with regard to the background and professional pathways of center directors. These administrators appear to come from an array of disciplines and therefore, it is unclear how or why faculty from various fields found their way into this role. This warrants continued research. Finally, it became apparent that the nature and structure of the Carnegie Classification application process that we incorporated for the survey included very few items regarding student leadership. As such, we came to realize that we have an incomplete picture of the role, responsibilities, and structures within centers for student leadership. Further research needs to include a broader and more comprehensive examination of this important component of campus centers.

So what are the next steps?

The answer is twofold. First and from an empirical context, further research is warranted to gain insight into these data. Respondents provided a "brush-stroke" of information regarding operations and program but the scope and structure of the survey did not afford ample space or opportunity for detailed elaboration. For example, while the vast majority of respondents reported faculty development as a key component of their programming and operations, details regarding structure, content, duration, and delivery of faculty development are not available in this study. Similarly, the professional pathway of center directors is worthy of continued exploration. As such, key elements identified in this investigation serve as a catalyst for further qualitative research. Likewise, it is unclear how (if at all) the responses from these centers with the Carnegie Classification of Community Engagement compare with those without the classification? The results of the reciprocal validation in this study revealed three factors or components not included in the professional literature (faculty leadership, outreach/communication, cross-campus collaboration) and therefore merit further exploration and discussion in the professional literature. Finally, it is worthy to consider additional investigation employing such a multiple regression analysis to identify components that predict or correlate with the Carnegie Classification.

Secondly and from an applied perspective, we also encourage center directors to convene an advisory group comprised of students, faculty, representatives from community agencies, and mid-level administration and review the results presented here. The group can identify which of these critical factors are currently in operation as well as determine priorities for those components not in place. This, in turn, may be useful in strategic planning. Likewise, it is our recommendation that newly formed centers incorporate and present these findings as a "wish list" to administrators to help in the implementation and maintenance of the center and its work. Finally, this initial work may be a foundation for creating useful assessment and/or program review tools that could be used to determine strengths and challenges of centers for continued development.

References

Battistoni, Richard. "Making a Major Commitment: Public and Community Service at Providence College." In *Successful Service-Learning Programs: New Models of Excellence in Higher Education*, ed. Edward Zlotkowski. Bolton, MA: Anker Press, 1998, pp. 169–188.

Bringle, Robert, and Julie Hatcher. "Implementing Service-Learning in Higher Education." *Journal of Higher Education* 67(2) (1996): 221–239.

Bucco, Diana, and Julie Busch. "Starting a Service-Learning Program." In *Service-Learning in Higher Education: Concepts and Practices*, ed. Barbara Jacoby. San Francisco, CA: Jossey-Bass, 1996, pp. 231–245.

Carnegie Foundation (2012). Community Engaged Elective Classification. http://classifications.carnegiefoundation.org/descriptions/community_engagement.php

Ellison, Julie, and Timothy Eatman. *Scholarship in Public: Knowledge Creation and Tenure Policy in the Engaged University*. Syracuse, NY: Imagining America, 2008.

Fisher, Irene. "We Make the Road by Walking: Building Service-Learning In and Out of the Curriculum at the University of Utah." In *Successful Service-Learning*

Programs: New Models of Excellence in Higher Education, ed. Edward Zlotkowski. Bolton, MA: Anker Press, 1998, pp. 210–230.

Furco, Andrew. "Institutionalizing service-learning in higher education. *The Journal of Public Affairs* 6 (2002): 39–68.

Hatcher, Julie, and Robert Bringle. "Developing Your Assessment Plan: A Key Component of Reflective Practice." In *Looking In/Reaching Out: A Reflective Guide for Community Service-Learning Professionals*, ed. Barbara Jacoby and Pamela Matuscio. Boston, MA: Campus Compact, 2010, pp. 211–230.

Holland, Barbara, and Mark Langseth. "Leveraging Financial Support for Service-Learning: Relevance, Relationships, Results, Resources." In *Looking In/Reaching Out: A Reflective Guide for Community Service-Learning Professionals*, ed. Barbara Jacoby and Pamela Matuscio. Boston, MA: Campus Compact, 2010, pp. 211–230.

Hollander, Elizabeth, John Saltmarsh, and Edward Zlotkowski. "Indicators of Engagement." In *Learning to Serve: Promoting Civil Society through Service-Learning*, ed. Maureen Kenny, Lou Ann Simon, Karen Kiley-Brabeck, and Richard Lerner, Vol. 7, Chapter 3. Norwell, MA: Kluwer Academic, 2002.

Jacoby, Barbara. *Service-Learning in Higher Education: Concepts and Practices*. San Francisco, CA: Jossey-Bass, 1996.

———. *Civic Engagement in Higher Education: Concepts and Practices*. San Francisco, CA: Jossey-Bass, 2009.

Jacoby, Barbara, and Pamela Mutascio. 2010. *Looking In/Reaching Out: A Reflective Guide for Community Service-Learning Professionals*. Boston, MA: Campus Compact.

Kecskes, Kevin, and Seanna Kerrigan. "Capstone Experiences." In *Civic Engagement in Higher Education: Concepts and Practices*, ed. Barbara Jacoby. San Francisco, CA: Jossey-Bass, 2009, pp. 117–139.

Kendall, Jane. *Combining Service and Learning: A Resource Book for Community and Public Service* (Vols. 1 and 2). Raleigh, NC: National Society for Internships and Experiential Education, 1990.

Paul, Elizabeth. "Community-Based Research: Collaborative Inquiry for the Public Good." In *Civic Engagement in Higher Education: Concepts and Practices*, ed. Barbara Jacoby. San Francisco, CA: Jossey-Bass, 2009, pp. 196–212.

Pigza, Jennifer, and Marie Troppe. "Developing an Infrastructure for Service-Learning and Community Engagement." In *Building Partnerships for Service-Learning*, ed. Barbara Jacoby. San Francisco, CA: Jossey Bass, 2003, pp. 106–130.

Rubin, Sharon. "Institutionalizing Service-Learning." In *Service-Learning in Higher Education: Concepts and Practices*, ed. Barbara Jacoby. San Francisco, CA: Jossey Bass, 1996, pp. 297–316.

Rue, Penny. "Administering Successful Service-Learning Programs." In *Service-Learning in Higher Education: Concepts and Practices*, ed. Barbara Jacoby. San Francisco, CA: Jossey Bass, 1996, pp. 246–275.

Saltmarsh, John, Matthew Hartley, and Patti Clayton. *Democratic Engagement White Paper*. Boston, MA: New England Resource Center for Higher Education, 2009.

Walshok, Mary. "Strategies for Building the Infrastructure that Supports the Engaged Campus." In *Colleges and Universities as Citizens*, ed. Robert Bringle, Richard Games, and Edward Malloy. Boston, MA: Allyn and Bacon, 1999, pp. 74–95.

Welch, Marshall, Peter Miller, and Kristen Davies. "Reciprocal Validity: Description and Outcomes of a Hybrid Approach of Triangulated Qualitative Analysis in the Research of Civic Engagement." In *Improving Service-Learning Practice: Research on Models to Enhance Impacts*, ed. Sue Root, Jane Callahan, and Shelley Billig. Greenwich, CT: Information Age Publishing, 2005, pp. 119–139.

Welch, Marshall. "Moving from Service-Learning to Civic Engagement." In *Civic Engagement in Higher Education: Concepts and Practices*, ed. Barbara Jacoby. San Francisco, CA: Jossey-Bass, 2009, pp. 174–195.

CHAPTER 14

"If you build it, they will come": Building a Structure for Institutional Change

Richard B. Ellis and Kristine Hart

Introduction

Every institution of higher education, whether public or private, large or small, two-year or four-year, has its own institutional and campus culture. While this culture is by no means static, it nonetheless is steeped in the history and traditions of the individual institution. With few exceptions, this tends to make many attempts to create institutional change a long-term endeavor rife with challenges that can, at times, make those involved feel like Sisyphus trying to roll the boulder to the top of the hill. In spite of this, colleges and universities across the country are being called to address the need to graduate civically engaged students from multiple arenas and stakeholders. For example, the American Democracy Project, a partnership established in 2003 between the American Association of State Colleges and Universities (AASCU) and the *New York Times*, has supported and encouraged its participating schools to graduate students who will be the "next generation of informed, engaged citizens for our democracy...involved citizens in their communities...[and] tomorrow's 'Stewards of Place.' "[1] However, it is not only academia that is sending out this call, but also students on campus who feel disconnected from their communities and their role as citizens.

This comes at a time when liberal arts education, including the civic behaviors of thinking critically and being part of an informed electorate, is under fire. Related to this, the power of a diverse yet collective student voice is being eroded through reduced access to higher education, the push for more online classes, which results in reduced student interaction, and the move to lessen degree requirements in order to produce good workers more quickly rather than developing good learners and good citizens. While not all institutions will heed the call to remain and strengthen public engagement, those that take on this challenge will find the benefits for the campus and the community invaluable.

In order to understand the progression of establishing a structure that supports a campus-wide culture of engagement, the authors have chosen to use a case study methodology. In a qualitative case study, the investigator is seeking a greater understanding of the uniqueness and complexity of the case. To sharpen the focus, it is essential that the investigator identify issues from which to draw and emphasize the intent and outcome of said issues.[2] Issue questions become the conceptual structure, rather than hypothesis or goal statements. In this case study, four pre-ordinate issue questions were identified:

- To what extent does student involvement direct the development of both the culture of community engagement and the creation of a campus center?
- How do fiscal constraints affect the growth of a culture of community engagement within the structure of an institution of higher education?
- How important are strong partnerships, both in the community and on campus, in the development of a culture of community engagement?
- What role does identity play in the establishment of a center for community engagement within an institution of higher education?

Washburn University as a Case Study

Washburn University, located in Topeka, Kansas, is one of the last remaining municipal universities in the United States. As such, the university's faculty, staff, and students hold, as one of their core values, a mandate to be engaged with the community outside the walls of the institution. However, it has only been in the past 17 years that an infrastructure has evolved to organize and expand this mission. The following sections will explore the development of this infrastructure within four themes: student leadership and direction, partnerships, building identity with students at the core, and fiscal needs and considerations.

Student Leadership and Direction

In a 1995 article, "The Youth Service Movement: America's Trump Card in Revitalizing Democracy," Matthew Moseley wrote:

> Remarkable change is occurring among American youth. An enormous resurgence of volunteerism and monumental efforts in rebuilding the civic structure of America are guiding the nation on a path toward revitalization and renewal.[3]

This resurgence of engagement saw students becoming involved in their communities in a significantly different way from previous generations. This new generation looked at service, rather than large-scale political activism, as the mechanism for social change.[4] In response, it became imperative for institutions to find ways to address this rising student movement through institutional support or new policies.

The modern institutional culture of community engagement at Washburn began in 1995 with the establishment of a student-directed service organization called Learning in the Community (LinC). While it had the support of a university faculty adviser, it was solely a registered student organization through the Student Activities and Greek Life Office. Operated by one student coordinator, the only goal was to involve other students in the community through volunteerism. Despite being relegated to a student club, the organization quickly attracted a sizable number of students. There is no doubt (in our minds) that some of the initial success of LinC was due to the luck of having a student coordinator who was highly motivated. However, more importantly, this initiative came at a time when college students across the country were yearning to be more involved. The true lesson that came out of this first year was that the success of the project was because of the fact that it was student driven. Without the participation of the broader student body, it would have likely been viewed as a "nice" project for a student intern that the institution could ignore.

Outside of encouraging and supporting the participation in community engagement by the student body, the student coordinator also spent time, with the faculty adviser, to carefully think about the sustainability of the project. This resulted in obtaining space for a "permanent" LinC office, developing a ten-year strategic plan for LinC, and recruiting multiple students to help run and expand LinC the following year. It was this recognition by the students that their initiative needed to have more structure than a regular cocurricular student organization in order to be a true resource for their peers. They also recognized the need for increased broad-based participation from across the campus in order to make the organization stand apart from traditional student clubs. Each group of student coordinators was aware of the strategic plan left by the original student coordinator and committed to moving her vision forward. This structure of student ownership provided a mechanism for accountability and inspired a commitment to the expansion of the project, thus giving them a collective voice about what they wanted their college experience to be.

When changing the structure of an institution toward campus-wide integration of service and civic engagement, it is essential to rely on students in the evolution of this process. In short, the service movement, as seen in the case of Washburn University, needs to be "owned" by students because they are the ones who do the work and in many cases will be the face of the institution as partnerships are formed and nurtured. Even in an era where more centers have become institutionalized, the need for sustaining active student leadership is critical to the success of centers.

Partnerships

While the energy and dedication of students is essential in the formation of a center, without building a network of close relationships with local, national, and international partners, there would be no avenue for students to become engaged in meaningful, high-impact ways. At the same time, just as it was imperative for students to have a strong role and voice in the development of a culture of engagement across campus, so too is it important that they be involved in developing strong partnerships. This is not just a philosophical approach, for it is students who often carry out the day-to-day structures of campus–community partnerships.

In the case of LinC, there has been a growth of partnerships from 2 in its inaugural year to over 100 today. While the expansion in number of partners may seem to have happened quickly, in reality, it was done very strategically and with a perceived purpose. In determining how to proceed in forming partnerships, it is important for the stakeholders (e.g., students, faculty, community agencies, etc.) to determine: (1) what the purpose of the engagement is; (2) what the desired outcomes will be; (3) whether it can be implemented well with current resources; and (4) whether it is sustainable. By following these partner-development principles, LinC has been able to create many strong, long-term, sustainable partnerships over multiple years. This is demonstrated by the partnership with the local domestic violence program. In the early phases of the development of this relationship, students, university staff, and representatives of the organization negotiated numbers of student participants, extent of responsibility, and most importantly what learning outcomes were expected. Over the years, this relationship has evolved to include greater numbers of participants and has enabled the partner to develop new programming while maintaining a long-term partnership with the university.

In many situations, the focus of partnerships is on connections with community organizations; however, there are partnerships that give structure to the organization. As an example, in 2001, Washburn University, through LinC, formed a partnership with the Bonner Foundation in Princeton, New Jersey. The Bonner Program provided a developmental model of service and leadership that lent structure to the program. This model guides students to increase the depth of their engagement while gaining an understanding of being stewards of place and deepen their roles as civically engaged citizens. This new relationship also afforded access to a national network of institutions of higher education that provided a wealth of information on how to incorporate engagement into the academic realm in a way that would raise the profile, respectability, and sustainability of LinC.

Institutions undertaking partnerships with national organizations must also carefully consider all aspects of what that partnership means for their center. Issues to consider are whether it requires more staff, more paperwork, matching costs, and restrictions on what must be done and cannot be done within the confines of the program's framework. In the case of Washburn and its partnership with the Bonner Foundation, the same process that took place with the local partners was again implemented in the development of this relationship. LinC staff and students met with the Foundation staff and students at other institutions to hear them talk about the program. When the opportunity came for Washburn to become a part of the Bonner network, the leadership and constituencies involved felt confident that it was a good fit for both organizations.

Building Identity with Student Leaders at the Core

The notion that student leadership was an integral component of the development of a culture of service drove the movement both nationally and on the Washburn campus. As student involvement grew, it became clear that there needed to be a unifying identity to secure a place in the structure of the institution.

Up to this point, the organization focused strictly on individual student volunteerism and short-term events with little or no reflection or purposeful knowledge and skill attainment. By establishing a relationship with the Bonner Foundation, LinC was not only able to offer scholarships to students, but also integrate and implement a developmental model of service and leadership into an organizational framework. In addition, the affiliation with the Bonner Foundation gave LinC an identity on campus. During this same time, the Washburn faculty member directing the Bonner program worked with the institution to bestow a university honor on students who successfully completed at least two years with the program. The honor of LinC Scholar/Bonner Leader is recognized at graduation and appears on each student's transcript along with departmental and Latin honors. This helped to increase the profile and image of LinC and this small action would be instrumental in eventually creating an academic arm of the center.

It is clear from reviewing this history that identity is a key factor in institutionalization of a program. While there was certainly an impact made on campus as a student organization, until LinC established a clear identity, it was not going to be acknowledged for the work that had begun. As with any enterprise, having an identity that guides the work of the organization is essential; however, it is also a way to structure outreach and marketing. This was apparent as LinC began to market itself.

One way this was accomplished was by incorporating the Bonner model and identifying itself and its programs from that perspective. By promoting the developmental leadership aspect of the Bonner model, a decision was made to purposefully recruit faculty, students, and staff for inclusion in the center's programs and initiatives from across campus. This allowed LinC to market itself both on campus and in the community as engaging a diverse cross-section of the university. This was a strategic move to broaden not only the scope and impact of LinC on campus and in the community, but to create broad support of the center's role within the institution.

Having a clear model to base the center's identity on also, in the end, provided not only a model for student development, but also for the development of the center itself. Table14.1 uses the Bonner Foundation's developmental model (the five E's) as a framework for this.[5] This model can also be found in Hoy and Meisel's (2008). Civic Engagement at the Center: Building Democracy through Integrate Cocurricular and Curricular Experiences, where its corollary model for an academically-connected minor or certificate can be found.

It is clear that without the identity as a unit representing all of the campus with a clear design and model that all students could identify with, there would have been no mechanism to reach out across campus. By clearly identifying itself as student directed with a leadership focus and a recognizable name, the expansion was easier. In short, having an identity may be the most important factor in the establishment of a center.

Table 14.1 Student development and campus center development

Developmental stage	Student development	Center development
Expectation	• Determine what the students' prior experience with engaged learning has been and introduce them to the concept of engaged learning as it fits with the institution and/or their academic program of study	• Determine whether the development of a center is consistent with the mission of the institution. • Determine whether the development of a center fits with the vision the administration has for the institution and whether such an initiative will be supported. • Determine whether an academic unit already exists on campus that can embrace the concepts of engaged learning or whether a center will have to be developed as a stand-alone entity
Explore	• Expose students to ways they can be engaged learners—this may take several forms, for example, a lead-in course such as a first-year seminar that incorporates high-impact engaged learning practices or direct exposure that leads to knowledge about the community and the issues the community faces (e.g., one-day service events or community panels) • Expose students to the concept of being civically engaged citizens who participate in the democratic process	• Determine what members of the institution (i.e., faculty, staff, and students) either already do with regard to engaged learning or have the desire and capacity to do. • Become knowledgeable about the agencies that exist in the institution's community and what their needs are • Expose and educate the institutional community to the benefits of having a center devoted to supporting engaged learning
Experience	• Actively involve students in democratic civic engagement where they become stewards of place with the purpose of enhancing their community (e.g., service-learning, internships, academic AmeriCorps, etc.)	• Actively involve members of the institution and community in developing the purpose and vision for a center and the role it will take in the institution and community. • Develop networks to guide the development of a center (e.g., Bonner Foundation, Campus Compact, etc.)

continued

Table 14.1 Continued

Developmental stage	Student development	Center development
		• Create partnerships with organizations that can provide high-impact engaged learning experiences and with institutional entities that can involve students in democratic civic engagement through their academic programs
Example	• Move students into leader/coordinator roles—this can take many forms from mentoring students who are at an earlier developmental stage to taking the lead in organizing data collection for a CBR project for developing and coordinating programming for an organization	• Move into being the single point of contact for engaged learning at the institution. • Establish meaningful, long-term partnerships between the center and community organizations • Offer knowledge and skill-based training and development opportunities to stakeholders to encourage high-impact partnerships
Expertise	• Encourage students demonstrate high-level connections between their academic field and engaged learning through capstones, academic research, and so on. • Encourage students to be future focused in connecting their democratic civic engagement work to their career and vocational goals as well as understanding their role as engaged citizens who will demonstrate lifelong involvement in their communities	• Develop center-based or center-academic unit civic and community engagement minors, majors, and/or certificates • Position the center as the expert for democratic civically engaged learning for the institution by connecting faculty and staff to community engagement projects related to their field and offering individual support and mentoring to develop these opportunities • Serve as a clearinghouse for engaged learning by making research, policy briefs, and so on, open and available for institution and community use • Encourage ongoing, high-level involvement by the institution by advocating for tenure and promotion consideration for faculty who incorporate engaged learning into the academic curriculum thereby fully integrating engaged learning throughout the institution

Fiscal Needs and Constraints

While the other three considerations in developing a center are important, fiscal issues can severely constrain the ability of a center to do the work it was designed to do. Having a budget that allows a center to hire the number of people and fund daily operational expenses and projects is one barometer of institutional support. Centers need to keep in mind that development of monetary resources will likely be an ongoing process rather than something to be done only in the first five years. In addition to funding operations of the center and its programs, many institutions must also consider the financial costs to students that may keep them from being involved in community engagement work. Integrating scholarships, work study funds, and stipends for students has been a key practice for us, especially to support the engagement of lower-income students in civic work.

From 1995 to 2006, LinC was classified as a student organization, which meant that institutional support was restricted to the US$2,000 that could be requested, but was not guaranteed, from the student government association as long as the beneficiary was the student organization. This hampered the organization's ability to grow; so in 2002, the faculty adviser secured an AmeriCorps VISTA position funded through outside sources to help with program development and fundraising. While that position was only a short-term solution, the AmeriCorps VISTA member and faculty adviser secured enough outside funding to support the continuation of that position until LinC was institutionalized as a center directly reporting to the vice president of Academic Affairs in 2006. Becoming an academic unit on campus, however, was not a solution to the fiscal constraints under which the center was working and fundraising has continued to be an ongoing priority. The center currently serves hundreds of students each year in addition to working with faculty and community partners with only two full-time administrators, an administrative assistant, and a grant-funded AmeriCorps VISTA director who solely handles the requirements of the VISTA grant. While obtaining the funds for more staff would be ideal, the majority of fundraising has been to support students.

The center found it imperative that a mechanism be found to fund student engagement initiatives on campus. This was especially important as a large portion of Washburn's student body is commuter based rather than residential with many having financial need requiring them to be employed in addition to their academic work. It should be noted that in today's economy, the issue of employment and affordability affects almost every student and every institution. This was addressed in several ways. First, the staff worked closely with Washburn's Financial Aid Office to establish a strong

Community-Based Federal Work Study Program, which allows students who qualify to earn money for high-level engagement in the community. Federal regulations mandate that institutions receiving federal work study money must designate at least 7 percent of those funds to employ students in community service jobs; Washburn currently uses 29 percent of these funds this way. This is important in increasing the breadth and depth of engagement across campus as it allows students with a desire to be engaged in their community the opportunity to do so. Additionally, with the support of the Bonner Foundation, LinC has been able to secure AmeriCorps education awards that provide scholarships to over 100 Washburn students each year who are engaged in high-impact work in the community. Again, without this support, students would not have access to these opportunities that support their academics while providing professional and personal benefits.

While the authors would like to be able to reassure individuals that "if they build it financial resources will come" in the same way that campus and community stakeholders do, to do so would underestimate the work that developing and maintaining a center entails in today's institutional climate. As an institution begins to develop or enhance its programs, continuous identification of innovative funding sources is essential. Looking at Washburn, it is clear that the development and expansion of the center was enhanced by creative funding and would have probably remained stagnant had these resources not been developed.

Conclusion

As the authors have looked at Washburn University and its development of a culture of engagement, it is apparent that the four issues identified played a significant role in the evolution from a student organization to an independent academic unit. Using this case study analysis, it appears that the essential elements for the success of a community engagement program include: (1) student involvement, not just as participants but as leaders in its development and growth; (2) strong partnerships within the community as well as partnerships with organizations that can provide direction as the center evolves; (3) a clear plan for addressing fiscal needs; and (4) an identity that can create the image the center wants.

Notes

1. "About ADP," American Association of State Colleges and Universities, accessed January 2, 2013, www.aascu.org/programs/ADP/.

2. Robert Stake, *The Art of Case Study Research* (Thousand Oaks, CA: Sage Publications, 1995), p. 16.
3. Matthew Moseley, "The Youth Service Movement: America's Trump Card in Revitalizing Democracy," *National Critic Review* 84, no. 3 (1995): 267.
4. Ibid., 270.
5. Ariane Hoy and Robert Hackett, "Student Development and Leadership," *Bonner Network Wiki*, last modified May 22, 2013, http://bonnernetwork .pbworks.com/w/page/13113175/Student%20Development%20and%20 Leadership. Please note that the student development model column in Table 14.1 is based on information from the Bonner Foundation development model and that the center development column is the authors' interpretation of how that translates into the development of a center. Additionally, this model is explored in the introduction of this book and in the publication *Civic Engagement at the Center: Building Democracy through Integrated Cocurricular and Curricular Experiences* by Ariane Hoy and Wayne Meisel.

References

"About ADP." American Association of State Colleges and Universities. Accessed May 22, 2013. www.aascu.org/programs/ADP/.

Hoy, Ariane, and Robert Hackett. "Student Development and Leadership." *Bonner Network Wiki*. Last modified May 22, 2013. http://bonnernetwork.pbworks. com/w/page/13113175/ Student%20Development%20and%20Leadership.

Hoy, Ariane, and Wayne Meisel. *Civic engagement at the center: Building democracy through integrated cocurricular and curricular experiences.* Association of American Colleges and Universities, 2008.

Moseley, Matthew. "The youth service movement: America's trump card in revitalizing democracy." *National Critic Review* 84, no. 3 (1995): 267–271.

Stake, Robert. *The Art of Case Study Research.* Thousand Oaks, CA: Sage Publications, 1995.

CHAPTER 15

Leveraging New Technologies for Engagement

Abby Kiesa and Ariane Hoy

The Digital Generation

Today's youth are a new digital generation. Traditional aged undergraduates, born after 1980, have been characterized as "digital natives" (Prensky, 2001, as cited in Bennett et al., 2009). Levine and Dean's *Generation on a Tightrope* (2012) reports that these Millennials are the most technologically oriented; in a 2009 survey, 42 percent cited the launch of the World Wide Web as the most significant event in their lives. They grew up with rapidly changing technologies. By kindergarten, texting, web browsers, smart phones, DVDs, Yahoo!, and the dot-com bubble were part of the American context; elementary school saw Google, Napster, music file sharing, and iPods spreading; and Middle school brought Skype, MySpace, and Facebook. Moreover, they are inheriting a world that is strikingly different from that of their parents:

> Today's college students are a more diverse, digital generation living in an information economy with an aging, increasingly immigrant, migrating population, a majority of whom reside in the South and West. Their world is flat, financially troubled, and inflamed by religious, economic, and political differences. (Levine and Dean, 2012, 7)

Howe and Strauss (2000) report that Millennials are breaking in key ways from Generation X; they are characterized as optimists, tolerant of diversity, team players who generally accept authority and follow rules, are the most watched over generation, and are also the most wired and technologically oriented. With parents who are often highly involved (Levine and Dean found that 41% are in touch with parents at least daily and 19% contact them three or more times a day), some of these youth are reported to need more support and guidance in developing independent problem-solving and decision-making skills. For those of us in academic community engagement, these youth bring many skills, proclivities, and talents we would be remiss not to tap.

Additionally, Millennials are helping to propel change in how we think of college itself, especially with respect to the integration of technology. The characteristics of these youth, many of whom are in college today, are prompting higher education to rethink teaching and learning. For digital natives, educational strategies must include 24/7, consumer-driven, active learning and hands on, concrete, multimedia, collaborative, and challenge-oriented projects (Howe and Strauss, 2000; Levine and Dean, 2012). This is the era of online faculty office hours, massive open online courses, competency badges, and learning analytics. Yet, technological change and its application in higher education, in many ways, is still in version 1.0. It is changing fast, but the pace is still slow, guarded by the overarching culture and structure of higher education. In a world where individual youth are making friends and sometimes defining their values and networking online (i.e., the average user spends on average 15 hours and 33 minutes on Facebook per month), those of us involved in promoting and organizing community engagement must find suitable ways to use these platforms and think about what learning and engagement are taking place there (as Bennett et al., 2009, suggest).

Community Engagement and Its Online Potentials

Although civic and political organizing can be done online, community engagement is also profoundly about *place*, real people, neighborhoods, and lived environments. Community engagement is a chance to invest in relationships and activities (such as tutoring, providing meals to the hungry, improving health care, building community programs, and lobbying for public policy changes) that involve face-to-face engagement. How can online activity lead to or inform offline engagement in a meaningful way? Or, vice versa? Research on social media and young people often focuses on who is online and what tools they use (the work of the Pew Internet and American Life Project; Edison Research, 2010), and has begun to investigate rates at which the Internet and social media are being used for explicitly civic or political purposes (Smith, 2011; National Conference on Citizenship [NCOC], 2008, 2009). Recent research into Internet usage has shown that online activities can increase young people's civic engagement, regardless of their prior motivations for going online (Kahne et al., 2011) and that online political activities are complements to offline activities (Cohen and Kahne, 2012).

Particularly in the field of community engagement, much of the efforts to use these technological tools to engage young people in civic life have been conducted outside of, or not directly connected to, formal educational institutions. Some K-12 civic education efforts have begun to build digitally learned lessons, like those of iCivics, which was recently found to have a positive impact on students' ability to write a civic-related essay (Kawashima-Ginsberg, 2012). Outside of education institutions, there are many organizations and initiatives like the League of Young Voters, Change.org, and issue-based groups that have developed key ways to reach youth and organize projects with the help of the Internet, particularly efforts to promote issue awareness and advocacy. Campus-based community centers are still experimenting with these platforms. Like higher education more broadly, many schools and their various departments and staff are trying to figure out how online tools and social media fit into their structured programs and how online tools and platforms can forward stated engagement goals. As Ratliff writes, "digital immigrants are now under pressure not only to adapt to new learning and communication styles of digital natives but also to restructure their own thought process to maximize student development" (2011).

What We Aimed to Do and Learn

In 2008, the Bonner Foundation and its network of campus-based programs received funding support from the Corporation for National and Community Service, which it utilized to create what was called the Serve 2.0 initiative (a meshing of Web 2.0 and service). Our network involves about 3,000 undergraduates annually, who are enrolled at diverse institutions (public and private, religiously affiliated and secular, large and small, and many of which are in the South). At its core, Serve 2.0 was about experimenting with the emerging and rapidly growing use of social media, including tools like Facebook, videos, wikis, and Twitter. The aim was to integrate this technology into an already established intensive, multiyear community engagement program—the Bonner Scholar and Leader Programs—and into the work of centers for community engagement more broadly.

Because the foundation and Bonner Network were already focused on a strategy for deepening community engagement work through enhancing issue-focused and team-oriented structures (described in other areas within this volume), the strategy adopted encouraged both breadth and depth. To promote breadth within the network as a whole, the foundation hosted trainings, and adopted and modeled the use of wikis and other tools for resource sharing and program management. To promote depth, a smaller subset of campuses engaged in a more vigorous application of a number of social media tools, oriented to benefit and enhance work with existing or new nonprofit partners.

The Center for Information and Research on Civic Learning and Engagement (CIRCLE) worked with the Bonner Foundation to understand and assess several aspects of the initiative, including:

(1) How the initiative leveraged new volunteers or greater levels of student engagement;
(2) How online tools played a role in building the capacity of nonprofit partners to achieve their missions and run high-quality programs;
(3) What impact the initiative had on helping campus staff and student leaders run stronger, more efficient programs, thereby increasing their own capacity and coordination with others on campus and in the community.

Using qualitative and quantitative methods, we sought to understand how social media tools were used on campuses and in communities. Data came from:

• Baseline and concluding surveys of the whole campus network;
• Biannual surveys of a subset of campus staff, community partners, and students on participating campuses; and
• Surveys of random samples of students from the whole network.

Mini-grant-Supported Campus Projects Focused on Deep Engagement

Mini-grant opportunities were created for campuses that then selected one or a few community partners and designed a strategy to integrate social media with the partners in ways that enhanced their work. Fifteen campuses were awarded sub-grants in this vein. This resulted in concrete partnerships with a number of different types of agencies in locales around the country. Each campus worked closely with its partner to define the projects and use of social media; these projects ranged in time from about one year to three years. The summary of some campus projects listed as follows provides some rich details about how programs integrated technology:

Concord University: focused on homeless serving organizations in West Virginia, creating and shared a series of videos, connected to service trips, to educate students and the public.

Davidson College: collaborating with the Lake Norman Community Development Council in Davidson, the college created training and capacity-building strategies for nonprofit agencies and their staffs.

Hamilton College: expanded services and economic opportunities for local refugee and immigrant populations in Uttica. Students and faculty conducted policy research, and created videos, a blog, and wiki to address the needs of this population.

Stetson University: focused on youth empowerment with CAUSE, a youth-led organization, in Spring Hill and Pierson. Facebook, wikis, and videos were utilized to raise funds, promote volunteerism, and enhance capacity.

The College of New Jersey: leveraged social media to increase faculty engagement through online project design spaces for community-based learning initiatives, 30 community engaged learning days (through which 1,600 freshmen complete eight hours of required service) in Trenton, and upper-division coursework.

University of California Berkeley: engaged graduate students in computer programming and a partnership with Volunteer Match, creating a visual mashup to drive broader student engagement with local California schools and youth.

University of Louisville: focused on arts, history, social justice, and diversity issues in partnership with Louisville's Frazier International History Museum, creating customized social media tools for interactive, educational activities.

Broader Efforts to Build Networked Capability

In addition to activities focused on respective local partners and communities, the Bonner Foundation and network experimented with social media platforms to increase the quality and efficiency of communication in a national, multicampus network. Prior to its application, campus staff and students (of which there are more than 150 and 3,000 respectively) had to rely on interactions with few foundation staff (numbering 8) to share resources, program models, and best practices. This dissemination of information and resources happened primarily through annual meetings, visits, and phone calls. By leveraging social media, the network could amplify one of its core tenets: *turn best practice into common practice.*

An example elucidates: Prior to Serve 2.0, the Foundation shared resources—such as trainings and reflection modules, event-planning guides, service immersion trip guides and partners, and staff handbooks—on a conventional website. This site was mainly static and did not provide an avenue for regularly communicating information and lessons learned by campuses. Four years later, the Bonner Network Wiki, created through the project, contains more than 4,500 pages of resource material and has had more than 800 people add and edit content. This allows for more rapid proliferation of information related to program development, management, and innovation, increasing program quality.

Social media also provided a way for students, staff, faculty, and alumni to connect with each other directly, and across campuses. For example, platforms like Facebook and LinkedIn are enabling the reconnection of Bonner alumni (now numbering more than 6,000) to reconnect with each other and current students. LinkedIn enables alumni—one-third of whom work for nonprofits, one-third in government, and one-third in for-profits or other careers—and students to network for jobs, internships, and issue-oriented projects. While not novel, these tools enhance the capacity of the Foundation and network to do more and do it better without significantly increasing staffing. When social media has been applied on the campus level, with the engagement of students in leadership roles, similar improvements in management and efficiency have been witnessed.

What We Learned

Our lessons learned are organized into the following areas: (1) What impact the initiative had on program capacity and coordination with others on campus and in the community; (2) how online tools played a role in building the capacity of nonprofit partners to achieve their missions and run high-quality programs; and (3) recruiting new volunteers and building greater levels of student engagement.

Program Capacity and Coordination

We wanted to know if using online tools could streamline program management and increase the capacity and exposure of campus programs. If students could access information about opportunities online, not in a binder, would more students get involved? As a result of different campus cultures and structures, uses looked different on each campus and students and staff played various roles.

Staff Perception and Use of Social Media Changed

There was trepidation among some staff (and some students) about using online tools. One reason was the conceptualization that Bonner program work is about *place* and some might fear that a choice was being presented: *online or offline*. The discussions and trainings were led by Heather Cronk, then at the New Organizing Institute, who encouraged staff and students to think about *purpose*, rather than a choice. Instead of a question of "online or offline," the discussion was focused on what a campus was trying to achieve, and how specific online tools may be helpful in forwarding the goal(s). While this reframing ended up being helpful for many staff, privacy and permission issues also needed to be dealt with on a campus and individual basis. For example, campuses that worked with youth or through local high schools or middle schools encountered new processes in order to get permission from partner schools and parents.

Campuses found that it was crucial not to use too many tools and confuse people. One staff member noted, "The main challenge in digital communication is that our campus is so inundated with digital and social media that it takes a lot to get their attention." Knowing the culture of the institution and how students and partners spend their time was important to use the most popular or already used social media sites. About a third of responding campuses reported that texting and Google tools are crucial to running their programs. One staff member stated, "We use texting all the time with our students. We find that they have their phones with them and it is much faster to get a response than email. Our campus email system is very cumbersome and not many students use it on a regular basis." Few campuses are using blogs; while many aspire to use this platform for reflection, it remains a more difficult tool.

Increasing Coordination On and Off Campus

Staff members told us that *coordination has increased* with other offices or programs on campus. In particular, almost all of the campuses said that coordination increased with non-Bonner students (89%) and with student organizations (78%). One campus wrote that this happened "Simply by getting our Bonner name out there and having more campus constituents understand and engage in our work and events."

> I think social media tools have helped us become more organized, market to a wider audience, and saved a significant amount of time with systems and reporting.

Students also agreed with this; roughly 70 percent of students randomly surveyed from the broader Bonner network agreed that social media tools being used by their Bonner program are increasing their coordination with other offices/programs on campus. There was a direct correlation between students who used online tools in connection to a Bonner project and belief that those tools were increasing coordination. In addition, those students who thought that social media and online tools are increasing coordination were also more likely to say that they themselves had done additional and better service because of these tools, and have engaged someone else with these tools.

> Again, the biggest challenge is participation. Some organizations/people discourage change and integration. This project is just that, a way to integrate people in a way that connects them and provides a constant flow of information. The best way we have been able to tackle these challenges is to continue to use the social media tools in ways that help organize and coordinate student projects.

In particular, Facebook was highly utilized. Students have used the platform extensively for a variety of community engagement activities, including planning a service event, planning a campus-wide event, and recruiting and collaborating with other student groups.

Promoting Campus-wide Engagement and Issue Awareness

Campuses have untapped potential for using social media to tell the story of their service work (told through blogs, wikis, videos, etc.); they have focused largely on these tools for management and coordination purposes. However, this is an area where third-party help (e.g., groups that specialize in producing recruitment videos) could be useful.

Campuses also used social media to promote student engagement in service, large-scale and campus-wide events, and awareness of issues. Students at College of Saint Benedict and Saint John's University created videos that highlighted homelessness in Minnesota and profiled the work of a local nonprofit partner, Place of Hope. They embedded videos on Facebook and on their center's website, and sent them along with e-mail blasts to invite students to a large event, Empty Bowls, that would benefit this and other local partners. Nearly a *third of the campus* turned out for this event. Reflecting on the usefulness of videos, a staff member noted:

> Videos provide a simple emotional response. Our campus utilizes and creates videos to communicate support for our nonprofits, social justice issues, and awareness at large.

Common Technology Applications for Partnerships

Sub-grantee campuses elected to focus on a relationship with a community partner and apply social media to benefit that work (Table 15.1). Over the course of three years, roughly 60 partners were involved in the projects by the 15 campuses. Descriptions of some of these partnerships were already shared, and the larger number of partners is the result of strategies that some campuses used to maximize information-sharing (e.g., University of California Berkeley's mash-up of school-based program opportunities) and capacity (e.g., Davidson and Stetson's training model).

Campuses working with low-income communities performed usage assessments to better understand levels of knowledge, and hardware and Internet access. This is one of the areas for innovation and where institutions can act as capacity builders. Others cited specific issues with introducing the social media tools to community partners. One reported: "There is a lot of hesitation from people that are first beginning to use specific social media tools. I think the best way to overcome this hesitation is to sit down one on one with

Table 15.1 Community engagement purposes of social media tools

Online tool/technology	Purposes campuses most often used the tool for
Facebook	Planning service and campus-wide events (i.e., posting news and ads); recruitment; communication or other work with community partners; alumni connections
Text messaging	Planning service and campus-wide events (i.e., texting meeting details); communication or other work with community partners
Videos	Recruitment (i.e., promotional videos); communication or other work with community partners; issue awareness/education (i.e., training for public education and advocacy)
Twitter	Used by individual faculty for courses (i.e., tweeting readings or reflections); used by student leaders to signal immediate news for organizing meetings and projects (with student participants following feed)
Online collaborative tools/Google tools	Collaborating on events/projects with faculty or other campus departments (i.e., workspace to design new courses)
Wikis	Planning service events; working on projects to benefit service site (i.e., featuring community partner profiles and student volunteer long-range plans)

them and show them how easy it can be to use." Another wrote: "Our community is still behind and feels the effects of the digital divide. As our state moves forward with technology we will see this gap move closer together."

Using Online Tools within Community Partnerships

Campuses had both excitement and trepidation about the idea of using online tools within a community partnership. Some staff were worried that almost any online activity would deter from relationship building and authenticity. In 2008, 92 percent of responding campuses in the Bonner Network had never used or tried Facebook, wikis, or videos to contribute to a relationship with a community partner. In 2011, 25 percent of campuses used Facebook to communicate with community partners either once a semester, monthly, or weekly; 10 percent via a wiki; and 12.5 percent were using videos with community partners at least once each year.

Sub-grantee campuses elected to focus on a relationship with a community partner and apply social media to benefit that work. Over the course of three years, roughly 60 partners were involved in the projects by the 15 campuses. Descriptions of some of these partnerships were already shared, and the larger number of partners is the result of strategies that some campuses used to maximize information-sharing (e.g., UC-Berkeley's mash-up of school-based program opportunities) and capacity (e.g., Davidson and Stetson's training model).

A different subsample of partners was surveyed each semester (by CIRCLE), and all partners surveyed at end of project. As noted previously, partners represented a diverse group of organizations: youth centers, schools, immigrant centers, museum, and an arts cooperative. Through this, 93 percent of community partners agreed that their "organization is better able to meet its mission because of the college student service related to this project." Students were asked, "To the best of your knowledge, how has your Bonner program's use of online tools or social media changed your service work or relationship to the community partner(s) that you worked with this year?" To this, 58 percent answered "Very positively" or "Positively." Moreover, the remaining students said "No Impact" and *no students at all* reported a negative impact.

We also tried to understand whether online tools facilitated more exposure for the partners. At the launch of the initiative, 67 percent of community partners said that the tools being used were "increasing your access to other students, staff/faculty, offices or programs on this particular campus." This decreased through the grant, though that makes some sense that the initial use would have the greatest impact. We also found that the online tools also increased some partners' access to those they did *not* already know (from the college or community); an average of 27 percent saying that they agreed or strongly agreed that the projects did this.

Student Engagement and Development

Much discussion about the Internet and young people focuses on how much time youth spend online and whether or not it is useful. This project took this question on to see how online tools could be leveraged for more and deeper engagement.

Student Leadership, Skills, and Competencies

Many campus staff reflected that student ownership in Serve 2.0 projects was critical. Some staff members thought that the skills students develop coordinating a project could be helpful in the future, providing them with marketable skills and an understanding of how tools can be leveraged for civic goals. A majority of students whom we asked also thought that they would be using online tools and social media in jobs after graduation. A staff member reflected that students needed to "think more about how [they are] communicating their message and be held accountable for that at a different level; develops a skill set that most college students don't as representing a program, not representing just self anymore. [They] have to look at it with a different lens."

A challenge, however, was finding and retaining the students interested in taking this on these roles. Many staff still felt that students were wary about using some social media, such as Facebook, for these purposes. This may have been an issue of exposure to organizational uses of online tools, or that some students were also cautious about how online tools would influence local relationships. A critical step is identifying leadership for this work:

> The biggest help is finding people who are excited and want to take on a piece of this initiative. The biggest challenge is deciding how to "market" (for lack of a better word) the initiative and maintain the motivation for it in the midst of so many other projects and tasks. Getting students to buy-in and be more involved in the process and creation. Many of the students in the program are averse to using the technology for work purposes.

A solution to student attrition (i.e., a talented senior builds the wiki and Facebook, but it is hard to recruit another when she graduates) that some campuses tried was to tie the work into an ongoing position (i.e., student internship). The need for special expertise (e.g., video-editing skills) made this more difficult than other hiring; however, staff members reflected that the payoff could be big for the program and students, making it time well spent:

> Students are very savvy in using social media tools and community partners need students to utilize these tools effectively. Students can be uniquely situated to help these partners learn and develop an understanding for how they can leverage online tools.

While already-engaged students were taking leadership, we also wanted to know if new outreach strategies recruited more volunteers. Roughly 28 percent of Bonner student respondents said that they engaged *someone else* (another student, another volunteer) in providing service as a result of using online/Internet programs or social media tools. More students reported engaging non-Bonner students in service *because of* using online/Internet programs or social media tools. On the whole, just less than half of the student respondents think that their campus has done *additional community service as a result* of using online/Internet programs or social media tools to organize service. Slightly more were neutral.

A similar dynamic was observed within campus Bonner Programs: 37 percent think that on the whole, their Bonner Program did additional community service as a result of using online/Internet programs or social media tools to organize service. A full fifth of respondents disagreed with this, suggesting that social media used by Bonner programs is affecting the larger campus service, rather than getting Bonner students to do more.

In addition to using social media to mobilize student awareness about issues and prompt volunteer commitments, programs have utilized these platforms to expand students' notions of and experience with civic engagement. Students at Macalester College created video trainings in preparation for students' involvement with public education and lobbying. Students at West Virginia Wesleyan College used YouTube, Facebook, and blogging to support the newly formed Main Street Arts Co-Operative in Upshur County as a community and economic development initiative involving local artists.

Conclusion

Was all of this effort to create videos, build and maintain wikis, manage and populate Facebook pages and groups worth it? In reflecting on the project and the results of our investigation and analysis, we would reiterate the following:

- Campus experiments suggest that social media and technology tools can be effectively leveraged to *increase the reach* of campus-based service and community engagement programs and efforts. They do this by reaching uninvolved students and other volunteers and by connecting engaged individuals with each other, with knowledge, and with information that builds their capacity and efficiency.
- *A focused, purpose-driven design works best.* While it is helpful to try a lot of tools, the purpose and needed function should drive the design, integration, and maintenance of these platforms. As a result, keeping online and offline efforts fairly integrated and streamlined is important.
- Programs (clubs, campuses, and partners) must think about *training and leadership development* in these roles. Students, staff, partners, and faculty have to be willing to spend time on the platforms and the constantly evolving technology and uses to keep them fresh, in order for them to contribute to the goal(s).
- The tools are *not a panacea for the challenges* common in offline community engagement. Having a solid vision, strategy, implementation plan, and attention to details is still important. While these tools may replace the two-inch binders in service centers, they are not a replacement for effective, professional, and continual communication, but a part of it. Online and offline strategies can reinforce each other, but face-to-face interaction is still an important part of most of our daily and weekly work.

We were encouraged by one finding suggested by our final student survey. We were curious if these platforms—known best for their social networking—would lead students to other forms of engagement, a sort of connecting the dots from their direct service work to understanding root causes, finding organizations or groups that delved deeper, or identified strategies for making systemic change. In fact, we found that for the most part, the students who have used online tools and social media as a part of Bonner also are *more likely to engage in the online political activities (our data suggest correlation, but not causation).* This suggests the need for more study and exploration in this learning context. New scholarship, such as EduCause's publication *Game Changers* (Oblinger, 2012), Christensen and Eyring's *The Innovative University* (2011), and Bowen's *Teaching Naked* explore the potential of new approaches for leveraging technology (open source, learning analytics, flipped courses, gaming, crowd sourcing, Massive Open Online Courses [MOOCs], etc.) to change and improve teaching, learning, and engagement. We are eager to continue finding strategies to leverage technology for deepening community engagement, especially in ways that involve intentional integration of deeper learning about the ways to achieve impact on the issues of education, health, poverty, economic development, and so on, where students and institutions are contributing and learning.

References

Bennett, W. Lance, Chris Wells, and Allison Rank. "Young citizens and civic learning: two paradigms of citizenship in the digital age." *Citizenship Studies* 13, no. 2 (2009): 105–120.

Bowen, José Antonio. *Teaching Naked: How Moving Technology Out of Your College Classroom Will Improve Student Learning*. San Francisco, CA: Jossey-Bass, 2012.

Christensen, Clayton M., and Henry J. Eyring. *The Innovative University: Changing the DNA of Higher Education from the Inside Out*. San Francisco, CA: Jossey-Bass, 2011.

Cohen, Cathy J., and Joseph Kahne. "Participatory politics: new media and youth political action." *Youth and Participatory Politics Network*, MacArthur Foundation (2012).

Edison Research (n.d.). Twitter Usage in America 2010. Retrieved from www.edisonresearch.com/home/archives/2010/04/twitter_usage_in_america_2010_1.php

Howe, Neil, and William Strauss. *Millennials Rising: The Next Great Generation*. New York: NY Vintage, 2000.

Kahne, Joseph, Lee, Namjin, and Jessica Timpany Feezell. "." Youth and Participatory Politics Network. Retrieved from http://ypp.dmlcentral.net/sites/all/files/publications/OnlineParticipatoryCultures.WORKINGPAPERS.pdf

Kawashima-Ginsberg, Kei. "Summary of Findings from the Evaluation of iCivics' Drafting Board Intervention." CIRCLE Working Paper #76 (2012). Retrieved from www.civicyouth.org/icivics-drafting-board-module-boosts-students-writing-skills/

Levine, Arthur, and Diane R. Dean. *Generation on a Tightrope: A Portrait of Today's College Student*. San Francisco, CA: Jossey-Bass, 2012.

National Conference on Citizenship (2008). Civic Health Index: Beyond the Vote. Retrieved from www.ncoc.net/97

National Conference on Citizenship. (2009). America's Civic Health Index: Civic Health in Hard Times. Retrieved from www.ncoc.net/2gp54

Oblinger, D. (2012). *Game Changers: Education and Information Technologies*. Washington, DC: Educause. Retrieved from http://www.educause.edu/research-publications/books/game-changers-education-and-information-technologies

Prensky, M. "Digital natives, digital immigrants." *On the horizon* 9(5) (2001): 1–6.

Ratliff, A. "Are they listening? Social media on campuses of higher education." *Journal of Technology in Student Affairs* (Summer 2011). Retrieved from http://studentaffairs.com/ejournal/Summer_2011/AreTheyListening.html

Smith, A. *The Internet and Campaign 2010*. Washington, DC: Pew Research Center, 2011.

CHAPTER 16

Strategic Planning for Centers: Fostering Pervasive, Deep, Integrated, Developmental Community Engagement

Ariane Hoy and Mathew Johnson

Strategic Planning in Higher Education

Strategic planning provides an opportunity to exercise a basic human capacity: to envision a future and strive toward that vision. As Dooris, Kelley, and Trainer (2004) note, planning enables *intentionality*, allowing individuals to apply an "ability to formulate goals and proceed toward them with direct intent." Strategic planning is a disciplined effort to produce fundamental decisions and actions that shape and guide what an organization is, what it does, and why it does it (Allison & Kaye, 2011). In higher education, long-range planning—which aligns the institution around its mission, vision, and values as well as articulates goals, logic, strategies, tactics, steps, and necessary resources—is more critical than ever. Most broadly, it allows institutions to clarify mission and purpose, recruit and retain students, attract hire and motivate faculty, plan and maintain facilities, strengthen their programs and student success, and remain financially solvent. Strategic planning witnessed an expansion in higher education through the 1960s, prompted in part by the founding of the Society for College and University Planning (SCUP), but was mainly dedicated to campus physical planning (Dooris et al., 2004). The 1980s saw institutional planning increase, especially following the 1965 and 1972 Higher Education Opportunity Acts, subsequent growth of institutions and enrollment in the 1970s, and rising costs. Publications such as George Keller's 1983 *Academic Strategy* heralded the emerging importance of strategic planning. Later, this practice was highlighted by accreditors, such as the 1998 Council for Higher Education Accreditation's Recognition Standards' requirement of "evidence of policies and procedures that stress planning and implementing strategies for change" (Dooris et al., 2004). Today, visioning is a part of the landscape for higher education, reinforced by accrediting bodies.

Has strategic planning been well utilized by centers of community engagement? When and why is it helpful or necessary? In our experience, which draws upon two decades' work with a national network of colleges and universities and their community engagement programs, strategic planning indeed supports a center and institution in pivotal ways. Long-range visioning supports program quality, helps clarify staff structure and roles, connects civic work to the institution's priorities and strategic plans, garners visibility, and secures financial and human resources. A third party, such as a foundation or higher education association, can play a critical role in helping to structure, guide, and facilitate these processes for campus centers, while informing and connecting this work with broader institutional trends and planning.

Strategic planning can also aid the institution in documenting its effective practices as well as aspirations for enhancing the quality of engagement. For the 2015 application of the Carnegie Classification for Community Engagement, a voluntary classification for which institutions of higher education apply to be recognized for their engagement work, evidence of the depth, pervasiveness, and integration of engagement will be needed. According to the Carnegie Foundation for the Advancement of Teaching, the application process involves "data collection and documentation of important aspects of institutional mission, identity and commitments, and requires substantial effort invested by participating institutions. Additionally, "The classification is not an award. It is an evidence-based documentation of institutional practice to be used in a process of self-assessment and quality improvement" (Carnegie Foundation, 2013).

Serving as an external source of networking, best practice sharing, and resource development has long been a function of the Bonner Foundation. Early in the Bonner Program's design, the foundation asked each institution to create a five- to ten-year plan for its program and center. In the mid-1990s, foundation staff partnered with other consultants, such as the Foundation Strategy Group, to distill the structures, institutional commitments, and best practices for institutionalizing (and endowing) campus centers. Most recently, this process has emerged from close working relationships with center staff as they navigate more complex decisions about the next stages of their work, including development of academic linkages, integration with student success, and restructuring centers. The recognition that community and civic engagement faces a critical moment—when strategies to make it *pervasive, deep, and integrated* across the institution are needed—has again fueled its importance. Planning supports institutions to enact their own *developmental* growth. Centers and programs today aim to increase meaningful campus-wide student engagement that is connected to the curriculum; carve their roles in fostering institutional learning outcomes such as citizenship, leadership development, and vocation; and cement integration of engaged learning and practice.

The Impetus for Strategic Planning for Community Engagement

Each year, administrators in the Bonner Network gather for planning, sharing best practices, and addressing core challenges surfacing at that time. These administrators are generally the directors of on-campus centers. Many of them teach, and a good number of them are also faculty members. Some centers reside under student life and others under academic affairs. In some cases, these centers fall under religious life or a chaplain's office, or in another unique entity (such as a broader consolidated center that focuses on civic engagement, diversity, and global experience or a dean of studies connected to both academic and student affairs). Regardless, each center must carve out and sustain relationships across campus with a range of other offices—academic departments, multicultural affairs, admissions, financial aid, development, and so on.

The Bonner Program and Foundation's approach to working with campuses is characterized as a long-range approach; relationships exist over multiple years and even decades. This allows for a *developmental* approach, not only for supporting students' learning but also for supporting the ongoing development of staff and faculty, as well as center and campus infrastructure. Hence, centers for community engagement can pursue large and ambitious visions, perhaps years away from implementation, but continue to make progress in building the capacity, structure, and resources needed to move toward that vision. This is important to deepening community engagement—for instance by systematically adding a high-level research and capstone component to students' four-year engagement or by increasing effective engagement of faculty across the institution in sustained, multiyear partnerships.

As we have surfaced and tackled challenges, one issue that repeatedly arises is the need for externally oriented long-rang strategic planning, connecting the center's work with the institution's plans. Most programs' staff engage in planning for a semester or even a year, but mapping out a three- to five-year strategy is not common. Moreover, staff want ways to concretely articulate the achievements, resource needs, and importance of their centers within a broader institutional context, especially to institutional and academic leadership. Staff want traction in moving civic work to the forefront and core of the institution's values, connecting it with academics and commanding more resources. Staff members also report that they often are so busy with the demands of day-to-day program management, student advising, and event management that making the time for critical but not urgent activities (like three- to five-year strategic planning) can be difficult. At times, this has led to a kind of "stuckness" where creativity and innovation is lost or diminished, perhaps because of prior difficulties or ingrained patterns. At times, this contributes to centers and programs sustaining initiatives that may no longer be productive. For example, what may have arisen (i.e., a campus-wide service day) due to the outstanding leadership of a group of students and staff becomes an annual project, involving hundreds of hours of staff and student labor but translating into little results in terms of generating new ongoing volunteers, community impact, or institutional support.

Making Better Use of Data and Experience

Through a partnership with Siena College's Siena Research Institute, campuses have participated in a nationally available assessment called the National Assessment of Service and Community Engagement (NASCE). (For more detailed information, see the chapter "An Untapped Reservoir for Student Community Engagement: What We Are Learning from the NASCE" in this volume.) After completing the NASCE, the institution receives a comprehensive report about institution-wide student engagement. These data provide an analysis of the levels of engagement and issue areas—youth development, working with the elderly, environmental work, and so on—where work is strongest and weakest. In addition, it paints a picture about the degree to which students' capacity for involvement has been tapped. Are 10 percent of students doing 80 percent of the service? Are the vast majority of students not involved in any way (despite large-scale service events)? When campuses took a hard look at these reports, their staff began to ask questions about the best way to move forward.

We were asked, then, to assist campus staff in making the best use of these data and others—such as the National Survey of Student Engagement (NSSE) or inventories of faculty involvement in service-learning. As a result, we designed a simple but powerful process for strategic planning. We drew on experience of other institutions of higher education that had conducted planning for civic and community engagement, researching effective methods. We opted for a strategy that could be accomplished in a condensed period of time, about a day and a half. We also opted for a strategy that could position and empower staff as agents of leadership and strategic direction within their own contexts. Campus staff act as convenors, inviting a core group of constituents including center staff, faculty members, community partner representatives, student leaders, and academic leadership (i.e., the provost or vice president of academic affairs). At times, alumni have also been involved, some of them who continue to work with the college and center as community partners.

The Process

In looking at the application of strategic planning in higher education, Dooris et al. found that three themes had arisen. First, they noted that "a rational-deductive, formulaic approach to strategic planning is being tempered with a cultural-environmental-political perspective" (2004, 7). Second, they found that effective planning is often more about learning and creativity, providing an opportunity to challenge assumptions and change structures and processes. It is characterized by synthesis. Third, they noted a growing emphasis on moving from "formulation to implementation, from plan to practice" (8). Indeed, our process mirrors these three themes. We rely heavily on collaboration, in which participants freely share their ideas and observations, and we as facilitators help guide them to synthesize and integrate insights, often involving structural or programmatic changes. The process involves visual planning, with large-scale posters and use of sticky notes. This process also emphasizes future-oriented visioning, dialogue to surface and claim prior successes, and reframing problems as opportunities to counter patterns of inertia or stuckness. With attention to the key constituencies involved in community engagement (students, staff, faculty, and community partners), we generally cover the following through a guided, interactive process:

- *Ground rules* and expectations;
- Sharing relevant program and institutional *history*;
- A *context map* activity that surfaces aspects of the community and institutional environment, especially regarding the needs of students, faculty, the institution, and the neighborhoods or places where institutional engagement is concentrated;
- An analysis of strengths, problems, opportunities, and threats;

- A review of *relevant data*, such as NASCE or NSSE data on student engagement;
- *Long-range visioning* for a three- to five-year period, drawing on the insights and analysis in order to articulate broad categories and detailed projects and plans;
- Revisiting the *mission and language* used to describe the center's and institutional aims for community engagement;
- *Action planning* and the creation of tangible work plans and timelines for implementation;
- At times, *a stakeholders' analysis*, in order to discuss how else the team might engage relevant constituencies for additional planning.

In addition, during these planning processes, *on the first day*, we document information generated into a structured, written plan. The draft of this plan is typically presented during the process, *on the second day*, so that the team involved *immediately* sees the results of their work *in writing* and in a format that can be shared more broadly. This written strategic plan generally includes the following:

- *Context* suggesting the history and achievements and laying the groundwork for broad far-reaching vision and goals;
- *Vision and/or mission statement* (for the center and/or institution related to community engagement);
- *Definition and description of the center* and its prominent programs and work (eliciting *action-oriented* verbs such as "engage," "inspire," and "connect" that describe what the center *does*);
- *Strategic initiatives*, with tangible and timed (i.e., six-month, one-year, three-year) objectives for each;
- *Detailed action plans* for each strategic initiative, generally in the form of a table including a break down by year (i.e., Year 1, Year 2, Year 3) with what needs to be done, costs, and responsible person/team.

For each strategic initiative, see Table 16.1.

Themes from the Planning

By 2013, we will have completed planning with 18–20 campuses (and had done so with 12 at the time of this article). In doing so, we have observed several themes that we share briefly, especially as they relate to deepening community engagement in higher education.

Table 16.1 Sample strategic plan: Initiative worksheet

Initiative (1) Create and implement a campus-wide vision for community engagement and social justice.

Outcome (a) Institution will have a community-wide recognizable identity for highly engaged students, faculty, and partners similar to the "athlete" identity.

Total estimated five-year cost: Estimate total cost here

Implementation plan	Year 1		Year 2		Year 3		Year 4		Responsible person/office	Benchmarks
	Do	Cost	Do	Cost	Do	Cost	Do	Cost		
Activity 1: Spell out the overall activity here.	Break it down into yearly pieces here.	Estimate or calculate the annual cost here.							Assign a person(s) responsible for leading the implementation of this activity here.	Specific, measurable, changes that will result from these activities.
Activity 2, etc.										

Coordination and Consolidation

At every campus, a key issue that surfaced is the need to better coordinate the work of community engagement, sometimes requiring structural changes. Many of the campuses are looking at deeper consolidation—for example bringing staff members in multicultural affairs into partnership with community engagement offices or moving the activities of community service, international study, and diversity into a coordinated center. Greater coordination is needed so that professional staff in centers can play important roles in managing sustained, multiyear, and developmental relationships with community partners. Community partners often express a desire for greater coordination with a center if they are working one-to-one with an individual faculty member for one course, but the agency would like to have sustained volunteers over the year or even multiple years.

Barriers to and Opportunities for Faculty Engagement

While the campuses generally have robust structures (many more than ten years old) for students' cocurricular engagement, a key interest is to forge new strategies for connecting engagement with curriculum. These interests range from institutional aims to create integrated student learning outcomes with civic dimensions to strategies for scaffolding courses that involve service-learning, community-based research, and high-impact practices. While many of the institutions have individual faculty members, in few or across many departments, which integrate community engagement, there is a common belief that academic community engagement can be deepened and scaled. Tackling barriers such as the reward structure or the frameworks for faculty tenure and promotion are common themes. Course load, the credit system, and faculty work load and governance frequently surface as areas where change may be needed. Even when some institutions have transformed tenure guidelines, lack of visibility or connections between faculty and center staff has emerged as a challenge.

Student Leadership and Engagement is Not Fully Tapped

These campuses generally have well-established Bonner Programs, which engage cohorts (usually 40–80 students) in the intensive, developmental multiyear program. Most of them also have a range of service clubs and organizations, such as fraternities or groups that plan and run one-time projects. Yet, they recognize that engagement across campus has the potential to grow and deepen. A key theme is the need for structural pathways for students, adequate training and support, and necessary rewards (i.e., including work study or financial aid). The data from the NASCE and NSSE often support this insight and help the planning team to set important goals—such as restructuring student leadership roles—that can support deepening their work. Additionally, centers must put attention on how to structure and grow supportive, empowering student leadership roles.

The Power of Connecting with Institutional Priorities

In all cases, those to whom the center staff directly report, often a Dean of Students, Vice President of Academic Affairs, or Provost, has been engaged in the planning. This provides an important opportunity for integration, giving the team a chance to understand how the outcomes of cocurricular engagement like increased retention and grades mesh with institutional goals. (Note: The Bonner Program's Student Impact Survey and Alumni Survey, discussed in the introduction, found that the *cocurricular* program supports these positive outcomes as well as skill development and postgraduate civic involvement.) Involved institutional leadership often sees that the work of the center builds the *success of the college*, and in response additional resources (such as staffing and increased budgets) have resulted from planning. In addition, this builds the capacity for strategic leadership by center staff, moving them into positions of institutional agency.

Community Partners See the Big Picture

One of the most interesting aspects of this planning has been the degree to which community partners provide critical information, for example, about the community context, economic needs, political issues, and suggested opportunities for the mutual benefit of college and community that can result. Moreover, even while planning has focused more on the needs of the institution than on the commuity, partners often bring critical insight, such as how to structure relationships with faculty or tackle the mismatched academic calendar and nonprofit calendars. We have observed that community partners offer innovative insights to administrators and faculty.

Lessons Learned

We asked that staff members involved in the strategic planning complete a survey in order to share their thoughts and insights about the process. The survey asked surfaced information about:

- The *process* of organizing individuals to participate in the strategic planning retreat we facilitated. For example, what were the challenges or surprises? How did staff get faculty, students, partners, and leadership involved?

- The *learning* that resulted from this process: What were the most helpful insights they had about your institution, center and/or program? What were the most useful components or discussions?
- The *impact* of the process: Did the plan influence institutional resources (budgets, allocation of funds, staffing, etc.)? How has the process or plan changed the operation or functioning of the center? Have there been subsequent meetings or the creation of committees or other structures to do more work on the plan and its implementation? How has the process or plan fostered organizational change?

In the following, we share some of the key insights from the staff. While at this point, this is not a large-scale research project (having involved just eight institutions), we believe that the information may be helpful to others who want to engage in strategic planning. Because of the small number of individuals involved, and concern for privacy, we keep the comments anonymous.

The Most Difficult Part is Getting People in the Room

A common difficulty faced by most of the campuses was that getting key stakeholders to participate could be challenging. Sometimes, this is a function of time (i.e., it is hard to get busy people to long meetings). As one team noted, "It is difficult and basically unrealistic to ask (or expect) faculty, administrators, students, community partners to dedicate that much time. We were lucky to get those stakeholders together for two or three hours." Other times, there are fears about the process, especially if the campus has participated in a lengthy planning endeavor.

Who was most difficult to involve, however, varied. Some found that getting faculty members to participate is challenging. One team noted:

One of the glaring pieces that was missing at our strategic planning retreat was our ability to identify faculty to be involved in the process. Even though our Center for Community and Civic Engagement directly reports to the Vice President of Academic Affairs, at the point we did the strategic planning retreat, we did not offer any academic courses and even though we offered services for faculty (e.g. assistance with developing service learning classes, incorporating CBR projects into the curriculum, etc.) we were rarely contacted to do so. Therefore, we were unable to identify any core faculty to assist us in this process outside of the Center's Director who is a tenured, full professor.

This is an area in which planning propelled change, as the team also noted:

> With the development of the civic engagement minor and our institution's inclusion in the Bonner High-Impact Initiative subsequent to the strategic planning process, we now have several faculty members who are highly involved in the Center's activities and partner with us to engage students in high impact practices. So, while we did not go into this with faculty we felt would be invested in the process, one of the direct results of the strategic planning process, and the way in which it caused us to rethink our mission and role, was to position ourselves to be more inclusive of campus-wide faculty participation and involvement in meaningful ways that benefited themselves and their students.

For another campus, engaging faculty members was easier because of the perception that planning would foster better campus-wide coordination. As the team noted:

> It was easy to get faculty involved because of the dedicated core of faculty we have working on community engagement and interested in the success of these endeavors. Also we have been engaged in strategic planning and curriculum reform, and so I drew on faculty already playing a role in those endeavors. Despite the fact that the time commitment was large, faculty felt a need to help out. Inviting faculty who were not able to come also helped to forge connections.

However, teams noted that the process was helpful in engaging previously uninvolved faculty. Some found that strategically involving faculty who were poised for leadership worked; as one noted, "We were able to get both a department head and long time faculty member involved who were incredibly useful."

The Challenges and Benefits of Partner Involvement

For some, targeting community partners proved difficult. Again, the difficulty depended on a few factors: (1) the level of infrastructure existing at the center; (2) the organization of community partnerships (i.e., teams); and (3) the way in which the process was explained. As one team noted:

> Possibly the most difficult piece, if one could really call it difficult, was thinking about which community partners to invite to the table because

while we have a large number of community partners, we knew going into the strategic planning process that we were going to want to address our relationships with them (i.e. making them deeper experiences for both the students and the agencies). Therefore, thinking about which long-term partners potentially had the capacity to think creatively about how the relationship might evolve became a priority in choosing the participants. This by no means meant that we intended to discount partners that engaged students in meaningful work, but lacked the current capacity to fully implement the developmental model or become high-level coeducators, just that we felt it was important to include individuals that would help us determine how to move these relationships forward and forward in a strategic, realistic way. In the end, we chose three partners that utilized our alumni as site supervisors with the anticipation that they would be able to look at the process from multiple lenses that took into account a variety of stakeholders."

For another campus where the program is relatively new and less well-developed, "deep partnerships" exist, the team noted:

We used the Outreach Office and Bonner Program connections with a variety of community partners, and our network of local educators in the public schools to get community members involved. This group, while limited, was excited about the possibilities to think of how to forge constructive relations between the University and community.

Yet, the process itself led to more commitment by many of the partners involved. One team stated, "Our partners surprised us by being excited to participate and coming up with ideas that actually increased their involvement and commitment to our program."

Importance of Outside, Neutral Observers (Who Can Provide Comparative Perspective)

Even when a campus team faced challenges with securing full participation in the strategic planning or had questions about the process, the team found that having an outside observer was helpful. At the same time, as facilitators we aim to both guide the process and also to help participants identify areas for integration and insights for transformation. In particular, teams were interested in learning about national trends, issues, and themes from across campuses. In addition, much of the usefulness had simply to do with freeing up individuals to reflect on their work without hangups about team roles and dynamics. As one team said:

> The first thing that I think it was important to come away with was that strategic planning is most successful when you have someone from outside your organization facilitate the process. There needs to be someone at the helm that does not have a vested interest in certain outcomes and does not hold a position of power over the members of the group in a way that intimidates or pushes them in a certain direction, but rather encourages full participation and candor in a respectful manner. There is also something about knowing that there are people outside of your organization who know what your final plan is that seems to give some level of accountability to do what you say you will do.

Incorporating the Perspectives and Needs of Institutional Leadership

In every case, center staff reached out to direct supervisors, usually a provost or VPAA, and solicited their involvement. The foundation acted as reinforcement, setting this expectation. While this individual did not participate the entire time and generally confined involvement to a few hours, this engagement proved highly beneficial. It connected the center's planning to institutional planning, as well as broader initiatives, such as accreditation review, a quality enhancement plan, and institutional learning outcomes and curriculum revision. One team noted:

> I asked the upper administration to support this, and they were happy to do this since it fit their ambitions to make community engagement one of the centers of their new strategic plan and ambitious desire to be able to project an image of the University on the move, putting itself at the forefront of higher education in specific ways. I had been working with various administrators on different aspects of the Bonner Program for a year, and used these forged connections to invite Administrators. The Provost's even limited presence was extremely important for setting the tone and expressing support.

Leveraging Institutional Data for Tangible Goals

Each of the campuses was asked to participate in the NASCE as well as to consult other relevant reports and studies, such as NSSE, studies of student retention, and inventories of academic community engagement. This allowed for institutions to set hard goals, for example, about how much they could increase student engagement. One team said:

> We have utilized the NASCE in several ways outside of the strategic planning retreat. One way is that we incorporated some of the data into our informational powerpoint that we use for presentations on campus and in the community. Specifically, one number that we highlight is that 39% of students are not satisfied with their level of engagement in the community at the university. We then connect it to what that means for students, faculty, the institution and the community and how the services we offer to students, faculty and the community can address this. In other words, it has become a part of the way we present and promote our Center as a resource. Another way we have used the NASCE is to support the information we presented in our recent five-year departmental review, especially with regard for areas of future growth and change.

A Written Blueprint Pays Off

As noted earlier, we designed the process so that written results of the group's work are immediately captured. This is gratifying. As one team noted:

> We were amazed and pleased when the facilitators revealed a fairly complete "template" of what we had talked about over the day and half of meetings... it was a great summary and way for us to start/continue the strategic planning that we have now begun to implement. The visioning and bold steps really helped us map out where we want to go as regional leaders. Our administration has taken notice of this and because of the intentionality of the process, has invested dollars and human resources to make it happen.

Moreover, the production of a written plan and its dissemination garner visibility and support. One team stated, "It has opened the door to the great campus community seeing our mission as beyond education to being a community asset with both obligations and responsibilities to the community."

A Jumpstart is Motivating, but Follow-up Is Critical

We found that the process, again collaborative in nature, generally allows the team to reflect on and celebrate institutional achievements. Even when followed by setting ambitious goals for the future, this opportunity to take stock of and note patterns of growth, change, and institutionalization often inspired the core staff team and others involved. One team declared: "We are doing more than we realized. This was an emotional shot in the arm and has really launched us into action...rather than just talking about the future. We're doing it!"

Morever, the teams appreciated having a supportive third party to offer trends, affirm plans, and conduct follow-up. By setting suggested dates for the completion of the written plan and a follow-up communication (generally by phone and/or e-mail, but in some cases a visit), plans were augmented, adding detailed timelines and leadership roles. One team noted: "We revisit it once a month to see where we are and to keep us accountable. Its sheer volume (40 pages) has impressed campus administration, and the intentionality in goals and action steps demonstrates we're serious about this." This has resulted in more institution commitment. That same team reported:

> The administration is now using our plan to help create a campus-wide professional development program to promote high-impact practice in the community engagement component of the new core curriculum. This has generated a new committee of deans and associate deans and a new cohort of faculty. It is helping shape the new core curriculum, legal logistics (MOUs, transportation policy, paying for background checks, etc.). Significant new funds have been allocated to help defray these costs that students used to pay for. We have gotten one new staff line and another is in discussion. The plan has also resulted in some one-time initiative dollars. It has had a huge impact on re-allocating resources for the new community engagement component.

Conclusion

For us as facilitators, the process of being engaged in the long-range strategic planning of many institutions has been rich and rewarding. Not only does it sharpen our own and participants' facilitation, communication, planning skills, observation, integration, and long-range visioning abilities, but it also allows participants and our network to discern *common* and *distinct* themes. Long-range visioning and strategic planning is a key component, we believe, to making community engagement and civic learning, and its power for student learning and community impact, more developmental, pervasive, deep, and integrated.

References

Allison, Michael, and Jude Kaye. *Strategic planning for nonprofit organizations: A practical guide and workbook*. John Wiley & Sons, 2011.

Carnegie Foundation for the Advancement of Teaching (2013). Classification Description: Community Engagement Elective Classification. Retrieved from http://classifications.carnegiefoundation.org/descriptions/community_engagement.php

Dooris, M. J., J. M. Kelley, and J. F. Trainer. Strategic planning in higher education. *New Directions for Institutional Research* 123 (2004): 5–11.

Keller, G. *Academic Strategy: The Management Revolution in American Higher Education*. Baltimore, MD: Johns Hopkins University Press, 1983.

Hoy, A. Personal communication. Survey of team leaders involved in Bonner High-Impact Initiative Cohort One, 2012.

PART V

Critical Insights and Reflections

CHAPTER 17

Transformation Is Just Another Word: Thinking through the Future of Community Engagement in the Disrupted University

Dan W. Butin

Near the end of their chapter about the results coming out of the National Assessment of Service and Community Engagement (NASCE), Johnson, Levy, Cichetti, and Zinkiewicz point out that "NASCE shows that in many areas, little service is done and few students are deeply engaged. This suggests that, rather than being at a ceiling, community engagement in college still has enormous potential to increase" (p. 75). As the Yiddish expression goes, from their lips to God's ears.

I strongly believe that community engagement (an umbrella term that for me denotes a wide range of interrelated practices and philosophies such as service-learning, community-based research, civic engagement, and participatory action research) is an important and oftentimes powerful model of teaching, learning, and research in the academy. However, as I have argued elsewhere (Butin, 2010, 2012a), we have indeed reached an "engagement ceiling" in higher education. Reading this important book has, unfortunately, only reinforced my perspective. Johnson and Levy thus have the facts right and the analysis wrong. And that is problematic for the future of community engagement in higher education if we do not come to better understand how to deeply embed powerful models of community-based teaching and learning in higher education.

I should be clear that the Bonner Foundation is probably one of the most respected organizations in higher education for those of us deep in the weeds of strengthening and institutionalizing civic and community engagement. For over 20 years, they have pushed for a systematic model to support student leadership around issues of community service and impact. Their Bonner Leaders and Bonner Scholar Programs can be found in close to 100 colleges and universities around the country; their linkages of community, curricular, and cocurricular programming is, to my mind, exemplary. As the Bonner Foundation moves toward a similar leadership model for community partnerships (Bonner, n.d.), it demonstrates the possibilities of campus–community partnerships that truly embody key aspects of respect, reciprocity, and relevance.

This makes my reflections about this book ever more difficult. This book contains some wonderful and important chapters full of inspiring programs, people, and results: Cochrane and Schill's chapter about student leadership; Meisel's reflections about Bonner's "journey"; Roncolato's insights about deeper partnerships. All of these and many other chapters are worthwhile reading to better understand what the Bonner Foundation has done and what more can be achieved. But at the same time, these chapters are, for me, primarily examples of the sheer tenacity, vision, and serendipity of individual rather than institutional endeavors. These are programs all too often run on shoestring budgets by overworked faculty and staff making the best of difficult times in institutions of higher education with competing and contradictory missions, policies, and practices around community partnerships.

This in no way diminishes what these programs have accomplished or Bonner's larger mission. Rather, it succinctly highlights how capacity building and organizational change are extremely difficult endeavors with very low success rates in postsecondary institutions (Hannan and Freeman, 1984; Meyer et al., 2007). It, moreover, points to the problematics of overextending our claims of impact (Butin and Saud, 2013; Etienne, 2012) to obscure the reality that campus–community partnerships require patience and perseverance, as does impacting higher education.

It is thus ironic that while most of us work in a field committed to process, we somehow wish that higher education could just be transformed as a product. Put formally, there appears to be a performative contradiction between our explicit scaffolding of students' identity formation and our implicit theories of institutional change. We deeply believe that students must do the hard iterative and dialogical work of action and reflection to come to understand the larger mechanisms and structures of institutional and societal inequities. Yet, at the very same time, we seemingly ignore that institutions of higher education are themselves always-already embedded within some of those same economic, historical, political, and sociocultural contexts. It is thus no surprise that Bonner's programs are powerful examples both of what can be done and the difficulty of doing so.

Let me offer a few examples. Schadewald and Aguilar-san Juan describe an interdisciplinary faculty development seminar—the Urban Faculty Colloquium—that they have been leading at Macalester College. It is a wonderful example of the deep work being done, as they note, to offer faculty a "learning community in which they are able to reflect on their roles on campus and on their place in the larger profession…as they develop themselves into 'civic professionals' " (p. 134). Importantly, they focus on reaching a broad swath of the faculty, since an "individual approach," they write, "risks only attracting the most interested and motivated faculty members. Without a base of support on their own campuses, they may not be able to develop their own interests or create a place for themselves within their institution or in the broader profession" (p. 133).

The seminar is structured around three broad and interlinked learning goals: "engaging the distinctions of 'place'; creating engaged learning opportunities; and supporting inquiries into faculty members' role as 'civic professionals' " (p. 138). Schadewald and Aguilar-San Juan paint a powerful picture of these goals and how faculty "somewhat surprisingly…evinced a hunger to discuss the mesh between and among their academic career paths, personal lives, and commitments to the common good" (p. 142).

Yet, even within this example lurks the omnipresence of the difficulties of success. The very structure of the seminar, they note, is predicated on counterbalancing "the transient nature of higher education, [where] faculty members may lack the knowledge of the local context in which they work" (p. 134). Even more problematically, especially for such a seemingly successful program, is their acknowledgment that the program's accomplishments have depended upon their president's commitment and funding: " 'soft money' has been the [program's] lifeline…Since external funding is never guaranteed, however, the precise future of our efforts is uncertain, and the degree to which various constituencies on campus will continue to work collaboratively is also unclear" (p. 136).

A similar dynamic can be glimpsed within Welch and Saltmarsh's excellent chapter on the key components and structures for community engagement on a college campus. Welch and Saltmarsh synthesize data from applications to the Carnegie Foundation's elective Community Engagement classification (Carnegie Foundation, 2012) with the extent literature to produce a list of key structures and formats for college-based centers focusing on engagement. These include institutional architecture/policy; center infrastructure; center operations; and center programs for faculty, students, and community partners.

Their survey of several hundred directors of such centers revealed how centers have "built upon and expanded" their cocurricular offerings to include "a significant shift and emphasis [towards] academic affairs, including a comprehensive campus-wide coordination of most community-based programming." As such, they argue, "what were once peripheral offices and services a generation ago have evolved into critical and more visible entities on campus with a specific role and mission" (p. 195). This is an important finding and their articulation of the "critical components and essential infrastructure" of such centers should be required for reading at Campus Compact offices around the country.

Yet, what is fascinating from my perspective is that even in their comprehensive review of the Carnegie data and literature review, "three additional items [within the 'Top Ten' list] emerged from the reciprocal validity process" (p. 189). In other words, center directors wrote in additional items not initially captured by Welch and Saltmarsh in their survey typologies. These three—"faculty leadership/buy in," "communication/ outreach," and "cross-campus collaboration"—are, to my mind, symptomatic of directors' worry about the perception of the institutional legitimacy of what they do and their need to signal their allegiance to and involvement in the academic enterprise (Gumport and Snydman, 2002; Meyer and Rowan, 1977).

It is interesting to note that such worries were not discovered in Welch and Saltmarsh's analysis of the Carnegie data and that survey takers actually took the time to write-in these additional components. These three components speak to the potentially peripheral status of such centers and the keen desire by the directors to reposition themselves to be more in line with the traditional epistemological center of the knowledge production and dissemination functions of higher education. The social movement literature, in fact, has long documented how such standard professionalization and formalization mechanisms of repositioning (Staggenborg, 1988) are used to offset the "tyranny of structurelessness" (Freeman, 1972) that bedeviled upstart activist movements. Welch and Saltmarsh may have thus unintentionally highlighted the precariousness of such centers at the very same time that they outline the key next steps for stabilizing these centers for future success.

Let me thus conclude my examples by highlighting Tal Stanley's chapter, since, as usual, Stanley offers a vivid and poignant articulation of the tensions embedded within meaningful community engagement work (see, e.g., Stanley, 2012; Stanley and Fisher, 2001). Stanley is the long-standing director of the Appalachian Center for Community Service at Emory & Henry College and the chair of its Public Policy and Community Service department. In that capacity, he has developed a comprehensive academic program, fostered major local and regional initiatives, and has long argued for a "comprehensive place-based model of education and service...[which] has as its goal the equipping of a citizenship of place with civic and intellectual skills."

This is powerful stuff, and Stanley has every right to be proud of his accomplishments. Yet, this is not where he stands; rather, he bemoans, we are all stuck at a "first order" superficial change as communities "face a loss of vitality and increasingly limited options for sustainable development" and as "the college is failing its 'democratic purpose'...Taken together, all of this suggests that at Emory & Henry we may have reached the limits of what we can accomplish through civic engagement" (p. 101).

In the chapter, Stanley offers a portrait of a difficult situation in one of his courses where community partners, students, and the faculty could not overcome a "thicket" of problems and silences and missed communicative moments. He uses this glimpse into "that January classroom with its walls and thickets" to suggest that perhaps it "demonstrated how unprepared all of us in educational institutions are for the processes required for democratic engagement and that we actually reified and reinforced all of the silences and divisions we were seeking to dismantle."

This is a deeply frustrating realization and Stanley demands that we search for an alternative: "The region needs leaders, citizens, critical thinkers to chart for us a way through the societal challenges it faces" and he as such looks toward better ways to bring together the academy and those outside of the walls. His chapter's focus on "co-educators and co-learners"— supporting both academics and community partners through "relational training and capacity building" (p. 102)—is a lovely reminder that there is a dire need for equal partners in the discussions, practices, and search for solutions to how to support and expand civic engagement.

This sounds exactly right. It suggests that deep community engagement practices such as those which the Bonner Foundation strives to foster are difficult to achieve. It is never easy or obvious how to link theory and practice or how to make what we do meaningful and sustainable to our local communities exactly because contexts and goals are all too often ill defined and the steps forward contestable. That in and of itself is not the problem, as this is what higher education is supposed to excel at: helping students gain the knowledges, skills, dispositions, and practices to make sense of and work within complex real-world domains through a "cognitive apprenticeship" (Barber, 2012; Brammer et al., 2012; Butin, 2012b).

The problem is that we seem to believe that it is possible to move beyond "first-order" superficial change by somehow flipping the NASCE data to suggest that we are on the brink of a transformational moment of moving civic engagement "from the periphery to the center" of higher education (U.S. Department of Education, 2012). But I am not so sure. And, to be honest, neither is this book. There are just enough hesitations, just enough blind spots, just enough "thickets" that I dare say that transformation is just another word. And that is a good thing, for ill-defined problems can only be solved through recharacterization (Lynch et al., 2009).

What I mean is that just as we do not believe that our students can be transformed in a moment, neither can our institutions nor our epistemologies. Rather, those destabilizing moments in the classroom and in the community are the openings of a long and far from stable process of development and discovery. The place-based learning that Stanley embraces is, I would argue, at a very deep level, all there is. They offer the opportunities and the doubts and the insights that become grist for exactly the kind of practices and partnerships that the Bonner Foundation has put at the heart of their goals. But that is all they are: opportunities, doubts, and insights that must be engaged with, deliberated on, and expanded upon.

This, for me, offers an opportunity for a profound grappling with the meaning of such place-based learning. Higher education as we know it is being fundamentally disrupted through demographic changes, market pressures, and technological advancements (e.g., Brint, 2009; Butin, 2013; Christensen and Eyring, 2011; Thille, 2012; US Department of Education, 2010). It has become clear that the monopoly of place-based institutions has been fundamentally shattered and their value propositions put into doubt. And it seems to me that once higher education splinters, so too does any singular or previously obvious notion of community engagement. What thus happens to community-based models of teaching, learning, and research in a postsecondary landscape focused on college completion and workplace readiness? Is there any longer a "place" within an online and automated learning environment? What does justice look like in such an educational space?

What this book suggests for me, to return to Johnson and Levy's phrasing, is that community engagement in college may, indeed, have enormous potential to increase. But I would suggest that it will do so not through the traditional models of service-learning and civic engagement. It will do so, instead, through the tenacity, vision, and serendipity of individuals finding new, dynamic, and powerful ways to make our education matter to our local and global communities. In that respect, the current disruption of the metaphorical and physical walls of the university may yet offer an opportunity to rediscover and recharacterize the very power of community engagement that the Bonner Foundation has put at the heart of its enterprise. From my lips to God's ears.

References

Barber, B. R. "Can we teach civic education and service-learning in a world of privatization, inequality, and interdependence?" *Journal of College and Character* 13, no. 1 (2012): 1–10.

Bonner Foundation. (n.d.). Building and maintaining community partnerships. Available at http://bonnernetwork.pbworks.com/w/page/13112252/Community %20Partnerships. Accessed on January 27, 2013.

Brammer, Leila, R. Dumlao, A. Falk, E. Hollander, E. Knutson, J. Poehnert, A. Politano, and V. Werner. *Core Competencies in Civic Engagement*. Andover, MA: Center for Engaged Democracy Publications, 2012. Available at http://scholarworks.merrimack.edu/ced_pubs/1.

Brint, S. "The Academic Devolution? Movements to Reform Teaching and Learning in US Colleges and Universities, 1985–2010." Research & Occasional Paper Series: CSHE. 12.09. *Center for Studies in Higher Education*, 2009.

Butin, D. W. *Service-Learning in Theory and Practice: The Future of Community Engagement in Higher Education*. New York, NY: Palgrave Macmillan, 2010.

Butin, D. W. "When engagement is not enough: building the next generation of the engaged campus." In *The Engaged Campus: Majors, Minors & Certificates as the New Community Engagement*, ed. D. Butin and S. Seider. New York: Palgrave Macmillan, 2012a, pp. 1–11.

Butin, D. W. "Rethinking the 'apprenticeship of liberty': the case for academic programs in community engagement in higher education." *Journal of College and Character* 13, no. 1 (2012b): 1–8.

Butin, D. W. "No Answers: Rethinking the Relevance of Higher Education in the Age of Learning Analytics." In *Higher Education in an Era of Relevance: How Relevant Should Colleges and Universities be to Society?*, ed. T. Simpson. Blue Ridge Summit, PA: Lexington Books, 2013.

Butin, D. W., and D. Saud. "Pushing back the rhetoric: a review of what community engagement can do." *Michigan Journal of Community Service Learning* (2013): 89–94.

Carnegie Foundation. Classification description: community engagement elective classification. Available at http://classifications.carnegiefoundation.org/descriptions /community_engagement.php. Accessed February 3, 2012.

Christensen, C. M., and H. J. Eyring. *The innovative university: Changing the DNA of higher education from the inside out*. San Francisco, CA: Jossey-Bass, 2011.

Etienne, H. *Pushing Back the Gates: Neighborhood Perspectives on University-Driven Revitalization in West Philadelphia*. Philadelphia, PA: Temple University Press, 2012.

Freeman, J. "The tyranny of structurelessness." *Berkeley Journal of Sociology* 17 (1972): 151–164.

Gumport, P. J., and S. K. Snydman. "The formal organization of knowledge: an analysis of academic structure." *Journal of Higher Education* 73, no. 3 (May/June 2002): 375–408.

Hannan, M. T., and Freeman, J. "Structural inertia and organizational change." *American Sociological Review* 49, no. 2 (Apr. 1984): 149–164.

Lynch, C., K. D. Ashley, N. Pinkwart, and V. Aleven. "Concepts, structures, and goals: redefining ill-definedness." *International Journal of Artificial Intelligence in Education* 19, no. 3 (2009): 253–266.

Meyer, J. W., and B. Rowan. "Institutionalized Organizations: Formal Structure as Myth and Ceremony." *American Journal of Sociology* (1977): 340–363.

Meyer, J. W., F. O. Ramirez, D. J. Frank, and E. Schofer. "Higher education as an institution." In *Sociology of Higher Education: Contributions and Their Contexts*, ed. P. J. Gum Port. Baltimore: Johns Hopkins University Press, 2007, p. 187.

Staggenborg, S.. "The consequences of professionalization and formalization in the pro-choice movement." *American Sociological Review* 53, no. 4 (Aug., 1988): 585–605.

Stanley, T. A. "Building In Place." In *The Engaged Campus: Certificates, Minors and Majors as the New Community Engagement*, ed. Dan W. Butin and Scott Seider. New York: Palgrave, 2012, pp. 153–170.

Stanley, T. A., and S. L. Fisher. "Partners, Neighbors, and Friends: The Practice of a Place-Based Education." *Practicing Anthropology* 23, no. 2 (2001): 19–23.

Thille, C. *Changing the Production Function in Higher Education*. Washington, DC: American Council on Education, 2012.

U.S. Department of Education (USDoE), Office of the Under Secretary and Office of Postsecondary Education. *Advancing Civic Learning and Engagement in Democracy: A Road Map and Call to Action*. Washington, DC: USDoE, 2012.

CHAPTER 18

Integrating Political Activities into Pathways of Engagement

*Abby Kiesa**

I t often seems that dialogue about civic engagement or community engagement—at conferences, trainings, and in research—is framed around a narrow definition of those terms, leaving out political engagement (electoral, policy- and issue-focused, and otherwise). Because our research at CIRCLE (a part of the Jonathan M. Tisch College of Citizenship and Public Service at Tufts University) defines civic engagement broadly and is fueled by ongoing research into youth voting, we are predisposed to think about many ways that youth can or do participate. Some in the field have tried to draw more attention to political engagement through individual sessions at conferences about civic engagement in higher education. For example, I recently participated in one such session at the 2012 International Association for Research on Service-learning and Community Engagement (IARSLCE) conference. Additionally, our colleague, Dean of Tisch College Nancy Wilson, was a speaker at one during the 2012 Association of American Colleges and Universities (AAC&U) annual conference (Hartley, 2012). These observations prompt me to draw attention to the importance of politics in civic engagement.

Several years ago, we collaborated with Nick Longo, Ross Meyer, and the Kettering Foundation to investigate the question. Longo and Meyer wrote a literature review on the topic, and then we conducted focus groups with students about the political system and political engagement.[1] At the same time, the Carnegie Foundation for the Advancement of Teaching and American Democracy Project (the national civic engagement effort of the

254 • Abby Kiesa

American Association of State Colleges and Universities) was working with faculty to study how a variety of courses could address political engagement (the Political Engagement Project), the findings of which were turned into a book.[2] And, recently, the conversation has come up again in reference to a proposed shift from "civic engagement" to "democratic engagement" as a guiding idea (Saltmarsh et al., 2009). In this chapter, I want to summarize and highlight recent data on political engagement and ask how best to promote one element of democratic engagement.

Why Care about Political Engagement?

Sometimes, the conversation about political engagement is framed as a problem about youth—that they just are not into politics, unlike youth of previous eras. The 2002 Campus Compact publication, *A New Student Politics*, suggested that students viewed community service as an "alternative politics" (p. VI), which may lead to additional politically related actions. However, explaining trends solely in terms of young people's opinions and preferences neglects the influence of opportunities and recruitment, which our own research and that of other scholars have found to be significant (CIRCLE, 2012; Godsay et al., 2012; Kahne and Middaugh, 2008; Kiesa et al., 2007). In fact, our focus groups found that students were looking for opportunities for discussion and for helping make sense of issues and the political system (Kiesa et al., 2007).

Several years ago, our focus groups suggested that opportunities for student political engagement were limited. It seemed that for students who are not political science majors, most of the opportunities to become politically engaged seem to come from student groups and organizations that are not directly a part of their college or university. During elections, some campuses do create opportunities for registration or for discussing the campaign, but those are not available at all campuses and rarely happen in nonelection years. Besides, voting is not the only form of political engagement. We learned from evaluating the Bonner Foundation Serve 2.0 initiative (Chapter 16) that students learn about politics outside of institutions, particularly online, by researching and discussing issues. Also, a few college-sponsored programs are described in this volume: The College of New Jersey's (TCNJ) work on local juvenile justice policy (chapter 7), and Emory & Henry College's investigation of local economic policy (chapter 6).

Campuses have found ways to institutionalize other forms of engagement, but less so political engagement. Campus Compact's 2011 annual survey reported that over three-quarters of responding campuses were working on 11 issues that had rather direct policy connections. Yet, our own observations suggest that these connections, and others related to political engagement, are relatively untapped. The state of politics, its hyper-partisanship and polarized positions, may make institutions concerned about how to deal with politics in a fair way and, as a result, many do not try. Saltmarsh, Hartley, and Clayton suggest that "partisan activities and political awareness and agency are being confounded" (2009, 5). But that means that students lose opportunities to learn about the influence of the political system on issues and communities and for high-quality political engagement, and miss alternative models of politics (an example of writing on alternative models is Boyte's *Everyday Politics*).

Many institutions claim that they want to build strong communities, encourage civic learning across disciplines, and support public service and democratic renewal for a strong democratic future. That requires taking into account the broader political context. As Bennett, Wells, and Rank suggest, civic education is lacking when it ignores what students learn elsewhere (2009). Since students learn about politics—in their own life, on social media, on television, in conversation—colleges and universities should help them think through their relationship to the political system.

Is it the Right Thing to Do?

Youth civic engagement is affected by differences in young people's life experiences and opportunities. Educational attainment is one of the most significant factors that influences engagement and is itself affected by families' economic situations (Godsay et al., 2012; Nover et al., 2010; for a comprehensive overview of this dynamic for all ages, see Verba et al., 1995). Our own analysis of many indicators of civic engagement shows that youth with "some college" are more engaged than their peers who have no college experience. Does that mean that when colleges boost their students' political engagement, they are only contributing to a gap in political participation?

Figure 18.1 shows the persistent gap in voter turnout by educational attainment. As noted earlier, voting is only one form of political engagement, and Figure 18.2 takes a broader view. It uses a large set of survey measures of civic and political activities asked by the US Census to divide young adults into six groups, including Political Specialists (engaged in electoral and nonelectoral political activities, but no community ones), Broadly Engaged (engaged in broad range of community but not necessarily political activities), Civically Alienated (participate in no civic activities), and Talkers (discuss issues but not engaged otherwise). Figure 18.2 shows patterns of engagement among 18-to-24-year-olds by whether or not they have any college experience and that young adults with some college experience,

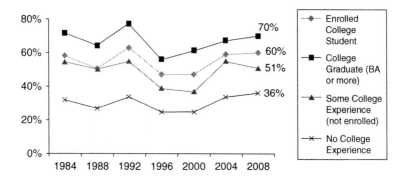

Figure 18.1 Voter turnout in presidential years among 18–24 year old citizens, by college enrollment status.

Source: CIRCLE analysis of Census Current Population Survey, November Supplements, 1984–2008.

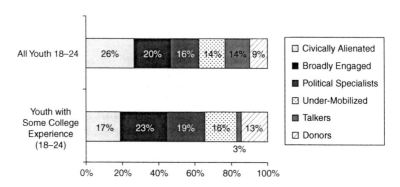

Figure 18.2 Youth civic engagement clusters in 2010 by college experience.
Source: Kawashima-Ginsberg and CIRCLE Staff, 2011.

including current students, are more likely to be Political Specialists or Broadly Engaged than their peers without college experience (Kawashima-Ginsberg and CIRCLE Staff, 2011).

Differences also arise on a single campus. Kawashima-Ginsberg performed a similar cluster analysis of Tufts students (2012) (Figure 18.3). In this case, students fell into the following groups: The Politicals were focused on political actions (including the promotion of voting), following the news, discussing it, and some did other civic and community activities. The Social-Change/Co-Curricular group saw their civic activities as furthering

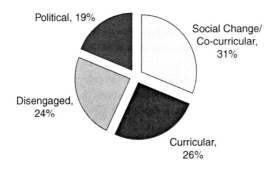

Figure 18.3 Tufts student engagement patterns.
Source: Kawashima-Ginsberg 2012.

social change and were engaged in noninstitutionalized programs (rather than classes). The curricular group did some kind of community service or community-based research through their classes, but often did not see this work as causing social change. The Political group scored high on parents' engagement and personal "sense of purpose," had the highest number of students with a mother with a graduate degree (50%), and were more likely to be male.

It ought to be a red flag that college students' engagement is so much higher than noncollege youth engagement, and that even on a highly engaged and well-resourced campus like Tufts, the politically engaged students are the most advantaged. It is not necessarily problematic for young people to choose their forms of engagement, and for some to make deliberate choices to engage in seemingly nonpolitical ways. However, the data suggest that many young people may not see ways to engage politically or have access to the full range of tools that can create change, including political tools. We ought to ask whether civic engagement programs may be reinforcing some of these patterns: by only serving college students, by drawing the most politically motivated students into political activities, and by offering seemingly nonpolitical, service-oriented alternatives for other students. These questions are especially pertinent for campus-based programs like those in the Bonner Network and others that focus on college access, civic engagement, and public policy.

Can Institutions Facilitate Political Engagement?

It can be difficult and time consuming to facilitate meaningful conversations without being perceived as promoting one party or ideology (as Saltmarsh et al., 2009, also suggest). At the 2012 AAC&U panel referenced earlier, University of Pennsylvania education professor Matthew Hartley suggested reasons why the civic engagement efforts in higher education have histori-cally tended to avoid politics. In his assessment, an "apolitical" movement was "safer"; it could more easily work itself into higher education; and funders were interested in it (Hartley provides context for this "safe strategy" in his chapter "Idealism and Compromise in the Civic Engagement Mosvement," 2011). Certainly, the Corporation for National and Community Service may not support political or partisan activities. In fact, research shows that it does not encourage politics, contrary to suspicions (Finlay et al., 2011). At that same panel, Adam Weinberg, former faculty member and campus adminis-trator and now president and chief executive officer of World Learning, sug-gested that it is a "myth" that funders would be discouraged from supporting student learning and engagement strategies that incorporate political learn-ing and engagement. He spoke of international service trips and the oppor-tunity for learning on those trips and upon return about foreign policy and US impact on the world. Both of these perspectives may hold true. A central factor may be how we explain and defend what we are doing.

A frame that many campuses use or try is what Megivern has proposed, that campus programs should be "political, not partisan" (2010). That is possible; recent data suggest that civic education at the high school level had no influence on students' partisanship or vote choice, which reinforces previous research (CIRCLE Staff, 2013; related to courses, see Colby et al., 2007 and Youniss and Yates, 1997). In seeking to be *non*-partisan, how-ever, colleges and universities should not become *anti*-partisan. Whether to view political parties positively or negatively is a student's choice. Certainly, party identification is strongly correlated with voting (Abramowitz, 2010). Inadvertently driving young people away from parties would most likely reduce political engagement.

Young people also need skills for current political engagement and to be equipped in the future, just as they do for other forms of engagement. Teaching those skills is an area institutions can contribute to, and it takes experience and training. Off-campus groups (such as Oxfam's CHANGE Leaders) often provide such training. I am not sure whether staff and fac-ulty on campuses also feel prepared to play that role. If not, it is a distinct barrier and need. Pedagogical models have been shared among members of American Democracy Project (the national civic engagement effort of the American Association of State Colleges and Universities), based on those who participated in the American Democracy Project's political engagement initiative, but that is a distinct subset of campuses in the United States. The Campus Electoral Engagement Project is attempting to build the capacity of campuses to engage students in major elections. If we are to adopt a full notion of civic learning, then faculty and staff need knowledge, skills, and ideas for how to make that happen.

What Do We Need to Support Institutions?

As with most efforts, the best strategies differ by campus, especially when they take a place-based approach, as at TCNJ and Emory & Henry College (in this volume). At the same time, it can be helpful for people from different campuses to share ideas, and as referenced earlier, provide opportunities for staff and faculty to learn. We can also work together to develop justifications and more models for campus-supported political engagement, perhaps best framed as "democratic engagement."

We should broadly leverage the lessons about campus political engagement already developed. This includes the curricular lessons from the Political Engagement Project, the Kettering Foundation's ongoing inquiry into higher education and democracy, and the ongoing politically focused work of American Democracy Project, in addition to other examples and lessons from individual campuses like some in this volume and elsewhere.

Using these resources, we need to talk about efforts to support student political engagement, and all the complexities, more often. This article raises many of the questions involved, but is not exhaustive of the potential local assets, barriers, and intricacies. More efforts in this area may exacerbate the gap in participation by college experience or cause ideological accusations that will need to be addressed. The solutions may be less difficult than trying to reverse decades of unintentional patterns that could be developing as a result of a lack of more opportunity. Including political learning and engagement into the broader civic work of higher education helps students make sense of civic and community life, provides students with more tools with which they could tackle problems, and more fully invests in the future of democracy. Those working on higher education civic engagement are likely accustomed to working with challenges. Certainly this is one challenge we are more than ready to take head on.

Notes

*I would like to acknowledge the feedback and advice of Peter Levine on this chapter.

1. Longo, Nicholas V., and Ross P. Meyer. 2006. CIRCLE Working Paper #46: College Students and Politics: A Literature Review. www.civicyouth.org/circle-working-paper-46-college-students-and-politics-a-literature-review/

2. Colby, Anne, Beaumont, Elizabeth, Ehrlich, Thomas, and Josh Corngold. 2007. *Educating for Democracy: Preparing Undergraduates for Responsible Political Engagement.* San Francisco, CA: Jossey-Bass.

References

Abramowitz, A. *The Disappearing Center: Engaged Citizens, Polarization, and American Democracy.* Yale University Press, 2010.
Bennett, W. Lance, Chris Wells, and Allison Rank. "Young citizens and civic learning: two paradigms of citizenship in the digital age." *Citizenship Studies* 13, no. 2 (2009): 105–120.
Boyte, Harry Chatten. *Everyday Politics: Reconnecting Citizens and Public Life.* Philadelphia, PA: University of Pennsylvania Press, 2005.
Campus Compact. *Deepening the Roots of Civic Engagement: Campus Compact 2011 Annual Membership Survey Executive Summary.* Boston, MA: Campus Compact, 2012.
CIRCLE. *Pathways to Leadership: A Study of YouthBuild Graduates.* Medford, MA, 2012.
CIRCLE Staff. What do Young Adults Know about Politics? Evidence from a National Survey Conducted after the 2012 Election [CIRCLE Fact Sheet], 2013. Available at www.civicyouth.org/high-school-civic-education-linked-to-voting-participation-and-political-knowledge-no-effect-on-partisanship-or-candidate-selection/
Colby, Anne, Elizabeth Beaumont, Thomas Ehrlich, and Josh Corngold. *Educating for Democracy: Preparing Undergraduates for Responsible Political Engagement.* San Francisco, CA: Jossey-Bass, 2007.
Finlay, Andrea, Constance Flanagan, and Laura Wray-Lake. The Impact of AmeriCorps on Voting [CIRCLE Fact Sheet]. 2011. Available at: www.civicyouth.org/impact-of-americorps-on-voting-study-finds-no-evidence-that-americorps-mobilizes-young-people-politically-non-voters-more-likely-to-enroll-in-program/
Godsay, Surbhi, Kei Kawashima-Ginsberg, Abby Kiesa, and Peter Levine. *That's Not Democracy: How Out-of-School Youth Engage in Civic Life and What Stands in Their Way.* Medford, MA: CIRCLE, 2012.
Hartley, Matthew. "Idealism and Compromise and the Civic Engagement Movement." In *"To Serve a Larger Purpose": Engagement for Democracy and the Transformation of Higher Education*, ed. John Saltmarsh and Matthew Hartley. Philadelphia, PA: Temple University Press, 2011.
Hartley, Matthew. "Where Is the Political in Civic Engagement?" (conference panel, American Association of Colleges and Universities Annual Meeting, Washington, DC, January 27, 2012).
Jonathan M. Tisch College of Citizenship & Public Service at Tufts University. *Typologies of Civic Engagement among Tufts Students: Civic Engagement and Psychosocial Well-Being Study.* Medford, MA: Kawashima-Ginsberg, Kei, 2012.
Kahne, Joseph, and Ellen Middaugh. *Democracy for Some: The Civic Opportunity Gap in High School.* CIRCLE Working Paper 59. Medford, MA: CIRCLE, 2008.

Kawashima-Ginsberg, Kei, and CIRCLE Staff. *Understanding a Diverse Generation: Youth Civic Engagement in the Unites States*. Medford, MA, 2011.

Kiesa, A., A. P. Orlowski, P. Levine, D. Both, E. H. Kirby, M. H. Lopez et al. *Millennials Talk Politics: A Study of College Student Political Engagement*. College Park, MD: University of Maryland, 2007.

Long, Sarah E. *The new student politics: The Wingspread statement on student civic engagement*. Providence, RI: Campus Compact, 2002.

Megivern, Laura E. "Political, not partisan: service-learning as social justice education." *The Vermont Connection Student Affairs Journal* 31 (2010): 60–71.

Nover, Amanda, Surbhi Godsay, Emily Hoban Kirby, and Kei Kawashima-Ginsberg. Electoral Engagement and College Experience [CIRCLE Fact Sheet]. 2010. Available at www.civicyouth.org/electoral-engagement-and-college-experience/

Saltmarsh, J., M. Hartley, and P. H. Clayton. *Democratic Engagement White Paper*. Boston, MA: New England Resource Center for Higher Education, 2009.

Verba, Schlozman, and Brady. Voice *and Equality: Civic Voluntarism in American Politics*. Cambridge, MA: Harvard University Press, 1995.

Weinberg, Adam. "Where Is the Political in Civic Engagement?" (conference panel, American Association of Colleges and Universities Annual Meeting, Washington, DC, January 27, 2012).

Youniss, J., and M. Yates. *Community Service and Social Responsibility in Youth*. Chicago, IL: University of Chicago Press, 1997.

CHAPTER 19

Critical Service-Learning as a Philosophy for Deepening Community Engagement

Tania D. Mitchell

D eepening community engagement speaks to our commitment to develop innovations in community-based learning and service that facilitate transformative experiences. These experiences are transformative for students who, through linking critical inquiry and community engagement, are gaining the knowledge, skills, and values to become "generative citizens," committed to actions that create more equitable systems for the future public good (Musil, 2003). They are also transformative for communities where, through partnerships with higher education institutions, innovative practices create new opportunities to address critical community concerns. Higher education institutions are also transformed as community engagement changes the ways faculty members teach and research, the ways students learn and develop, and the ways lines between campus and community are blurred and reconfigured.

Following the advocacy of Robert Rhoads (1997) for "critical community service" and Cynthia Rosenberger (2000) for "critical service learning," I sought to outline the elements of a critical service-learning pedagogy (Mitchell, 2008). Through a review of the literature, I found that attention to social change, work to redistribute power, and the development of authentic relationships were the particular strategies central to enacting a community-based pedagogy with explicit aims toward social justice.

Lee Ann Bell (2007) defines social justice as both a process and a goal. She presents a vision of the world where the rights of all are valued, respected, and accepted and when access to the opportunities and resources necessary to be your best self is unrestricted. With regard to community engagement, when I think of social justice as a goal, I think about the actions that are needed to move us closer to that vision. But when I think of social justice as a process, I think about the behaviors, the relationships and encounters, we practice every day that remind us how and who we need to be if that goal is ever to be realized.

I would like us to view community engagement with the same process and goal understanding as Lee Ann Bell brings to her conception of social justice. To identify and work toward a vision of our communities that can be seen as *just* while simultaneously working each day to treat each other justly and model relationships and interactions indicative of a more *just world.*

I have considered a critical service-learning pedagogy as a tool for transforming courses and individual experiences of community engagement. However, after reviewing the essays for *Deepening Community Engagement*, I am inspired to think about the possibilities of a critical service-learning framework as a philosophy for institutionalizing community engagement in higher education. In particular, what are the possibilities for institutions of higher education to approach community engagement from this critical perspective? How might our institutional approach to community engagement be shaped by intention and action that bring attention to social change, work to redistribute power, and develop authentic relationships?

To bring attention to social change from an institutional view means that our campuses work with community members to identify assets, concerns, needs, and opportunities that can be leveraged in ways that positively impact the community. Our faculty are encouraged to focus their teaching on concepts, theories, and issues that can be explored and applied in real-world contexts, providing students with the knowledge to recognize structural injustice and the skills to respond. In planning community work, we identify activities, experiences, and interventions that address root causes. And when the service work we do does not target the roots of problems, then we have open and honest conversations about the limits of service to bring us closer to that vision of justice.

This attention to social change can be seen in the commitment to sustained, prolonged engagement that is central to many of the programs described in the chapters of this volume. To deepen community engagement, providing opportunities to lengthen the time students spend in community with a single community agency creates the time to truly understand the issues and assets of the agency, to explore the limits and possibilities of work responsive to the structural conditions that the agency exists to address, and to build the commitment to lifelong engagement in service of social change. The focus on social change is evident in the way Macalester College works to prepare faculty for engaged scholarship and teaching (Aguilar-San Juan and Schadewald, chapter 9, this volume), and in the various classroom conversations that utilize reflexive discourse to create spaces for students to understand their responsibility to improve community conditions. It is evident in the commitment of Allegheny College and University of Minnesota to locate outreach and engagement centers in the community. Through these "community-centered" centers (Roncolato, this volume), community members have access and agency to seek out support and assistance, and campus partners gain insight and access to the neighborhood, its assets, concerns, and possibilities. Campuses create interdependent centers where social change can be visualized, practiced, and hopefully realized.

Actively taking steps to disrupt traditional hierarchical structures in community-engaged scholarship—from making decisions about the kinds of work that will be done in the community to organizing classrooms in ways that honor the knowledge and experience of community members, students, and diverse constituents too often ignored—are key aspects of work to redistribute power. Moving from recognizing power to naming it and from naming power to challenging it brings a critical service-learning lens to community engagement.

As our institutions commit to deepening community engagement, the differential access to power that shapes traditional service relationships requires analysis, dialogue, and discussion. But, it also requires a reconfiguration of community work in order to challenge the "residual legacies" of inequality and interrupt the reproduction of oppressive interactions that can be an unintended consequence of service (Musil, 2003).

We must seek to limit the legacy of disruption that is too often a natural occurrence of community engagement and service-learning. Our emphasis on the academic calendar and on student schedules mean that community agencies are regularly asked to conform their programs to fit what is, at best, a temporary engagement. Roncolato's (chapter 5, this volume) example of the soup kitchen overwhelmed by short-term service-learning volunteers is demonstrative of the harm we can do when we fail to consider power relationships in community engagement. Giving community agencies the space and opportunity to define what a commitment to their organization must look like and being respectful and responsive to those requirements are the very minimum we must do. A longer-term commitment to partnership that is not beholden to the academic calendar and that involves campus partners (students and faculty) in work that has been identified by the community and for which campus partners are adequately prepared can do much to put the power of the service relationship in the hands of community members who should benefit most from the exchange. Creating a role for community members in governance goes even further. The development of advisory boards that involve community members (agency representatives as well as clients and constituents) in leadership and consulting roles that guide campus efforts at community engagement gives the community voice and power in experiences that directly target their work, environment, and lives.

Work to redistribute power means that we should move away from expectations for service commitments in terms of hours in the community. It should mean that we develop meaningful, sustained partnerships where campus partners are able to enter and exit with sensitivity and respect. Where service relationships are not reliant on a single course or experience, but community partners are an institutional priority. To limit the legacy of disruption means that we work to complete the agreed-upon tasks regardless of the time it takes.

Work to redistribute power requires that we honor the expertise community partners bring to engagement experiences and recognize them as coeducators. I agree with Stanley (chapter 6, this volume) that to invite a community partner into the classroom without extending an honorarium "extend[s] the class silences" and reifies unequal power structures (p. 99). Work to redistribute power in a campus–community partnership requires valuing all constituents and their contributions, and remembering that fair compensation is sometimes the best way to do that.

Classroom work to redistribute power shows up in the texts we choose— lifting marginalized voices to introduce concepts, theories, and lived experience, and in the ways learning is facilitated and assessed. Utilizing multiple forms of assessment that involves students (for themselves and for their peers), faculty, and community partners can be a powerful and practical opportunity to engage all parties about the work done, the knowledge created, the understanding developed, and the relationships experienced. Similarly, sharing responsibility for facilitation honors and makes space for the knowledge and lived experience people bring with them to community-engaged learning. It demonstrates that we are all teachers and learners in these experiences, and that we all have something to share and gain through our collective work.

I have seen community engagement experiences where community members (not agency representatives, but the clients and constituents the agency represents) are recognized as learners alongside those college students considered as "official participants." The exchange of ideas and experiences, conversations about texts, and shared work in the community upset expectations and assumptions of those serving and served, those teaching and taught. These efforts demonstrate work to redistribute power and make real the process of social justice—affirming and exercising, in the *present*, the society we want to work toward.

Developing and practicing authentic relationships using a critical service-learning framework as a philosophy for deepening community engagement require us to practice receptivity (Coles, 2011). We must move beyond listening to one another and aim for understanding, committing to the dialogic work necessary to ensure that it can happen. To build authentic relationships means building relationships that are not dependent on one person; committing to relationships that continue beyond the confines of the academic calendar; ensuring relationships disrupt the server–served dichotomy; and allow participants to shift between roles as teacher, student, and person in need. Authentic relationships respect personal histories and build solidarity.

The work (described in this volume) that campuses are doing to organize longer-term service relationships that engage students in progressively deeper and different work for multiple years creates important time to develop authentic relationships. The trust that is developed between campus and community partners as they witness students and faculty return week after week and year after year shifts our work from performance to authentic engagement, demonstrating a willingness to be genuinely and deeply engaged and to be vulnerable to learn. From an institutional perspective, we move from being *in* the community to *part* of the community. We recognize ourselves as interdependent—that the concerns of the community impact our campus and our lives, and that the assets and resources we hold and develop should be shared with our community for the benefit of us all.

The cohort experiences that campus programs have developed for community engagement are another important aspect of authentic relationship building. Cohorts, as a mechanism for engagement, afford opportunities for sensemaking, as knowledge is a product of social action (Weick, 1995). Through the cohort, students (and faculty, as per the Macalester College example offered in this book) work together to make meaning of their experiences and to grow individually and collectively through an environment rich with confirmation, contradiction, and continuity (Kegan, 1994).

Because the relationships provide continuity, cohort members have the time to develop trust and authenticity, which creates an environment for sharing, challenge, and support. Community engagement experiences often create contradiction, by challenging students to test their frames for meaning construction against the reality of current US society. As students encounter experiences with injustice (be it poverty, violence, unequal education), their notions of how the world *is* versus *should be* come into conflict with each other. Cohorts create spaces to process those conflicts, identify strategies to manage and work through them, and develop allies committed to working for change. Confirmation in cohort experiences creates spaces for members to affirm one another in both difficult and positive places. Confirmation honors each cohort member and the experience he or she brings to community engagement—supporting his or her journey and pushing his or her growth. Cohorts create a safe space for members to process, to be vulnerable, to fail miserably, and to be triumphant. It is another effort, through intentional community, to exercise the process aims of social justice.

Developing authentic relationships for community engagement means we develop a shared agenda, acknowledge the power relations implicit in our interactions, and recognize the complexity of identity, understanding that our relationship within the community engagement context is further complicated by societal expectations. It means that despite the complexity, we continue to be in relationship, learning as we go, building solidarity, to realize a vision for community that honors the agenda we have created.

Tony Robinson (2000) once described service-learning as a "glorified welfare state," suggesting that the service work we most often choose for community engagement experiences sustains rather than challenging the status quo. As many campuses near 30 years of community engagement (and some campuses have been doing this work longer than that), what lasting, meaningful change can we contribute directly to our work in communities? What impact do we hope to have that transforms our students, our faculty, our institutions? How do we want the communities where we live, work, and serve to be different?

I believe that deepening community engagement by making our commitments to social justice explicit in our practice and our relationships is the work that we must do if community engagement is to fulfill its promise as a transformative practice in higher education for community and student development. "[S]ocial justice...takes the concerted effort of interdependent stakeholders" who have decided together to work for a more equitable society (Schulz, 2007, 34). A philosophy of critical service-learning that brings attention to social change, works to redistribute power, and develops authentic relationships can support our community engagement efforts to realize more just relationships by empowering communities, educating students, and engaging all of us in work for a better world.

References

Bell, Lee Ann. "Theoretical Foundations for Social Justice Education." In *Teaching for Diversity and Social Justice: A Sourcebook, Second Edition*, ed. M. Adams, L. A. Bell, and P. Griffin. New York, NY: Routledge, 2007, pp. 1–14.

Coles, R. *Cultivating Pedagogies for Civic Engagement and Political Agency: Reflections for Discussion of the Theory and Practice of Democratic Transformations in Higher Education*. Dayton, OH: Kettering Foundation, 2011.

Kegan, Robert. *In Over Our Heads: The Mental Demands of Modern Life*. Cambridge, MA: Harvard University Press, 1994.

Mitchell, Tania D. "Traditional vs. critical service-learning: engaging the literature to differentiate two models." *Michigan Journal of Community Service Learning* 14, no. 2 (2008): 50–65.

Musil, C. M. "Educating for citizenship." *Peer Review* 5, no. 3 (2003): 4–8.

Rhoads, Robert A. *Community Service and Higher Learning: Explorations of the Caring Self*. Albany, NY: SUNY Press, 1997.

Robinson, Tony. "Dare the school build a new social order." *Michigan Journal of Community Service Learning* 7 (2000): 142–157.

Rosenberger, Cynthia. "Beyond empathy: developing critical consciousness through service learning." *Integrating Service Learning and Multicultural Education in Colleges and Universities* (2000): 23–43.

Schulz, David. "Stimulating social justice theory for service-learning practice." In *Race, Poverty, and Social Justice: Multidisciplinary Perspectives through Service Learning*, ed. José Z. Calderón. Sterling, VA: Stylus Press, 2007, pp. 13–30.

Weick, Karl E. *Sensemaking in Organizations*. Vol. 3. Thousand Oaks, CA: Sage Publications, Incorporated, 1995.

PART VI

Conclusion

Future Possibilities: High-Impact Learning and Community Engagement

Ariane Hoy and Mathew Johnson

The High-Impact Community Engagement Practices

As we complete this volume, we also embark on Year 2 of the Bonner High-Impact Initiative, a strategy through which colleges and universities are joining a national learning community to link engaged learning with community-driven practice. Each institution is bringing together faculty, partners, students, and staff to craft initiatives that scale and deepen high-impact practices (HIPs), tying them to community engagement. These teams are participating in long-range strategic planning, attending a summer institute during which they plan high-impact projects, and implementing innovative projects and curricula. In the first year of the initiative, nine institutions participated. Another nine institutions are joining in 2013, and a third cohort will join in 2014. Each commits to at least three years' involvement, after which the project will become a standing initiative of the Bonner Foundation and Network.

The High-Impact Initiative leverages promising research about engaged learning presented in the Liberal Education and America's Promise Report and *College Learning for the New Global Century*, as well as subsequent publications *High-Impact Educational Practices* and *Five High-Impact Practices*. Moreover, the strategy aims to capture and spread best practices of community engagement, drawing on two decades of experience of programs connected to the Bonner Network that have collectively graduated more than 6,000 alumni, most from low-income and underrepresented backgrounds. As the Student Impact Survey and Alumni Survey suggested, the model of a multiyear, intensive, developmental experience in community engagement produces positive results in students' learning, skill development, retention, and completion. Creating an analog to the HIPs, we have begun to articulate high-impact community engagement practices (HICEPs), which can act as multipliers for engaged learning. Thus far, these include:

- *place*—the engagement focuses on understanding and responding to the history, assets, needs, politics, economics, and other facets of the community (i.e., partner, neighborhood, city, polity) where work is occurring
- *humility (co-knowledge)*—the engagement approach affirms that each stakeholder or involved individual (student, faculty member, community partner, elected leader, etc.) brings valuable knowledge and experience to bear for the work
- *integration*—the engagement is created and carried out in ways that fundamentally build across and break down boundaries (such as curricular and cocurricular; disciplinary; or town/gown) and leverages the contributions of stakeholders to achieve learning and change
- *depth*—the engagement fosters pathways for students to carry out multiyear projects tied to their studies, for partners to engage in and benefit from multiyear strategic agreements including capacity building, and for institutions to make sustained commitments through partnerships toward impact
- *development*—the engagement is informed by an understanding of appropriate student and organizational (partner and campus) developmental needs and capabilities, which change and progress over time
- *sequence*—the engagement is structured to include a progression of projects or roles (i.e., for students and faculty) over time (multiple terms) or calendar years; scaffolding both learning and doing
- *teams*—the engagement involves multiple participants (such as student volunteers, staff members, and faculty) with roles and positions that include multiple levels (i.e., direct service, research, capacity building, project coordination, etc.)
- *reflection*—the engagement involves regular structured and unstructured reflection in oral, written, and innovative formats (such as digital storytelling or blogging)
- *mentors*—the engagement involves dialogue and coaching with peers, partners, staff, and/or faculty that contributes to the analysis and synthesis of learning and experience
- *learning*—the engagement involves collaborative and responsive teaching and learning, as well as a philosophy that promotes continuous learning by all those involved

- *capacity building*—the engagement involves work that can build or enhance the organization, school, or agency over time, its ability to achieve its mission, and its resource base (i.e., training, program evaluation, board development, fundraising)
- *evidence*—the engagement involves integration of evidence-based or proven program models that enhance the organization, school, or agency's effectiveness and that leverage the institution's ability to provide relevant research or information to serve community needs
- *impact*—the engagement aims to identify and achieve specific and measurable outcomes, design strategies for evaluation, and find ways to document and show long-term (qualitative and quantitative) impacts.

In practice, the HICEPS are generally clustered as they are structured into and play out within a particular relationship with a community partner; for example, the integration of a site-based team involving freshmen, sophomores, juniors, and seniors serving at a local school or youth development program may enable a focus on *place, humility, depth, sequence, mentors, and capacity building.* Nonetheless, it is helpful to pull these apart and articulate them as a set of best practices to which sustained campus–community engagement can aspire and connect with parallel pathways of academic study.

The High-Impact Teams—again comprised of partner, student, faculty, and staff members—will create and carry out initiatives, over a three-year (or longer) period through which they systematically link practices such as by connecting a first-year seminar with *place* and *mentors*, designing course-based internships that involve *capacity*-building projects and *learning*, linking undergraduate research with a policy analysis assignment utilizing *evidence* of a proven program model, or engineering a senior capstone program where a student assists with evaluation for *impact*. While it is too early to provide a full report from the first cohort, already the campuses involved are creating and implementing innovative and transformational projects, such as:

- place-based first-year experience programs and seminars with semester-long engagement that introduces students to pathways through the undergraduate experience;
- new texts authored through community listening projects incorporating community partners' voices and perspectives that can be linked with academic coursework;
- upper-division research seminars and centers that build and offer institutional capacity for public policy research and support to nonprofit organizations;

- community and economic development initiatives that can create a hub for involvement by multiple programs, faculty, and departments as "stewards of place"; and
- deliberative democracy forums facilitated by student leaders that involve public and community leaders and ignite greater campus involvement in a given neighborhood or issue.

In carrying out these initiatives, campuses will seek to achieve both internal (institutional) and external (community) change; design, implement, and scale effective community engagement initiatives that reach more students in meaningful ways; and maximize meaningful engagement and impact for communities. The High-Impact Initiative is working to foster institutional transformation—including reward structures, tenure and promotion changes, long-range strategic planning, and the inclusion of community partner voice in institutional decision making. The initiative aims to make more pervasive academic community engagement, connected strategically and developmentally with cocurricular engagement, and informed by discernable (and proven) best practices in engaged learning and community engagement.

As a national learning community—also involving support and consultation from the Association of American Colleges and Universities, the New England Resource Center for Higher Education, and other groups—collectively we hope to pave new avenues for civic engagement in higher education that move it from partial and peripheral to pervasive, deep, and integrated. As noted in the section on faculty and staff, this work is also helping our network to collectively explore and surface an analog to HIPs, what we call HICEPs. These principles can be helpful not only for short- and long-range planning but also for learning outcome design and assessment. They can act as magnifiers for engaged learning, especially because they provide a way for students and faculty to live the mission of public engagement in a tangible way, tied to a real community and the potential for impact. In the following, we share some questions and structures that may inform or elucidate these principles, guiding planning and implementation work of campus–community partnerships:

Place

- Is the community engagement systematically informed by an understanding of the place and community voice (i.e., roles in program and institutional decisions)?
- Are community assets and needs systematically informing the community engagement?

- *Relevant structures*: Community Asset Mapping; Community Advisory Boards; town-hall meetings and forums; community representation as Trustees.

Humility (Co-valuing Knowledge)

- Does the campus (involved members and more broadly) demonstrate that the knowledge of the partner and community is valued as key assets?
- Is the knowledge of all stakeholders (community and campus) valued and incorporated as assets in the partnership and projects?
- *Relevant structures*: Community Asset Map results; detailed inventories; integration of data in making focused choices; knowledge sharing; coeducator roles; learning circles.

Integration

- Does the community engagement include both the student development insights of cocurricular experience and the contextualization of academic learning?
- Are the positions through which we partners involve students and faculty leveraging the academic knowledge and skills available?
- *Relevant structures:* faculty members with long-term relationships to partner sites and teams of students; placements that are embedded in coursework.

Depth

- Is the community engagement embedded within a structure of strategic developmental sustained partnerships?
- Have the organization and the college agreed to build and implement a multiyear, developmental partnership?
- *Relevant structures*: multiyear partnership agreements; strategic plans with partners; detailed job descriptions for VISTAs (Volunteers in Service to America); community learning agreements; and positions that involve multisemester evolution for students.

Development

- Is the community engagement developmentally appropriate for the stage of the undergraduate (or graduate) student or other volunteer?

- Is the organization able to specify the developmental needs of each position and able to match volunteers appropriately?
- *Relevant structures*: developmental placements; outcome-oriented job descriptions for volunteers who also show growth over time.

Sequence

- Could the community engagement project and/or courses be offered and linked across multiple semesters and experiences?
- Can the organization work with the college to access volunteers and resources year round?
- *Relevant structures*: programs that operate year round (i.e., summer internships/fellowships/programs); course sequence opportunities for students; academic programs with sequences; shared campus–community calendars.

Teams

- Is the community engagement structured to maximize the effective use of student learning, collaboration, and leadership (i.e., site/issue teams)?
- Can the organization integrate team-based management and student leadership such that the positions offer developmental work and opportunities?
- *Relevant structures:* site- or issue-based teams; management approaches that involve student leadership or VISTAs at sites; volunteer management strategies that engage volunteers at multiple levels.

Reflection

- Does the community engagement involve structured (and unstructured) rigorous reflection?
- Do the volunteers participate in reflection through which they understand the community context?
- *Relevant structures*: structured and unstructured reflection opportunities; trainings and facilitation that support ongoing reflection; blogs; vlogs; journaling; e-portfolios; course-based reflection assignments.

Mentors

- Does the community engagement involve dialogue and guidance (from faculty, staff, and partners) as supervisors, participants, and facilitators?

- Are there opportunities for the volunteers (students and faculty) to be mentored, including by partners, faculty, students, and others with knowledge and experience to share?
- *Relevant structures*: Bonner Buddies (pairings of upper-class and under-class students; families [groups of students across class years used during meetings and trainings]; retreat programming; shadowing of new Bonners with veterans; required 1-to-1 meetings; advising structures; faculty and dean mentors (often tied to cohorts, sites, or classes).

Learning

- Is there an intentional opportunity for stakeholders (faculty, staff, students, and partners) to reflect on, share, and articulate their own learning (learning approaches and outcomes) as they engage in collaborative community-based initiatives, reflect upon and assimilate content, meaning, and action?
- Is the learning process co-constructed; is it inclusive of both community and campus constituents as authentic collaborators as teachers, learners, and scholars?
- *Relevant structures*: engaging partners as coeducators; engaging partners in helping students process their learning and growth through reflection; partners teaching in classroom contexts

Capacity

- Is the community engagement focused around capacity-building needs of the partner or constituency in ways that contribute to enhancing its work (i.e., program design, CBR and policy research, assessment, resource development, organizational development)?
- Can the partnership result in increased capacity by both the institution and community constituents to address and solve problems?
- *Relevant structures*: community-based research projects and community-based participatory research; policy research assignments for the partner and the production of issue briefs; issue-oriented capacity-building initiatives such as when a campus conducts a community health index study for the local area; board development (utilizing campus resources or individuals); fundraising and resource sharing; community economic development projects; new program design; the integration of proven program models to improve service delivery and/or organizational capacity.

Evidence

- Is the community engagement informed by evidence-based practice and proven program models?
- Can the partnership help the organization or community constituency identify relevant program models, approaches, or evidence to inform, enhance, or deepen its work?
- *Relevant structures*: the production and integration of proven program models; research on behalf of a partner/agency; community-wide educational settings (i.e., town-hall meetings and forums); deliberative democracy forums that integrate dialogue about effectiveness; issue-based gatherings of nonprofit partners to foster coalitions.

Impact

- Is the community engagement organized to achieve measurable community impact (i.e., qualitative and quantitative)?
- *Relevant structures*: community-listening projects that work with partners to identify intended outcomes and then find or create measures for them; capacity-building metrics and rubrics; evidence-based program design and implementation; logic modeling; strategic planning with community partners to share community indicators; outcome-based program design.

Conclusion

As noted, this work, while drawing on more than 20 years' experience, in many ways, is just beginning to provide a foundation through which to turn the focus of campus–community partnerships and the centers that manage them toward strategies for collective and measurable impact. We believe that this is the next frontier of the higher education community engagement movement, one that offers promise for inspiring challenges and successes ahead. Undoubtedly, these constructs and their application will be tested, refined, and even refuted over the next several years. Nonetheless, we believe that both the concepts, their application, the nuances, and the stories of lived experience accumulated by the campuses and communities engaged can and will offer a valuable contribution to the field of higher education community engagement. We aspire to create future avenues to share this work as we press on, making the way by walking as lifelong students, educators, and activists.

References

Brownell, Jayne Elise, and Lynn Ellen Swaner. *Five High-Impact Practices: Research on Learning Outcomes, Completion and Quality.* Washington, DC: Association of American Colleges & Universities, 2010.

Crutcher, R. A., R. Corrigan, P. O'Brien, and C. G. Schneider. *College Learning for the New Global Century: A Report from the National Leadership Council for Liberal Education and America's Promise.* Washington, DC: American Association of State Colleges and Universities, 2007.

Kuh, George D. *High-Impact Educational Practices: What They Are, Who Has Access to Them, and Why They Matter.* Washington, DC: Association of American Colleges & Universities, 2008.

Contributors

Editors

Ariane Hoy is Vice President for program and resource development at the Bonner Foundation. Ariane attended Stanford University, where she worked to connect her studies with community engagement in East Palo Alto, designing a credit-bearing course co-taught by students and partners involving community-based internships. She was awarded a John Gardner Fellowship. Focusing a career on civic engagement, Ariane served as program director and senior trainer for City Year; director of the Echoing Green's fellowship for social entrepreneurs; vice president for Program at Jumpstart; and executive director of Campus Outreach Opportunity League (COOL). Ariane serves as a member of the advisory boards for Association of American Colleges & Universities (AAC&U)'s *Diversity & Democracy* and the Center for an Engaged Democracy. As a member of the AAC&U VALUE project national advisory board, she participated in faculty teams to create rubrics for civic engagement and integrative learning. She is the author of more than sixty trainings in Bonner's Civic Engagement Curriculum. She coauthored an AAC&U publication "Civic Engagement at the Center" and contributed to *The Engaged Campus: Certificates, Minors, and Majors as the New Community Engagement.*

Mathew Johnson is an associate professor in Sociology and Environmental Studies at Siena College. He earned a PhD in Sociology from Brandeis University and a Bachelor's of Science from Siena College. Dr. Johnson is the founding director of Academic Community Engagement office and its programs including the Siena VISTA Fellows Program, the Siena Bonner Service Leaders Program, the Academic Service Learning/Community Based Research Program, the Academic AmeriCorps Program, and International Service Internship Program. These programs combine to bring more than US$3 million of state, federal, and private investments in community development partnerships throughout New York's Capital Region annually. Dr Johnson is author of numerous publications and contributed to *The Engaged Campus: Certificates, Minors, and Majors as the New Community Engagement.*

Authors

Karin Aguilar-San Juan earned her PhD in Sociology at Brown University and is an associate professor of American Studies at Macalester College. She is an urban sociologist who teaches and publishes in Asian American Studies. She also teaches classes on and is engaged with the schools to prison pipeline. She is the editor of *The State of Asian America: Activism and Resistance in the 1990s* (South End Press, 1994) and *Little Saigons: Staying Vietnamese in America* (University of Minnesota Press, 2009). Since 2005, she has been the codirector of the Urban Faculty Colloquium.

Ellen Alcorn is the assistant director of Community-Based Learning at Harward Center for Community Partnerships at Bates College. In this role, she facilitates community-based placements, projects, and research with local public schools and other youth-serving organizations. She also serves as the Director of the Bonner Leader Program.

Kelly Elizabeth Behrend is a Bonner Scholar alumnus of the University of Richmond and former staff member of the Bonner Foundation, where she led the design and implementation of the Bonner International Partnerships Initiative. Her undergraduate thesis in International Peace and Conflict Studies was awarded with the James W. Jackson Award for Excellence in Library Research in the Social Sciences and a nomination for Best Undergraduate Paper in Political Science at the Midwest Political Science Association National Conference. Kelly's experiences in strategic partnerships for social change through higher education have since inspired her to pursue similar work with the private sector. Kelly is a Rotary International Ambassadorial Scholar at EOI Business School Madrid, where she is studying for a Master's degree in Sustainable Development and Corporate Responsibility. Kelly also presently serves as director of Corporate Responsibility for the Peacework Development Fund.

Suzanne Bonefas is the director of Special Projects in the Office of External Programs at Rhodes College, where she works with community partners on projects that are mutually beneficial to Rhodes and to the broader Memphis community. She also assists faculty and staff in the cultivation of ideas into proposals and by identifying potential funding sources. She has also served as the director of Technology Programs for the Associated Colleges of the

South since 1996. In 1999, she helped establish the ACS Technology Center at Southwestern University.

Dan W. Butin is an associate professor and founding dean of the school of education at Merrimack College and the executive director of the Center for Engaged Democracy. He is the author and editor of more than seventy academic publications, including the books *Service-Learning in Theory and Practice: The Future of Community Engagement in Higher Education* (2010), which won the 2010 Critics Choice Book Award of the American Educational Studies Association, *Service-Learning and Social Justice Education* (2008), *Teaching Social Foundations of Education* (2005), and, most recently with Scott Seider, *The Engaged Campus: Majors, Minors and Certificates as the New Community Engagement* (2012). Butin is an Associate Editor of the Michigan Journal of Community Service Learning and a board member of the Journal of College and Character. Butin's research focuses on issues of educator preparation and policy, and community engagement. He blogs at the Education Policy Blog and at the Huffington Post. Prior to working in higher education, Butin was a middle school math and science teacher and the chief financial officer of Teach For America.

Pete Cichetti is the assistant director of the National Assessment of Service and Community Engagement (NASCE) for the Siena College Research Institute (SRI), where he organizes and facilitates the implementation of each participating college or university's NASCE survey. Previously, Pete served as the coordinator of Community-Based Research at SRI through the Siena College AmeriCorps VISTA Fellows Program. He received his BA in International Affairs from The George Washington University.

Ashley Cochrane is the director of the Center for Excellence in Learning through Service (CELTS) at Berea College. She directs the Bonner Scholars Program and the Service-Learning Program. Ashley received her Bachelor's of Arts degree in Sociology and Religious Studies from the University of Virginia and her Master's of Science degree in Education (Counseling Psychology) from the University of Kentucky. Her professional experiences include work as a community organizer and mental health counselor in rural Appalachian communities.

Stephen Darr is the founder and chief executive officer of Peacework, an international nonprofit organization focused on community-driven development in over 20 countries around the world. Peacework manages partnerships between organizations with unique resources and communities and villages in developing countries, often between academic institutions or corporations in a variety of fields that match local development standards and objectives. Steve has a BA degree from the University of Arkansas, an MDiv from Duke University, and additional studies at Georgetown University and Virginia Tech. He has authored or coauthored numerous articles related to international development and service in the *Journal of Business Research*, *Organization Management in Construction*, *International Educator*, and several academic journals. Steve lives in Blacksburg, Virginia.

Patrick Donohue is the assistant provost for Community Engaged Learning Programs and Partnerships at The College of New Jersey. Patrick earned his undergraduate and graduate degrees from Rutgers University, where he was the student vice-chair of the US Public Interest Research group. Before joining the staff at The College of New Jersey (TCNJ), Patrick was a political science professor at Middlesex County College, where he also founded Democracy House, the oldest replication Bonner Leader program in the country. He is past board president of Isles Inc., a nonprofit partner in Trenton, New Jersey.

Richard B. Ellis is the director of Learning in the Community (LinC) at Washburn University, where he has taught since 1992. Dr Ellis received his PhD from Kansas State University in Family Studies and Human Services. He is a full professor who teaches in the Human Services Department, previously served as the chair of the Human Services Department, and oversees the Civic Engagement Poverty Studies minor.

Patrick Gruber is the Bonner Scholars Coordinator at Carson-Newman University. He is a graduate in Sociology and Economics from West Virginia Wesleyan College. Patrick worked in upstate New York with local nonprofits through AmeriCorps VISTA and as a VISTA Leader for the Siena College AmeriCorps VISTA Fellows Program. He cochairs the High-Impact Initiative team that is working on projects for economic development in Jefferson City, Tennessee.

Robert Hackett is the president of the Bonner Foundation, where he has served since 1992, first as vice president and director of the Bonner Scholars Program. Earlier, Mr Hackett worked at the Telesis Corporation, an affordable housing developer in Washington, DC. He also served as the managing director of the COOL during its first three years, 1985–1988. Mr Hackett has been associated in various capacities with the Youth Policy Institute, a Washington, DC-based nonpartisan organization that researches and reports on policies and programs relating to young people. Mr Hackett received his Bachelor's degree from Harvard University and a Master's degree in public and private management from Yale University's School of Organization and Management.

Kristine Hart is the associate director of LinC, where she has served since 2001. She has experience as an AmeriCorps VISTA, Jumpstart site manager, and Washburn's community service coordinator. As associate director, she manages and engages 100+ Washburn student AmeriCorps members each year in long-term (12–60 months), meaningful service that utilizes a developmental model. Kristine also teaches Introduction to Poverty Studies, the first seminar in Washburn's Civic Engagement Poverty Studies minor.

Emily W. Kane is a professor of Sociology and also serves in the Women and Gender Studies Program at Bates College. She teaches courses on gender, family, childhood, social inequality, research methods for sociology, public sociology, and community-based research.

Abby Kiesa is a youth coordinator and researcher at the Center for Information and Research on Civic Learning and Engagement (CIRCLE), where she focuses on research about young people, youth-serving organizations, and educators. Previous to CIRCLE, Abby organized students around the country as part of a national campaign of Campus Compact to increase youth involvement in public life. She has contributed to several publications and coedited "Raise Your Voice: A Student Guide to Making Positive Social Change." In 2007, Abby was named an emerging leader in Service-Learning, a two-year experience designed to elevate and prepare a new, culturally diverse generation of service-learning leaders committed to working with traditionally underserved populations, schools, and communities. Abby earned a Master of Arts degree in American Studies at the University of Maryland College Park. Abby currently serves on the board of directors of IARSLCE (the International Association for Research on Service-Learning and Community Engagement), the American Democracy Project Implementation Committee (a project of the American Association of State Colleges and Universities), and is on the Leadership Team of the Generational Alliance.

Holly Lasagna is the associate director for Community-Based Learning at the Harward Center for Community Partnerships at Bates College. Her work entails day-to-day operations of academically based community engagement, new initiatives such as outcomes assessment, as well as long-term development of community-based learning and research.

Dr Donald P. Levy is the director of Siena Research Institute with prior experience as the director of the Institute for Social and Community Research (ISCR) at West Virginia Wesleyan College, and director of Research at the Center for Population Research (CPR) at the University of Connecticut. Dr Levy holds a PhD in Sociology from the University of Connecticut and a BA degree from Yale University. He has conducted numerous local, regional, and national studies; presented his research in scholarly and popular venues; and has been interviewed for the *New York Times*, *Fortune*, and National Public Radio.

Thomas G. McGowan is an associate professor of Sociology and chair of the Anthropology and Sociology department at Rhodes College, where he has taught for his entire career. He was a service-learning pioneer at Rhodes and continues to conduct research and curriculum workshops related to service-learning at Rhodes and throughout the southeast. He spearheaded the development of an intergenerational service-learning program that helped students deconstruct their assumptions regarding aging through interaction with Memphis elders. The Life Histories Project produced qualitative research data exploring ontological change. Thomas earned a PhD in Sociology from the University of New Hampshire and a Bachelor's in Communications and Master's in Social Research from Hunter College, the City University of New York (CUNY).

Heather McNew Schill is the assistant director for the CELTS at Berea College. She attended Berea, earning a degree in Psychology with an emphasis on Sociology and Child and Family Studies. Heather oversees the student-led community service programs and the Bonner Scholars Program. Heather holds a Master's of Education in College Student Affairs from Azusa Pacific University.

Wayne Meisel is the founding president of the Bonner Foundation, where he served between 1989 and 2010. Meisel currently serves as the director of Faith and Service at the C.F. Foundation in Atlanta, Georgia. As a presidential appointee to the Commission on National and Community Service, Meisel served as one of the architects of the AmeriCorps programs and also as a charter board member of Teach for America. Wayne is a graduate of Harvard College and Princeton Theological Seminary. In 1985, he founded COOL, which became a national platform for student voice and leadership to expand campus–community partnerships and the service movement. He is an ordained minister in the Presbyterian Church.

Tania D. Mitchell is an assistant professor in the department of postsecondary teaching and learning at the University of Minnesota's college of education and human development. Her teaching interests include social justice theory, civic discourse, public service and service-learning, diversity in higher education, and college student development. Much of her research focuses on service-learning as a critical pedagogy to explore civic identity, social justice, student learning and development, race and racism, and community practice.

Tania D. Mitchell received her doctorate in education from the University of Massachusetts Amherst in 2005. From 2002–2007 she served as Assistant Professor for Service Learning Leadership at California State University Monterey Bay where she developed the minor in Service Learning Leadership and directed the Student Leadership in Service Learning Program, a nationally recognized peer education program. In 2012, Mitchell received the Early Career Research Award from the International Association for Research on Service-Learning and Community Engagement (IARSLCE).

Georgia Nigro is a professor of Psychology and recently completed a term as the interim director of the Harward Center for Community Partnerships at Bates College. She has taught courses involving community-based learning since coming to Bates in 1983.

Michelle Nix is the Youth Services officer for the Jefferson County Juvenile Court, a key community partner to Carson-Newman University. Michelle has worked with youth and community development programs, including through the Department of Children Services in the State of Tennessee. Michelle is the founder of The Journey Program, a successful alternative program for truant youth. She trains and supervises many ongoing student volunteers, including Bonner Scholars, from Carson-Newman, and is currently pursuing her Master of Arts in Applied Social Justice with a focus on Social Entrepreneurship.

David Roncolato is the director of Community Service and Service Learning at Allegheny College. An Allegheny alumnus David majored in History and Religious Studies. He worked for 20 years for the Roman Catholic Church prior to taking his current position. He received a Master's degree in Christian Spirituality from Creighton University and a PhD in Catholic Social Ethics, from Duquesne University. His dissertation was on the ethics of US–Cuban relations. In addition to other responsibilities at Allegheny, David coordinates the Values Ethics and Social Action minor and directors of the Bonner Program.

Nicole Saylor is the director of the Bonner Center for Service Learning and Civic Engagement at Carson-Newman University. In this capacity, she has developed a Quality Enhancement Plan (QEP) on Service-Learning and strengthened community engagement programs campus-wide with a focus on student development. She earned degrees in Psychology, Sociology, and Adolescent Development at the University of Tennessee, a Master's and PsyD in Clinical Psychology from Wheaton College, Wheaton, Illinois. Nicole is a licensed clinical psychologist. Her areas of service interest include Christian Community Development, youth development, and women's issues.

Paul Schadewald earned his PhD in History from Indiana University and is the associate director of the Civic Engagement Center at Macalester College. Since 2005, he has been the codirector of the Urban Faculty Colloquium at Macalester and supports academic civic and urban engagement. He helped facilitate the partnership between the MN Historical Society and Macalester College that created the 2007 exhibit, "Right on Lake Street" at the MN History Center. He was the cochair of the 2011 national Imagining America Conference, "What Sustains Us?" and is currently co-leader (principle investigator) on Imagining America's "Engaged Undergraduate Education" research group.

John Saltmarsh is the codirector of the New England Resource Center for Higher Education (NERCHE) at the University of Massachusetts, Boston, and a faculty member in the Higher Education Administration Doctoral Program. He leads the project in which NERCHE serves as the partner with the Carnegie Foundation for the Advancement of Teaching for Carnegie's Community Engagement Classification.

Anthony C. Siracusa is the Community Service Coordinator in the Bonner Center for Faith and Service at Rhodes College. He earned a Bachelor's degree in History from Rhodes. Subsequently, he traveled the world as a Thomas J. Watson Fellow studying bicycling cultures and cycling policy. Siracusa serves on the Memphis Metropolitan Planning Organization's Bicycle and Pedestrian Advisory Committee. He also serves on the board of directors for the Greater Memphis Greenline Inc., Bike Walk Tennessee, and the Memphis Hightailers.

Marshall Welch is the director of Saint Mary's Catholic Institute for Lasallian Social Action since 2007. Marshall has been in higher education for 25+ years as a faculty member and director of the Lowell Bennion Community Service Center at the University of Utah. His disciplinary background is in teacher education. Marshall has taught service-learning courses and has been involved at the local, regional, national, and international levels with publications, presentations, workshops, and consultation.

Craig Zinkiewicz is a graduate research fellow at the Siena College Research Institute. He received his BA in Psychology from Siena College in 2007 and his Master's degree in Educational Psychology from The College of Saint Rose in 2012. He has worked on the NASCE project since January 2011 and his primary responsibilities include creating variables, working with the data set and producing the executive summary reports for the participating schools.

Index